THE GREEK NEW TESTAMENT ISSUE

How It Affects English Translations

G. Michael Cocoris

© 2009/2022 by G. Michael Cocoris

All rights reserved. This publication may not be reproduced (in whole or in part, edited, or revised) in any way, form, or means including, but not limited to electronic, mechanical, photocopying, recording, or any kind of storage and retrieval system *for sale*, except for brief quotations in printed reviews, without the written permission of G. Michael Cocoris, 2016 Euclid #20, Santa Monica, CA 90405, (310) 463-2361 michaelcocoris@gmail.com, or his appointed representatives. Permission is hereby granted, however, for the reproduction of the whole or parts of the whole without changing the content in any way for *free distribution,* provided all copies contain this copyright notice in its entirety. Permission is also granted to charge for the cost of copying.

Unless otherwise indicated, all Scripture quotations are taken from the New King James Version ®, Copyright © 1979, 1980, 1982 by Thomas Nelson, Inc. Used by permission. All rights reserved.

TABLE OF CONTENTS

PREFACE 1
Chapter 1 SOURCES OF THE GREEK NEW TESTAMENT 7
Chapter 2 THE TEXTUS RECEPTUS 19
Chapter 3 THE WESTCOTT-HORT TEXT 27
Chapter 4 THE TRADITIONAL TEXT 39
Chapter 5 THE CRITICAL GREEK TEXTS 55
Chapter 6 METHODS OF TEXTUAL CRITICISM 59
Chapter 7 AN EVALUATION OF THE TEXT TYPES 69
Chapter 8 THE MAJORITY TEXT 113
Chapter 9 THE BYZANTINE TEXT 121
Chapter 10 FAMILY 35 139
Chapter 11 WHAT DIFFERENCE DOES IT MAKE? 147
Chapter 12 ENGLISH TRANSLATIONS 209
CONCLUSION 227
APPENDIX I: THE WESTCOTT-HORT THEORY 275
APPENDIX II: RULES OF TEXTUAL CRITICISM 289
APPENDIX III: SINAITICUS AND VATICANUS 293
APPENDIX IV: PAPYRUS 301
APPENDIX V: TR AND MT DIFFERENCES 305
BIBLIOGRAPHY 325

ABBREVIATIONS

CT	Critical Text: Nestlé-Aland Text and United Bible Society text
f^{35}	Family 35, the Greek text edited by Pickering
HF	The Majority Text, the Greek text edited by Hodges and Farstad
MSS	Manuscripts (plural)
MS	Manuscript (singular)
NA	Nestlé-Aland Greek text
NT	New Testament
NU	Nestlé-Aland/United and Bible Society texts,
𝔓^{115}	A Papyrus manuscript
RP	The Byzantine Text, edited by Robinson and Pierpont
TR	Textus Receptus
USB	United Bible Society Greek Text
WH	The Westcott-Hort Text, edited by Westcott and Hort

PREFACE

My first exposure to the issue of New Testament Greek texts was in college. The dispute was between the Textus Receptus and the Westcott-Hort theory. I sided with Westcott and Hort. In seminary, I was taught the Critical Text approach to the New Testament Greek text. So, when I graduated, I put it into practice.

Then, five years after graduating from seminary, I stumbled upon the book *The Last Twelve Verses of Mark* by John Burgon. Burgon's book prompted me to reconsider the issue of the New Testament Greek text. I spent several months revisiting and researching a subject I thought I had settled on as far back as my college days. As a result of that study, I changed my mind. (In the Preface to the article I wrote entitled "The Translation of the Bible," I explain in more detail my experience with the New Testament Greek text; see it at insightsfromthrword.com under Advanced Courses)

In the early 1980s, I wrote "Why So Many Versions?" In it, I explained the textual issue. In the late 1980s, I spoke to several groups of pastors for Thomas Nelson Publishers about why I use the New King James Version. As part of that presentation, I summarized the textual question. In 2004, I made a video for Thomas Nelson that included material on this subject. (intro at https://www.youtube.com/watch?v=QzdBtZllKK8&t=10s.)

In the meantime, over the years, I collected notes and articles on the New Testament Greek text issue. Most of that material was scattered across several folders on my computer. Then, on a Sunday afternoon in

February 2022, I made an unplanned and unprepared presentation on the New Testament Greek text problem to a small group of friends. The next day, out of curiosity, I decided to see what I had collected on the subject. As I surveyed the folders and files on my computer related to this subject, I discovered a wealth of unorganized material and thoughts. I decided that the information needed to be organized and presented clearly and concisely, explaining the issue with the Greek New Testament text. Hence, this presentation.

The issue of the Greek New Testament is complex. It is complex because there are thousands of New Testament Greek manuscripts, and their wording differs. Thus, when Greek manuscripts have differences, the first issue is which difference is to be translated. The explanation of the various answers to that question is the subject of this material.

First, several observations are in order. Although there are thousands of differences among the thousands of Greek New Testament manuscripts that exist today, *no central doctrine of Christianity is affected.* All scholars agree with that. Except for fragments that do not address these issues, all New Testament Greek manuscripts teach the Trinity, the deity of Christ, the death and resurrection of Jesus Christ, salvation by grace through faith, etc.

Second, while there are differences among the Greek New Testament manuscripts, the vast majority of them are of no significance! Daniel Wallace, an authority on Greek manuscripts, points out that there are about 400,000 variants ("variation in the wording") in the New Testament, but 99% make no difference whatsoever because they are differences 1) in spelling, 2) in the presence or absence of an article ("the" appears 20,000 times in the NT, 1 out of every seven words), and 3) in word order. In

Greek, "John loves Mary" can be said in 96 different ways. (Wallace, https://www.youtube.com/watch?v=qMWGloVfMF0).

Third, there are differences among the Greek New Testament manuscripts that do not change the meaning. White says these include changes, additions, and subtractions. On the next page is a chart created by White that provides examples of some differences that do not affect the meaning of the passage. For instance, in some passages, some manuscripts have the word "Jesus," and others have "Jesus Christ." (The titles "Critical Text" and "Byzantine Text" in the following chart will be explained later in the book.)

Reference	Critical Text	Byzantine Text
Matthew 4:18	He	Jesus
Matthew 12:25	He	Jesus
Mark 2:15	He	Jesus
Mark 10:52	He	Jesus
Luke 24:36	He	Jesus
Acts 19:10	The Lord	The Lord Jesus
1 Corinthians 16:22	The Lord	The Lord Jesus Christ
Acts 19:4	Jesus	Christ Jesus
1 Corinthians 9:1	Jesus	Jesus Christ
2 Corinthians 4:10	Jesus	Lord Jesus
Hebrews 3:1	Jesus	Christ Jesus
1 John 1:7	Jesus	Jesus Christ
Revelation 1:9	Jesus	Jesus Christ
Revelation 12:17	Jesus	Jesus Christ
1 Thessalonians 3:11	Jesus our Lord	Our Lord Jesus Christ
2 Corinthians 5:18	Christ	Jesus Christ

Acts 15:11	The Lord Jesus	Lord Jesus Christ
Acts 16:31	The Lord Jesus	Lord Jesus Christ
1 Corinthians 5:4	The Lord Jesus	Lord Jesus Christ
2 Corinthians 11:31	The Lord Jesus	Lord Jesus Christ
2 Thessalonians 1:8	The Lord Jesus	Lord Jesus Christ
2 Thessalonians 1:12	The Lord Jesus	Lord Jesus Christ
2 John 1:3	Jesus Christ	The Lord Jesus Christ

Taken from White, pp. 45-46 (except the titles are changed)

Fourth, relatively few differences among the Greek manuscripts make a meaningful difference. Wallace says it is ¼ of 1%.

Specifically, 99% of 400,000 is 396,000 differences that make no difference whatsoever because of differences in spelling, the presence or absence of an article, or word order. That leaves 4000 differences. Those 4000 differences include changes, additions, and subtractions that do not change the meaning. If only ¼ of 1% makes a meaningful difference, there are only 1,000 such problems.

Philip Schaff estimated that only 400 variants affect the sense of the passage, and only 50 of these are important. He assessed that not one affects "an article of faith or precept of duty which is not abundantly sustained by other undoubted passage, or by the whole tenor of Scripture teaching" (Schaff, cited by White, p. 39).

The bottom line is that while there are multiplied thousands of differences among the Greek manuscripts of the New Testament, the vast, vast majority make no difference whatsoever (e.g., differences in spelling), many do not change the meaning (Jesus versus Jesus Christ), and only a relatively small number change the meaning of a passage, but no central doctrine or duty of Christianity is affected.

Be all that as it may, a relatively small number of differences affect a passage's meaning. What are they? Later in this presentation, many of them will be explained, but some of the more well-known *passages* that are affected include the last 12 verses of Mark (Mk. 16:9-20), the story of the woman taken in adultery (Jn. 7:53-8:11; known as the Pericope Adulterae), and the reference to the Trinity in 1 John (1 Jn. 5:7-8; called the Comma Johanneum). Those passages are omitted from some manuscripts. Were those passages part of the original New Testament? Should they be in the Bible?

In some cases, a *word* or *phrase* is not in some manuscripts. For example, in some manuscripts, Mark 9:29 reads, "Jesus said, 'This kind can come out by nothing but prayer and fasting.'" Other manuscripts omit the last two words. In this case, there is a meaningful, practical difference. Did Jesus say that this kind comes out by prayer, or did He say this kind comes out by prayer *and fasting*? When those kinds of differences occur in the manuscripts of the Greek New Testament, the question becomes, "How does one determine which variant reading is correct?"

What follows is an attempt to clarify this complex subject. Regardless of which position on the issue you choose to adopt, exposure to this information will make you aware of some of the differences in English translations and the reasons behind them. The practical result will be which English translation you choose for serious Bible study.

G. Michael Cocoris
Santa Monica, California

Chapter 1

SOURCES OF THE GREEK NEW TESTAMENT

The original manuscripts of the New Testament, known as "autographs," no longer exist; however, they were copied, and those copies were copied, and those copies were copied, and so on. Thousands of those handwritten copies have survived. Beyond those copies of the New Testament, there is a massive amount of material in ancient translations of the New Testament and the writings of early Christian authors. Here is a brief explanation of the sources of the New Testament's wording.

The Greek Manuscripts of the New Testament

A *manuscript* is a handwritten copy. In 2013, Daniel Wallace stated that 5,824 complete or partial Greek manuscripts have survived, comprising 2.6 million pages (see bibliography for his YouTube speech). A more recent count puts the total over 6000. These manuscripts come in "different shapes and sizes."

Today, a Bible is a leather-bound **book** printed on **paper**, often featuring a **Times New Roman font.** Before the invention of printing, Scripture was typically found in the form of a **scroll** (Old Testament) or **codex** (New Testament), handwritten on **papyrus** or **parchment** in either

uncial or **minuscule** script. What do codex, papyrus, parchment, uncial, and minuscule mean?

Rather than a book, the form was either a scroll or a codex. A scroll was a roll of pages. It was typically 12 inches tall and varied in length to over 35 feet. A codex was pages stacked and bound along one side (precursor to a book). "Apparently, from the beginning, Christians did not use the scroll format for their writings, but rather the codex" (Aland, p. 75).

Rather than paper, the material on which the New Testament was written at first was papyrus. Papyrus was made from the papyrus plant. See "papyrus" in Job 8:11. New Testament manuscripts were written on papyrus from the 1st to the 8th century. Parchment was a writing material made of animal skin, chiefly sheep, goats, and calves. (Vellums are calf skins.) See "parchments" in 2 Timothy 4:13. The name was derived from the city of Pergamum, where parchment was developed in the 2nd century BC (Metzger, p. 4). Beginning in the 4th century AD, parchment became a popular writing material (Aland, p. 76). The Chinese invented paper in the first century AD, but did not gain popularity in the West until the 12th century (Aland, p. 77).

Rather than Times New Roman font, the script was either uncial or minuscule. Uncial script (a.k.a. majuscules) was handwriting in all capital letters with no SPACEBETWEENWORDS. That was not easy to read. For example, what does GODISNOWHERE mean? It can be "God is nowhere" or "God is now here" (Metzger, p.13; see for NT examples). The minuscule script was written in lowercase, *cursive* letters.

All New Testament *papyrus* codices are written in capital letters (uncials) and dated from the 2nd to the 8th centuries. There are no papyrus minuscules. New Testament *parchment* codices were written in capital letters (uncials) and date from the 4th to the 10th century. At the beginning of the 9th century, the minuscule script was initiated and became popular almost immediately (Metzger, p. 9).

Papyrus codex in uncial script   2st _____ 8th
Parchment codex in uncial script   4th _____ 10th
Parchment codex in cursive script   9th _____ 15th

Greek New Testament manuscripts are designated as papyri, uncials, minuscules, and lectionaries, and are numbered as follows: papyri (1-140), uncials (01-0323), minuscules (1-2965), and lectionaries (ℓ-2412). An index of these Greek manuscripts can be seen at http://textus-receptus.com/wiki/D._A._Waite.

Papyrus Codex in Uncial Script Papyri are named using the Gothic letter P ($\mathfrak{P}$) followed by a number ($\mathfrak{P}^{66}$). As of 2021, about 140 papyri have been found.

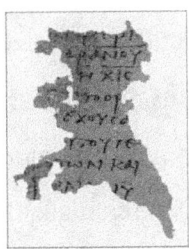

$\mathfrak{P}^{115}$ of Revelation 13:18
(It reads 616 instead of 666.)

𝔓⁴⁵ contains two small leaves of Matthew 20-21, 25-26, portions of Mark 4-9, 11-12, Luke 6-7, 9-14, John 4-5, 10-11, and Acts 4-17. 𝔓⁴⁵ is from the first half of the 3rd century and is the oldest manuscript of Mark (AD 200).

𝔓⁴⁶ contains Romans 5–6, 8-15, all of Hebrews, Ephesians, Galatians, Philippians, Colossians, virtually all of 1 and 2 Corinthians, and 1 Thessalonians 1–2, 5. It is the oldest manuscript of Paul's letters (*ca.* AD 200). Note: Hebrews is after Romans.

𝔓⁴⁷ contains Revelation 9-17, the oldest manuscript of Revelation (3rd century).

𝔓⁵² contains John 18:31-33, 18:37-38, dated AD 90-150 (Wallace, speech; Aland: 125, p. 84). It is the size of a credit card and is the earliest extant Greek manuscript.

𝔓⁶⁶ contains a large portion of the Gospel of John.

𝔓⁷⁵ contains most of Luke and John and a partial codex of Acts

Parchment Codex in Uncial Script New Testament uncial manuscripts are named by capital letters. Alexandrinus is "A." Vaticanus is "B." Bezae is "D," etc. Greek and Hebrew letters are also used. Sinaiticus is the Hebrew letter א. The uncials were assigned numbers by Caspar René Gregory (1884-1894), but to distinguish them from minuscules, which are also numbered, the numbers of the uncials are preceded by a 0: Sinaiticus is 01, Alexandrinus is 02, Vaticanus is 03, Bezae Cantabrigiensis is 04, etc. There are 267 uncial manuscripts.

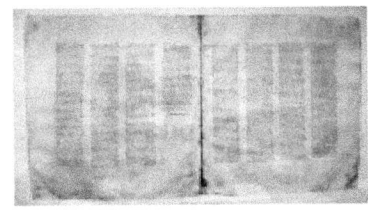

Codex Sinaiticus

Codex Sinaiticus (א or 01) is a fourth-century manuscript containing about half of the Greek Old Testament, the complete New Testament, the Epistle of Barnabas, and portions of the Shepherd of Hermas. Parts of it are in four libraries, but most of it is in the British Library in London, where it is on public display.

Codex Alexandrinus (A or 02) is a fifth-century manuscript containing most of the Greek Old Testament and Greek New Testament. It is one of the earliest and most complete manuscripts of the Bible. It is from Alexandria and is in the British Library.

Codex Vaticanus (B or 03) is a fourth-century manuscript containing the Gospels, Acts, the General Epistles, the Pauline Epistles, and the Epistle to the Hebrews (up to Hebrews 9:14); it lacks 1 and 2 Timothy, Titus, Philemon, and Revelation. It is in the Vatican Library, where it has been since the 15th century.

Codex Ephraemi Rescriptus (C or 04) is a fifth-century manuscript containing six Old Testament books and every New Testament book except 2 Thessalonians and 2 John. The reason those two are not in Codex C is not known. (This codex is not intact.) The name of Codex C is Ephraemi Rescriptus because the parchment on which it is written has been recycled. Originally, it was inscribed with the biblical texts. Then, the pages were washed and reused for another text. Recycled pages are called palimpsests, a term meaning "scraped again." The Council of Trullo (AD

692) condemned using manuscripts of Scripture for other purposes. In the case of Codex C, the "upper" text consists of treatises composed in the 12th century. The "lower" biblical text was deciphered by Tischendorf (1840-1843).

Codex Bezae Cantabrigiensis (D^{ea} or 05) is a fifth-century manuscript in Greek and Latin, containing most of the Gospels, Acts, and a small fragment of 3 John. A digital copy is available on the Cambridge University Library's website. As many as eleven people made corrections between the sixth and twelfth centuries. Its origin is debated; it is probably from France. It was given to Beza, who passed it on to Cambridge University. It contains abbreviations; for example, ΧΡΣ for Χριστος, Christos. It includes one of the longer endings of Mark, the Pericope Adulterae (Jn. 7:53-8:11), and the text of Acts is nearly 8½ % longer than the Textus Receptus (Metzger, p. 294). John 5:4 is omitted.

Parchment Codex in Minuscule Script During the ninth and tenth centuries, the minuscule (cursive) script replaced the uncial script. Thus, minuscule manuscripts are later than papyri and uncial manuscripts. Arabic numbers designate them, but the system is more complicated than simple Arabic numbers. For example, there are 18^{evv}, 113^{Acts}, and 132^{Paul}. The Institute for New Testament Textual Research (INTF) in Münster has cataloged 2911 minuscule codices.

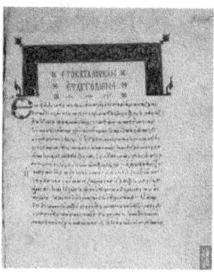

Minuscule 481 of Luke 1:1-7a

#1 is a 12th-century manuscript containing the Gospels, Acts, Pauline Epistles, and the General Epistles.

#2 is an 11th/12th-century manuscript containing the Gospels.

#3 is a 12th-century codex manuscript containing the New Testament, except for the book of Revelation. It is one of the manuscripts used by Erasmus.

#7 is a 12th-century manuscript containing the New Testament.

#35 is an 11th-century manuscript containing the New Testament. It is significant because of what Pickering did with it. See the Chapter on Family 35.

Some other minuscule manuscripts contain the entire New Testament, including #18 (1384), #61 (16th century), #141 (13th century), #175 (10th/11th century), #201 (A.D. 1357), #241 (11th century), #242 (12th-century), #367 (1331), #386 (14th century), #582 (1334), #986 (14th century), #2136 (17th century), #2494 (1316), etc.

Lectionaries New Testament lectionaries contain selected passages used for public reading. In ancient Jewish synagogues, passages from the Law and the Prophets were read every Sabbath. When "Paul and his party" (Acts 13:13) were in the synagogue on the Sabbath day at Antioch in Pisidia (Acts 13:14), "after the reading of the Law and the Prophets, the rulers of the synagogue sent to them, saying, 'Men *and* brethren if you have any word of exhortation for the people, say on'" (Acts 13:15). The *Encyclopedia Britannica* says, "The early Christians adopted the Jewish custom of reading extracts from the Old Testament on the Sabbath. They soon added extracts from the writings of the Apostles and Evangelists."

Thus, a Christian lectionary is "a book containing portions of the Bible appointed to be read on particular days of the year.... At first, the lessons were marked off in the margins of manuscripts of the Scriptures. Later, special lectionary manuscripts were prepared, containing the appointed passages in proper sequence" (see the complete article at the website https://www.britannicacom/topic/lectionary).

Lectionaries are named by the abbreviation "lect" or a cursive letter "𝑙," for example, Lect. 30. Lectionaries are written on papyrus, parchment, vellum, and paper in all capital letters or cursive letters. The INTF in Münster has cataloged 2484 lectionary manuscripts.

Lectionary 187 (cursive)

Lect. 1 (10th century) contains the Gospels in all capital letters.

Lect. 6 (1265) contains the Gospels and apostles in cursive.

Lect. 197 (15th century) contains Matthew 25:1-13, Mark 5:24-34, Luke 1:1-25, 57-68, 76, 80, Galatians 4:6-7, 1 John 4:12-19 in cursive.

Lect. 1416 (13th century) contains 1 Peter 1:1-9, 13-19, 2 Peter 2:11-24 in cursive.

The papyri, uncials, minuscules, and lectionaries were written from the 2nd century to the 16th century. The chart on the next page displays the distribution of Greek manuscripts by century, showing the number of various types of Greek manuscripts produced in each century.

The chart on the next page is from *The Text of the New Testament: An Introduction to the Critical Editions and to the Theory and Practice of Modern Textual Criticism by* Kurt and Barbara Aland. It is from 1995. The number of manuscripts has increased since 1995; nevertheless, this chart illustrates the distribution of manuscripts throughout the centuries.

Century	Manuscripts			Lectionaries	
	Papyri	Uncials	Minuscules	Uncials	Minuscules
2nd	2				
2nd/3rd	5	1			
3rd	28	2			
3rd/4th	8	2			
4th	14	14		1	
4th/5th	8	8			
5th	2	36		1	
5th/6th	4	10			
6th	7	51		3	
6th/7th	5	5		1	
7th	8	28		4	
7th/8th	3	4			
8th	2	29		22	
8th/9th	-	4		5	
9th	-	53	13	113	5
9th/10th	-	1	4		1
10th	-	17	124	108	38
10th/11th	-	3	8	3	4
11th	-	1	429	15	227

11th/12th	-	-	33		13
12th	-	-	555	6	486
12th/13th	-	-	26		17
13th	-	-	547	4	394
13th/14th	-	-	28		17
14th	-	-	511		308
14th/15th	-	-	8		2
15th	-	-	241		171
15th/16th	-	-	4		2
16th	-	-	136		194

The Center for the Study of New Testament Manuscripts (CSNTM) has many digital photographs of New Testament Greek manuscripts on its website (https://www.csntm.org/). So do many other websites.

The Translations of the New Testament

In addition to Greek manuscripts of the New Testament, there are more than 10,000 Latin manuscripts of the New Testament that date back to the second century, as well as 9,300 manuscripts in various ancient languages, including Syriac, Slavic, Gothic, Ethiopic, Coptic, and Armenian.

The Ancient Writings that Cite the New Testament

The writings of Christians in church history contain quotations and references to the New Testament that provide data concerning its wording. Wallace states that there are more than 1 million quotations, and the entire New Testament could be reconstructed from them (Wallace, speech; see also Metzger, p. 86). Problems with quotations include 1) whether the author intended to quote or paraphrase the passage verbatim, 2) whether the author consulted a manuscript or relied on his memory, and 3) whether he cited it once or many times. Origen is notorious for not quoting a passage twice in precisely the same words (Metzger, p. 87).

Summary: The original autographs of the New Testament no longer exist; however, a vast amount of material is available in manuscripts, translations, and the writings of early Christian authors.

Portions or complete copies of the New Testament are preserved in 140 papyri, 267 uncials, 2911 minuscules, and 2484 lectionaries. There are about 60 manuscripts of the complete New Testament and about 150 more that do not have Revelation (Pickering, p. 203 fn. 1). The available information concerning the text of the New Testament is far more extensive than any other ancient book. For example, "Homer's *Iliad* is preserved in 457 papyri, 2 uncials, and 188 minuscules" (Carson, p. 18).

The oldest manuscript, $\mathfrak{P}52$, is dated in the first half of the second century. Metzger observes, "Just as Robinson Crusoe, seeing a single footprint in the sand, concluded that another human being with two feet was present on the island with him, so $\mathfrak{P}^{52}$ proves the existence and use of the fourth Gospel during the first half of the second century in a provincial town along the Nile, far removed from the traditional place of composition (Ephesus in Asia Minor)" (Metzger, p. 39).

That is an enormous amount of material, but it has a problem. As you can imagine, those handwritten copies do not perfectly agree with each other. A simple example is that some manuscripts of 1 John 1:4 read "that *your* joy may be full" (KJV; NKJV, italics added) and other manuscripts read "that *our* joy may be full" (NASB; NIV; ESV, italics added). Which word did John originally write, "your" or "our?"

If such an immense volume of the Greek New Testament is available, and those sources do not agree, how will the original wording be determined? The following chapters explain the various answers to that question. They are in chronological order.

Chapter 2

THE TEXTUS RECEPTUS

Until the invention of printing in about AD 1450, all copies of the New Testament were handwritten *manuscripts*. The first printed *text* of the Greek New Testament was published in 1516. Four men edited that initial printed text until it was named Textus Receptus in 1633.

Erasmus

Desiderius Erasmus (1466-1536), a Catholic priest and popular author, produced the first printed Greek text in March 1516. He published five editions, each an improvement over the last.

First Edition (1516) Erasmus's first edition included a Greek text, a Latin translation, a preface for each gospel and epistle, and notes. For example, in 1 Corinthians 14:19, he wrote, "St. Paul says he would rather speak five words with a reasonable meaning in them than ten thousand in an unknown tongue. They chant nowadays in our churches in what is an unknown tongue and nothing else, while you will not hear a sermon once in six months telling people to amend their lives" (Harrison, pp. 66-67). He was aided by two scholars, Nikolas Gerber and Ioannes Oecolampadius, who later became an aid to Zwingli. Oecolampadius looked up all the references to the Hebrew text of the Old Testament because Erasmus did not know Hebrew (White, p. 54).

As Erasmus traveled, he examined manuscripts in England and Europe (White, p. 54), "but only used a few" (Wilkerson in Fuller, p. 143). "The manuscripts which Erasmus used differed, for the most part, only in small and insignificant details from the bulk of cursive manuscripts" (Wilkinson in Fuller, p. 144). Erasmus did not use Codex D, which was available in Basel, Switzerland, where he did his work. The seven manuscripts he did use were 1^{eap} (entire NT, except Rev.), 1^{rK} (Rev), 2^e (Gospels), 2^{ap} (Acts and epistles), 4^{ap} (Paul's epistles), 7^p (Paul's epistles), 817 (Gospels). Five were from the 12th century and two were from the 15th century.

Erasmus only had one manuscript of Revelation (Minuscule 1^{rK}, later renamed 2814 by Aland). Since it lacked the last six verses of Revelation, he translated the Latin Vulgate version of those verses back into Greek. Thus, his editions have "book of life" instead of "tree of life" in Revelation 22:19. He also introduced material from the Vulgate elsewhere. For example, the words "And he trembling and astonished said, Lord, what wilt thou have me to do?" (Acts 9:6) are not in any Greek manuscript. Metzger states that Erasmus imported them from the Vulgate, but they are also found in Acts 22:10 (Metzger, p. 100). Revelation 17:8 has καιπερ εστιν (and yet is) instead of και παρεσται (and shall come). Revelation 17:4 has created the Greek word ἀκαθάρτητος (instead of τὰ ἀκάθαρτα). There is no such Greek word.

Erasmus began his work on the Greek New Testament in August 1515. It was published in Basel on March 1, 1516. The first edition was filled with "innumerable errors." Erasmus later said it was "thrown together rather than edited" (Aland, pp. 3-4).

Second Edition (1519). Erasmus used Minuscule 3 (the entire NT, except Revelation), changed the text in about 400 places (most, but not all, were typographical errors), and added a few erroneous readings. Martin Luther used this edition as the basis of his German translation.

Third Edition (1522) This edition differed from the second in 118 places. In 1521, Erasmus consulted Paulus Bombasius at the Vatican Library as to whether the Codex Vaticanus contained the Comma Johanneum (1 John 5:7-11). Bombasius supplied a transcript of 1 John 4:1–3 and 1 John 5:7–11 to show that it did not (from the article at https://en.wikipedia.org/wiki/Codex_Vaticanus). Nevertheless, when Erasmus was accused of omitting 1 John 5:7-8, he promised that if those verses could be found in any manuscript, he would include them in his next edition. When they were found in a single manuscript (61 from the 16th century), he did as he promised, inserting them in the third edition. In a lengthy footnote, he expressed his suspicion that the manuscript was prepared for him (Metzger, p. 101). Harrison says, "It got into the Latin by mistaking one of Cyprian's comments as part of the text of Scripture" (Harrison, p. 67). Tyndale used this edition to translate the first complete English translation ever printed (1526, Farstad, p. 11). It was the basis for Stephanus' editions in 1546 and 1549 and was used by the translators of the Geneva Bible (1557).

Fourth Edition (1527) The last two editions included some changes from the Complutensian Polyglot (Harrison, p. 67). A polyglot contains several languages. The Complutensian Polyglot was produced at Alcala in Spain. It was the first printed polyglot of the entire Bible, published in 1520. The Hebrew, Septuagint, Greek, and Latin Vulgate texts appeared alongside each other. Based on the Complutensian Polyglot, Erasmus altered Revelation in about 90 passages (Metzger, p. 102).

Fifth Edition (1535) Wilkinson says that if Erasmus had desired a transcript of Vaticanus, he could have had it (Bissell's *Origin of the Bible*, p. 84; see Wilkerson in Fuller, p. 170). In 1533, Juan Ginés de Sepúlveda of the Vatican Library "cross-checked all places where Erasmus's New Testament differed from the Vulgate and supplied Erasmus with 365 readings" (taken from https://en.wikipedia.org/wiki/Codex_Vaticanus; Tregelles. *On the Printed Text of the Greek Testament*, p. 22). The only one we know about is the name of the island in Acts 27:16, καυδα (Cauda), not κλαυδα (Clauda), but he did not make the change. (The current edition of the TR contains κλαυδα, but the Westcott-Hort text, the NIV, and the ESV have καυδα.) The fifth edition also discarded the Vulgate.

Simon Colinaeus

A printer in Paris, Simon Colinaeus (1480-1556), published an edition of the Greek New Testament in 1534. It contained "numerous differences" from Erasmus's five constantly revised editions because of the use of the Complutensian Polyglot and other manuscripts (Aland, p. 6). This work was never reprinted.

Stephanus

Robert I. Estienne (1503-1559; a.k.a. Latin, Stephanus and Stephens), son-in-law of Colinaeus, was also a printer in Paris. He was a Catholic who became a Protestant late in his life. As a result of the opposition he received from Catholic theologians due to his printing of Bibles with commentaries, he and his family fled to Geneva, where he published many of John

Calvin's works. He published four editions of the Greek New Testament in 1546, 1549, 1550, and 1551.

First Edition (1546) Stephanus's first edition was printed in Paris. It was largely a compound of the Complutensian Polyglot and Erasmus's additions (Carson, p. 36).

Second Edition (1549) Like his first edition, Stephanus's second edition was also printed in Paris and was essentially a combination of the Complutensian Polyglot and Erasmus's additions.

Third Edition (1550) In 1538, Francis I requested that Stephanus put a copy of every Greek book he had ever printed in the royal library. Hence, his third edition, also printed in Paris, was called the royal edition. It followed the text of Erasmus's 1527 and 1535 editions. Stephanus also included variant readings from the Complutensian Polyglot and 15 Greek manuscripts, including minuscules 4, 5, 6, 2817, 8, 9, Codex Bezae (D), and Codex Regius (L). This has been called the first critical edition (Carson, p. 36).

Fourth Edition (1551) Having fled to Geneva in 1550, Stephanus's fourth edition was printed in Geneva. It was a reprint of the 1550 text. For the first time, verse divisions were included in the text. The same verse divisions are used today. Metzger says, "It has often been stated that Stephanus marked the verse divisions while journeying 'on horseback' and some of the infelicitous divisions arose from the jogging of the horse that bumped his pen into the wrong place. Stephanus' son asserts that his father did the work while on a journey from Paris to Lyons, but the most natural inference is that the task was accomplished while resting at the inns along the way" (Metzger, p. 104).

Beza

Theodore Beza (1519-1605), the successor to John Calvin (1565-1604), published nine editions of the Greek text, but only four of them were "independent editions (1565, 1582, 1588-89, and 1598)" (Metzger, p. 105). He "drew upon Stephanus's listings of variant readings and added many more of his own, drawing from important manuscripts in his possession. He also immediately placed the information on the variant readings under the text, using the same style as modern critical editors (White, p. 65). At the time, he owned Codex Bezea and Codex Claromontanus but "made relatively little use of them" (Metzger, p. 105).

"The translators of the King James version relied largely on Beza's editions of 1588-1589 and 1598" (Carson, p. 36). In their Preface to *The Greek Text" The Greek Text Underlying the English Authorized Version 1611* (KJV), the Trinitarian Bible Society says, "The editions of Beza, particularly that of 1598, and the two last editions of Stephens, were the chief sources used for the English Authorized Version of 1611."

The Elzevirs Printers

Bonaventure Elzevir (1583-1652) and his nephew Abraham Elzevir (1592-1652) published editions of the Greek text at Leyden in 1624, 1633, and 1641. In the Latin introduction of their 1633 edition, they said that this text was the *"textum ab omnibus receptum"* ("text received by all"). That expression was shortened to Textus Receptus or Received Text (Farstad, p. 107). In their Preface to *The Greek Text* (see the previous paragraph), the Trinitarian Bible Society says, "The editions of Stephens, Beza, and the Elzevirs [that is, the Textus Receptus] all present substantially the same text and the variations are not of great significance and rarely affect the sense."

Later, the name Textus Receptus was applied to the Stephens text of 1550. Hence, the Greek text of the King James Version has been referred to as the Textus Receptus (Farstad, p. 107), even though the term was not coined until over a hundred years after the first Greek text was printed and *more than twenty years after the King James Version* was published.

Summary: The first printed Greek text of the New Testament was edited by four men, after which it became the primary text for the translation of the King James Version, and later, it was known as the Textus Receptus.

Although they are all basically the same, there have been about 30 editions of the Textus Receptus (Pickering and Freitas, p. 179).

The Textus Receptus was used for the translation of the King James Version (1611, 1613, 1629, 1664, 1701, 1744, 1762, 1769, 1850), Tyndale New Testament (1526-1530), Cloverdale Bible (1535), the Geneva Bible (1560-1664), Bishops' Bible (1568), Douay-Rheims Bible (1582, 1610, 1749-52), English Dort Version (1657), the New King James (1982), the Modern English Version (2014), and many others.

A free copy of the Textus Receptus is at e-sword.net. For more information on the Textus Receptus, see the article at the website https://www.skypoint.com/members/waltzmn/TR.html.

Nevertheless, the Textus Receptus has been severely criticized. The criticism started early. Even before Erasmus published his work, a man named Dorp wrote to him, "For it is not reasonable that the whole church, which is always used this edition [the Latin Vulgate] and still both approves and uses it, should for all the centuries have been wrong.... If, however, they contend that a sentence as rendered by the Latin translator varies in point of truth from the Greek manuscript, at that point, I bid the Greeks goodbye and cleave to the Latin" (White, p. 56).

In an August 13, 1521 letter to Peter Beberius, Erasmus wrote, "I did my best with the New Testament, but it provoked endless quarrels. Edward Lee pretended to have discovered 300 errors. They appointed a commission that professed to have found barrels of them. Every dinner table rang with the blunders of Erasmus. I requested particulars and could not have them" (Froude, p. 267, cited by Wilkerson in Fuller, p. 143).

A typical comment today is like that of Carson, who says it was based on "a small number of haphazardly collected and relatively late minuscule manuscripts. In about a dozen places, no known Greek manuscript witness attests its reading" (Carson, p. 36). Eventually, the Textus Receptus became the text *not* received by all! What happened? That is the subject of the next Chapter.

Chapter 3

THE WESTCOTT-HORT TEXT

After 1633, the Textus Receptus was the "Received Text," but it was criticized. Over the next approximately 250 years, three developments led to its dethronement: the emergence of textual criticism, the discovery of two Greek manuscripts, and the Westcott-Hort Textual Theory.

Textual Criticism

Secular Textual criticism is a process used to determine the text's original wording. It originated among the ancient Greeks. As Metzger explains, many versions of it developed because those who recited the Iliad and the Odyssey in public occasionally altered the text to suit the occasion. There were even "City Editions." As a result, a critical study of Homer was pursued at the library in Alexandria. Zenodotus of Ephesus (*ca.* 325-*ca.* 234 BC), a librarian at Alexandria, was the first to compare many manuscripts of the *Iliad* and the *Odyssey* to restore the original text. He made four kinds of corrections: 1) He eliminated verses he regarded as suspicious. 2) He marked some verses as doubtful but left them in his editions. 3) He transposed the order of some verses. 4) He introduced some new readings (Metzger, p. 149).

In an article on textual criticism in general, rather than specifically on New Testament manuscripts, the *Encyclopedia Britannica* provides an overview of the history of textual criticism (see the article at https://www.britannicacom/topic/textual-criticism/History-of-textual-criticism). Here are some of the highlights gleaned from that article.

"The systematic study and practice of the subject [of textual criticism] originated in the 3rd century BCE with the Greek scholars of Alexandria…. The aim of the librarians … was to collect and catalogue every extant Greek book and to produce critical editions of the most important ones together with textual and interpretative commentaries…. The copyist was expected to reproduce his exemplar [the MS being copied] as exactly as he could, and corrections were based on comparison with other copies, not on the unaided conjectural sagacity of the scribe. Such was the practice of the best monastic scriptoria."

The Britannica article then jumps to 1350, when, to make material from "classical antiquity" readable, "texts were corrected freely and often arbitrarily by scholars, copyists, and readers…. For the most part, the correction of texts was a purely subjective display of taste, sometimes right but much more often wrong, and resting as a rule on nothing more solid than a superficial sense of elegance." The Britannica article says advances took place "slowly and unsystematically…. The accepted method was to correct the text (i.e., the text of the last printed edition) … with the aid of the manuscript and printed sources and the critic's own ingenuity."

The Britannica article adds that "the first important departure from this pattern" was by J. J. Scaliger (1577). ["He was the first to lay down and apply sound rules of criticism and emendation, and to change textual criticism from a series of haphazard guesses into a 'rational procedure subject to fixed laws' (Mark Pattison);" see the entire article at https://www.geni.com/people/Joseph-Scaliger/6000000043234717569].

The Britannica article explains that Scaliger used "the genealogical method," that is "all the extant copies are derived from a lost manuscript."

Scripture The Britannica article says, "Meanwhile, New Testament criticism was being developed on scientific and historical lines." The article lists J. A. Bengel, J. J. Wettstein, and J. J. Griesbach, but others need to be added.

John Mill (1645–1707) collated textual variants from 82 Greek manuscripts. Daniel Whitby (1638–1725) attacked Mill's work, insisting that the text of the New Testament had never been corrupted and that the text of the Textus Receptus equated the autographs.

Johann Albrecht Bengel (1687-1752) was the first to categorize manuscripts into text types, a group of manuscripts that tend to agree with one another. In 1740, he divided manuscripts into Asiatic (later) and African (ancient). He also favored the principle that "the more difficult reading is, the stronger."

Johann Jakob Wettstein (1693-1754) produced an apparatus (footnotes listing various readings) fuller than any previous edition. He introduced the designation of ancient manuscripts with Roman capital letters and the later ones with Arabic numerals.

J. S. Selmer (1725-1791) divided the New Testament manuscripts into three groups in 1767. He expanded Bengel's two groups (Epp in Black, p. 36).

J. J. Griesbach (1745-1812) combined the principles of Bengel and Wettstein. He enlarged the apparatus by considering more citations from ancient authors and translations. He categorized Greek manuscripts into three groups, known as "families" or "text types": Western, Alexandrian, and Byzantine Recensions. (An individual manuscript may have one text type, or it may have several. If it has several, it is said to be "mixed.")

Karl Lachmann (1793-1851) utilized the oldest known Greek and Latin manuscripts to create a text that he believed would have been read around AD 380. Burgon says he "virtually originated the principle of the recurring exclusively to a few ancient documents to the exclusion of the many" (Burgon, *The Revision*, p. 21). "His edition of the Greek New Testament (1831; 2nd ed. 1842–50) was intended primarily as a vindication of the principles of Bentley and Bengel and a demonstration that the *textus receptus* must be finally rejected" (from the Britannica article mentioned above). By the way, he invented the priority of Mark.

These men are important because, as Moses Silva, who is "an unrepentant and unshaken Hortian," says, Hort was not an innovator. "His starting point was the achievement of previous scholars, preeminently the work of Bengel and Griesbach, but closer to him in time advances made by Lachmann, Tischendorf, and Tregelles" (Silva in Black, pp. 142-143).

Two Manuscripts

Sinaiticus Constantin von Tischendorf (1815-1874) spent his career at the University of Leipzig, where J. G. B. Winer influenced him to use the oldest manuscripts to compile a text of the New Testament as closely as possible to the original. "His first major accomplishment was to decipher Codex Ephraemi Syri Rescriptus (C), a Greek New Testament manuscript written in the fifth century but later washed clean (i.e., a palimpsest) and its text replaced with treaties by the Syrian Church Father Ephraem.... He also discovered on his travels in the Orient, sponsored by Czar Nicholas I, numerous other uncial manuscripts (twenty-one, to be precise).... He further made a careful examination of a number (twenty-three?) of other neglected uncials" (Aland, p. 11). He is the one who discovered Codex Sinaiticus.

In 1844, while visiting St. Catherine's Monastery at the base of Mount Sinai, Tischendorf discovered 43 parchment sheets containing an ancient copy of the Greek Old Testament in a trash basket filled with trash to start fires. The monks gave Tischendorf the 43 pages as a gift.

In 1853, Tischendorf revisited the monastery but made no discoveries. He returned in January 1859. On the last day of his visit, he was shown a Greek manuscript of the complete New Testament and parts of the Old Testament dating to the 4th century. He persuaded the monks to present the manuscript to Tsar Alexander II of Russia, who paid to publish it (1862). It is appropriately named Sinaiticus. In 1933, Russia sold the Sinaiticus to the British Museum for 100,000 pounds.

Vaticanus There was another manuscript stored in the Vatican, at least since 1481, appropriately named Codex Vaticanus.

"Simply because of their antiquity, many scholars regarded them [Sinaiticus (א) and Vaticanus (B)] as better copies of the original autographs and, thus, more authoritative than the later manuscripts on which the Textus Receptus was based" (Farstad, p. 107).

Westcott and Hort

Their Book Westcott and Hort published their Greek text in 1881. A year later, they published *Introduction and Appendix*, which explained their theory. They both claim responsibility for the content of the second volume, but Hort wrote it. Since Hort was the author, his name alone will be in the following references. Page numbers after his name are from Volume II. From their *Introduction and Appendix*, the following is a brief summary of their theory regarding the Greek text. (See Appendix I for a more detailed overview.)

Methods The Westcott and Hort methods of textual criticism include: 1) Internal evidence of readings, that is, determining the corruption in the text made by the copyist (Hort, pp. 19-30). 2) Internal evidence of documents, that is, determining the trustworthiness of the individual document (Hort, pp. 30-39). "The most prominent fact known about a manuscript is its date" (Hort, p. 31). 3) Genealogical evidence, that is, determining the genealogical tree (historical relationships) of the manuscript (Hort, pp. 39-66).

In all capital letters, Hort declares, "ALL TRUSTWORTHY RESTORATION OF CORRUPTED TEXT IS FOUNDED ON THE STUDY OF THEIR HISTORY" (Hort, p. 40). He explains that the history of a manuscript is gained by comparing it with other manuscripts (Hort, p. 46) and the clearest evidence is the presence of "conflated" readings, that is, a combination of readings from two other manuscripts (Hort, p. 53). He claims, "The preservation of a comparatively small number of documents would probably suffice for the complete restoration of an autographed text" (Hort, p. 57). Yet, he says, "Personal judgment inevitably takes a large part in the final decision," and "personal discernment would seem the sure ground for confidence" (Hort, p. 65).

Sources Hort discusses the Greek manuscripts (Hort, pp. 74-78), versions and translations (Hort, pp. 78-86), and Church Fathers' quotations (Hort, pp. 87-89).

Text types According to Westcott and Hort, there are four text types (Hort, pp. 120-135). Text types are an important concept in textual criticism.

1. The Western text type is characterized by *changes* in words, clauses, and even sentences "with astonishing freedom" (Hort, p. 122) and *additions* (Hort, p. 123).

2. The Neutral text type is the purest. "That a purer text should be preserved at Alexandria than in other churches would not in itself be surprising. There, if anywhere, it was to be anticipated that, owing to the proximity of an exact grammatical school, a more than usual watchfulness over the transmission of the writings of apostles and apostolic men would be suggested and alive, but the rapid total extinction of comparatively pure text in all of the places would undeniably be a riddle hard of a solution" (Hort, p. 127). The Neutral text type is in Vaticanus, Sinaiticus, L, 1, and 33. The "four great early Bibles [are] ℵBAC" (Hort, p. 141).

3. The Alexandrian text type is derived from other manuscripts originating from Alexandria. "The only documentary authority ... [is] quotations by Origen, Cyril of Alexandria, and occasionally other Alexandrian Fathers and two principal Egyptian versions, especially that of Lower Egypt" (Hort, pp. 130-131).

4. The Syrian text type is a late, edited text type. Hort says, "New interpolations ... are abundant, most of them being due to harmonic or other assimilation, fortunately, capricious, and incomplete" (Hort, p. 135). [Note carefully: Syrian text type is another name for Griesbach's Byzantine text type.]

Conclusion When Westcott and Hort considered their 1) methods of textual criticism (the variances, the document, and the genealogy), 2) the applications of their method to the Greek manuscripts, versions, and the Fathers, 3) resulting in four text types (Western; Neutral; Alexandrian; and Syrian), their theory boiled down to two basic concepts, the inferiority of the Syrian text type (their name for the Byzantine text type) and the superiority of what they call the Neutral text type (Vaticanus, Sinaiticus, etc.).

Hort said there is a "strong indication" that the Syrian text was deliberately revised. "The final process was apparently completed by 350 or thereabouts. At what date, between 250 and 350, the first process took place is impossible to say with confidence.... Whether, however, Lusianus [martyred in 311] took a leading part in the earlier stage of Syrian revision or not, it may be assigned with more probability either to his generation or that which immediately followed than to any other" (Hort, pp. 136-137). Also, "The first point to decide with respect to each reading is whether it is Pre-Syrian or not" and if it is, it is "to be rejected at once as proven to have a relatively late origin" (Hort, p. 163). In short, the Syrian text type *is a late, edited text type* and, therefore, *inferior.*

The first evidence that the Syrian text type is "late" (compared to the Western and Neutral text types) is the presence of conflated readings. Hort gives eight examples of conflated readings in the New Testament: Mark 6:33, 8:26, 9:38, 9:49 and Luke 9:10, 11:54, 12:18, 24:53 (Hort, pp. 95-107).

A second piece of evidence that the Syrian text type is late is the writing of the Fathers. Origen does not exhibit any "clear and tangible traces of the Syrian text" (Hort, p. 114). "An overwhelming proportion of the variants common to the great mass of cursive and late uncial Greek MSS are identical with the readings followed by Chrysostom" (ob. 407)" (Hort, p. 91). In other words, the fact that the Syrian text is not found in Origen (AD 250) but in Chrysostom (AD 407) demonstrates that it is a late text. "It follows that all distinctively Syrian readings may be set aside at once as certainly originating after the middle of the third century, and, therefore, as far as transmission is concerned, corruptions of the apostolic text" (Hort, p. 117).

A third piece of evidence that the Syrian text type is late is the translations. "The only versions, besides the Italian and the Vulgate Latin, in which the complete Syrian text is clearly and widely represented are definitely known to be the fourth century or later centuries, that is, the Gothic, Aethiopic, Armenian, and Harklean Syriac" (Hort, p. 159).

Another indication that the Syrian text type is late is the presence of individual readings. "The first point to decide concerning each reading is whether it is Pre-Syrian or not," and if it is, it is "to be rejected at once as proven to have a relatively late origin" (Hort, p. 163).

To summarize, the Syrian text type is a late, edited text type. The proofs are: 1) Conflated readings. 2) No ante-Nicene Father quotes the Syrian text type. 3) ancient translations. 4) The readings that claim to be original disappear compared to other readings. The bottom line: "All distinctively Syrian readings must be at once rejected" (Hort, p. 119).

On the other hand, "B very far exceeds all other documents in the neutrality of text ... and a long interval after B, but hardly a less interval before all other MSS stands א." As for other manuscripts, the ones having the "most Alexandrian readings usually have also [the] most neutral readings" (Hort, p. 171). "It is our belief (1) that readings of א B should be accepted as the true reading until strong internal evidence is found to the contrary, and (2) that no reading of ℵ B can safely be rejected absolutely, though it is sometimes right to place them only on an alternative footing, especially where they received no support from Versions or Fathers" (Hort, p. 225). In short, the Neutral text type is the far superior text type.

As you can see, Hort's explanation is complex. Pickering, an expert in textual criticism, said, "I have read every word of Hort's 'Introduction,' all 324 difficult pages of it [I had to read some pages two or three times to be more or less sure that I had understood]" (Pickering, p. 24).

In his book *The Identity of the New Testament Text IV* (2014), Pickering summarizes Hort's view. He says Hort's basic approach starts by assuming that the New Testament is to be treated like any other book. Hort applies the principles of textual criticism used for all ancient texts. No new principles are needed. There are no signs of deliberate falsification for dogmatic purposes. Such a position allowed Hort to employ the family-tree method, also known as genealogy, which involves analyzing the ancestors of the texts. The genealogical method enabled Hort to reduce the massive number of manuscripts to four voices: neutral, Alexandrian, Western, and Syrian, thus justifying handling the Syrian text type as one witness.

Pickering quotes Colwell's explanation of Hort's genealogical method, which he used to reduce the vast majority of New Testament manuscripts to a single one. "As the justification for the rejection of the majority, Westcott and Hort found the possibilities of the genealogical method invaluable. Suppose there are only ten copies of a document and nine are all copied from one. Then, the majority can be safely rejected. Or suppose that the nine were copied from a lost manuscript and the lost manuscript and the other one were copies from the original; then the majority vote would not outweigh that of the minority. These are the arguments with which W. and H. opened their discussion of the genealogical method.... They show clearly that most manuscripts are not **necessarily** to be preferred as correct. It is this *a priori* possibility Westcott and Hort used to demolish the argument based on the numerical superiority of the adherents of the Textus Receptus" (Colwell, "Genealogical Method," p, 111, bold print his; cited by Pickering, p. 19).

Pickering explains that by justifying the handling of the mass of late manuscripts as one text, Hort proves that the late manuscripts are inferior and even inconsequential. His first proof is conflated readings. His second proof is quotations from the Ante-Nicene Fathers. His third argument is based on internal witnesses, and his explanation for how those readings came into existence is that there was an organized revision of the text, probably by Lucian, who died in AD 311 (Pickering, 2014, pp.18-26).

In his book, *The Revised Version of the First Three Gospels Considered in Its Bearings upon the Record of Our Lord's Words and of Incidents in His Life* (1882), Frederick Charles Cook said, "I will ask the reader to compare these statements with the views set forth, authoritatively and repeatedly, by Dr. Hort in his 'Introduction.' Especially in reference to the supreme excellence and unrivaled authority of the text of B—with which, indeed, the Greek text of the Westcott and Hort is, with some unimportant exceptions, substantially identical, coinciding in more than nine-tenths of the passages which, as materially affecting the character of the synoptic Gospels, I have to discuss" (Cook, p. 6, cited by Wilkinson in *Which Bible?* p. 211).

Indeed, Hort himself wrote, "So many readings of B by itself commend themselves on their own merit that it would be harsh to reject any hastily, though undoubtedly not a few have to be rejected at last" (Hort, p. 238). Hoskier concluded, "Westcott and Hort's text is practically B" (Hoskier, *Genesis of the Versions*, p. 416, cited by Wilkinson in Fuller, p. 212).

Summary: Westcott and Hort dethroned the Syrian text and enthroned the Neutral text, which rests on two manuscripts, Vaticanus and Sinaiticus.

All of Westcott and Hort's works, including their Greek text, are available at http://www.westcotthort.com/bookshelf.html.

Chapter 4

THE TRADITIONAL TEXT

Westcott and Hort had a contemporary opponent named John Burgon (1813-1888). Burgon graduated from Oxford, spent his adult life at Oxford as a Fellow of Oriel College, was vicar at St. Mary's (the University Church), and was Gresham Professor of Divinity. In 1876, he was made Dean of Chichester, an ecclesiastical position, not an academic title, and, as a result, is known as Dean Burgon. Burgon was "an ardent defender" of the text type found in most Greek New Testament manuscripts. He named this text type the Traditional Text (Hills, Introduction to *The Last Twelve Verses of Mark* by Burgon, p. 20; hereafter Introduction). Note carefully: The text type Burgeon called the Traditional, Griesbach called the Byzantine, and Westcott and Hort called the Syrian. It has also been referred to as the Majority Text.

Burgon devoted the last 30 years of his life to textual criticism. "In 1860, for instance, he traveled to the Vatican Library to personally examine Codex B. And in 1862, he traveled to Mt. Sinai to inspect the many manuscripts there. Later, he made several tours of European libraries, examining and collating NT manuscripts everywhere he went. At the same time, he was compiling his massive index of the NT Quotations in the Church Fathers, which is deposited in the British Museum, but never published" (from Edward Hill's article on John Burgon in *The Encyclopedia of Christianity*, cited by Green, p. 17).

Burgon's books on textual criticism include *The Last Twelve Verses of Mark* (1871) and *The Revision Revised* (1883, a reprint of three articles in the *Quarterly Review* against the Revised Version of 1881 and a reply to an article written against those three articles). He amassed material for a definitive defense of the Traditional Text but did not live to complete the project. After his death, E. Miller pieced together the fragments Burgon left and published them in 1896 in two volumes: *The Causes of Corruption of the Traditional Text of the Holy Gospels* and *The Traditional Text of the Holy Gospels Vindicated and Established.* In 1978, D. A. Waite (Th.M., Dallas Theological Seminary; Ph.D., Purdue) founded The Dean Burgon Society (http://deanburgonsociety.org).

The Last Twelve Verses of Mark

In Chapter 1, Burgon states the case for the last twelve verses of Mark, namely that the manuscript evidence is overwhelming, that no church Father says the verses are suspicious, and that the argument derived from internal consideration is baseless (Burgon, p. 79).

In Chapter 2, Burgon shows that the rejection of the last twelve is recent. Mill (1707), Bengel (1734), Weston (1751-2), and Birch (1788) accepted the passage, and Griesbach (1796-1806) was the first to insist that the concluding verses of Mark are spurious (Burgon, pp. 83-84). Codex B was the solitary manuscript omitting the passage (Burgon, p. 85; Codex ℵ had not yet been discovered). Lachmann originated the new principle of deference to a few arbitrarily selected ancient documents (1842), followed by Tischendorf, Tregelles, Dean Alford, and Westcott and Hort (Burgon, pp. 86, 91),

In Chapter 3, Burgon appeals to the early Fathers. 1) Papias (AD 100) says Justin drank poison (Mk. 16:18). 2) Justin Martyr (AD 151) quotes part of Mark 16:20. 3) Irenaeus (AD 180) quotes Mark 16:19. 4) Hippolytus (AD 190-227) quotes Mark 16:17-18 and alludes to verse 19. 5) Vincentius quotes two verses from Mark 16:9-20. 6) The Gospel of Nicodemus (3rd century) contains Mark 16:15, 16, 17, and 18. 7) Apostolic Constitution (3rd or 4th century) quotes Mark 16:16. 8 & 9) Eusebius (AD 325) "largely" discusses these verses and records Marinus asking a question about them. 10) Aphraates (AD 337) quotes Mark 16:16, 17, 18. 11) Ambrose (AD 374-397) quotes verse 15 four times, verses 16, 17, and 18 three times, and verse 20 once. 12) Chrysostom (AD 400) quotes Mark 16:19, 20, adding, "This is the end of the Gospel," and elsewhere has an unmistakable reference to Mark 16:9. 13. Jerome (AD 331-420), although supposed to be a witness for the opposite side, put these verses in the Vulgate. 14) Augustine (AD 395-430) quotes these verses and discusses them repeatedly. 15 & 16) Nestorius quotes Mark 16:20 and Cyril of Alexandria, except for this quotation, adding a few words of his own (AD 430). 17) Victor of Antioch (AD 425) gives the most conclusive testimony (see Chapter 5). 18). Hesychius of Jerusalem (uncertain date, maybe the 6th century) appeals to Mark 16:19 and quotes it at length (see Chapter 5). 19) *Synopsis Scripturae Sacrae* (an ancient work much older than any of the late uncials) rehearses in detail the contents of Mark 16:9-20. Burgon mentions seven others that could be cited and points out he has cited three from the second century and four from the third century, etc. (at least seven are more ancient than the oldest of the extant Gospels), who come from every part of the ancient church from Antioch to Rome.

In Chapter 4, Burgon examines the early versions. The following contains Mark 16:9-20. 1) the Syriac Peshitta (2nd century). 2) Curetonian Syriac (3rd century, vastly more ancient than either B or ℵ). 3) Philoxenian Syriac is a revision of the revised translation. 4) the Vulgate (A.D. 384). 5) Vetus Itala (2nd century), an old Latin version of African origin. 6) Gothic (A.D. 350). 7 & 8) Egyptian versions" Memphitic (4th or 5th century) and Thebaic (3rd century). These versions are from Syria, Macedonia, Africa, Italy, Palestine, and Egypt.

In Chapter 5, Burgon demonstrates that the alleged hostile evidence is the product of the critics' imagination. Critics, such as Tregelles and Tischendorf, claimed that Mark 16:9-20 is absent from Eusebius, Gregory of Nyssa [AD 335-395], Victor of Antioch, Severus of Antioch, Jerome, etc. Burgon responds that Clement of Alexandria does not refer to the last Chapter of Matthew's or Mark's Gospel. Clement of Rome does not quote from Mark's gospel at all! Burgon then examines the ancient authors involved one by one. He concedes that at the time of Eusebius, there must have been many copies of Mark's Gospel that were without the 12 concluding verses (Burgon, p. 129), but see his explanation of Eusebius' quotation (Burgon, pp. 119-129, 142) and Jerome's inclusion of these verses in the Vulgate (Burgon, p. 134).

In Chapter 6, Burgon shows that the manuscript testimony is overwhelmingly in favor of Mark 16:9-20 (this is Part I). Those verses are not in B or ℵ, but in 18 other uncials and about 600 cursives, including A, C, and D^2 (Burgon, p. 149).

In Chapter 7, Burgon shows that the manuscript testimony is overwhelmingly in favor of Mark 16:9-20 (this is Part II). ℵ and B omit "in

Ephesus" in Ephesians 1:1, but they "stand quite alone among MSS" (Burgon, p. 169). According to Tischendorf, the evidence for the omission is that Marcion (AD 130-140) did not find the words "at Ephesus" in his copy. The same is true of Origen (AD 185-254); Basil the Great (who died in AD 379) affirmed that those words were lacking in *old* copies (Burgon, p. 171).

The basis for saying Marcion omitted these verses is that Tertullian said certain heretics (he specifies Marcion) had given Ephesians the unauthorized title of "the epistle to the Laodiceans," which proves that Tischendorf's inclusion is invalid (Burgon, pp. 171-172). Epiphanius, who lived about a century and a half later than Marcion and who "for many years made Marcion's work his study, says that Ephesians is one of the ten epistles of Paul, which Marcion retained and the epistle to the Laodiceans Marcion put as number eleven, which means that Tischendorf's point is without foundation (Burgon, pp. 172-174). Burgon concludes that both Origen and Basil are just saying that "in Ephesus" is omitted in some copies (Burgon, pp. 174-177). Furthermore, the words "in Ephesus" are in all copies (except ℵ and B), all versions, and if the words are omitted, the text is "all but *unintelligible*" (Burgon, p. 177, italics his).

In Chapter 8, Burgon shows, "*The twelve verses ... are found in every copy of the Gospels in existence with the exception of Codices B and ℵ*" (Burgon, p. 194, italics his).

In Chapter 9, Burgon argues that internal evidence demonstrates the reverse of the unfavorable treatment of these verses. He discusses style and phraseology. He points out how "exceedingly dissimilar" is the style of Revelation and the Gospel of John (Burgon, p. 220). The same is true in Matthew, Luke, and the Gospel of John (Burgon, p. 172). Moreover, the style of Mark 1:9-20 is not different from that of Mark 16:9-20 (Burgon, pp. 223-224; see also pp. 261-270). After examining in detail words and phrases in Mark and Luke, Burgon concludes, "The grounds of suspicion vanish out of sight" (Burgon, p. 250). Tregelles wrote, "I am well aware that arguments on *style are* often very fallacious and that *by themselves* they prove very little" (Tregelles, italics his, cited by Burgon, p. 249).

In Chapter 10, Burgon demonstrates that the lectionaries are "absolutely decisive as to the genuineness of these verses" (Burgon, pp. 271-291). "It is, in fact, universally received that the Eastern Church has, from a period of even Apostolic antiquity, enjoyed a lectionary—or established system of Scripture lessons—of her own" (Burgon, p. 273). "It is at least quite certain that in the ivth century (if not long before), there existed a known Lectionary system alike in the Church of the East and the West."

Cyril of Jerusalem (AD 348) speaks of "appointed lessons." In the latter part of the 4th century, Chrysostom spoke of the "sections of the gospel" that the congregation was to hear in church. Eusebius, Origen, and Clemens of Alexandria habitually used a technical term for ecclesiastical lection (Burgon, pp. 275-276). Hesychius (d. *ca* 450) said the conclusion of Mark's gospel was one of the lections for Easter (Burgon, p. 284).

Burgon concludes. "That Lessons from the New Testament were publicly read in the assemblies of the faithful according to a definite scheme, and on an established system, *at least* as early as the fourth century,—has been shown to be a plain historical fact" (Burgon, p. 287, italics his). Then, he again cites Cyril at Jerusalem, Chrysostom at Antioch, Constantinople, and Augustine in Africa He adds, "In other words, there is found to have been *at least at that time* fully established throughout the churches of Christendom a lectionary, which seems to have been essentially one and the same in the West and the East" (Burgon, p. 287, italics his).

In Chapter 11, Burgon says the explanation for the omission of Mark 16:9-20 is that the lectionary concluded with Mark 16:8 (Burgon, p. 293). He contends that where the lectionaries stop explains the omission in numerous cases in the New Testament.

In Chapter 12, Burgon summarizes the evidence. He repeats that the last 12 verses of Mark are in every known manuscript except two, B and ℵ, and in B, there is a vacant column for it, *"the only vacant column in the whole codex"* (Burgon 331, italics his).

For a detailed discussion of *The Last Twelve Verses of Mark*, see https://cdn.ymaws.com/www.tbsbibles.org/resource/collection/156A9AA2-2086-4C4E-BE0A-08A4508415DA/The-Last-Twelve-Verses-of-Mark-16.pdf. For a more recent defense of this passage, see William R. Farmer, *The Last Twelve Verses of Mark*. New York: Cambridge University, 1974.

The Revision Revised

Burgon's *The Revision Revised* is a reprint of three articles that first appeared in the *Quarterly Review* and an answer to a pamphlet written against two of his articles.

The first article, "The New Greek Text," analyzes the Westcott-Hort Greek text and B and ℵ in particular. Burgon shows the fallacy of following the new Greek text in passage after passage. In the process, he says, "Textus Receptus needs Correction" (Burgon, 21 Fn.) and "In Not A Few Particulars, The Textus Receptus Calls For Revision (Burgon, p. 107, capitals his). "We know that Origen in Palestine, Lucian at Antioch, Hesychius in Egypt, 'revised' the text of the NT" (Burgon, p. 29). He says his book *The Last Twelve Verses of Mark*, which was written a decade before, "has never yet been answered" (Burgon, p. 36). Compared to the Traditional Text, B omitted 2877 words from the four Gospels alone, ℵ eliminated 3455 words, and D eradicated 3704 (Burgon, p. 75).

The second article, "The New English Version," critiques The Revised Version, the English translation based on the Westcott-Hort Greek text. Again, as in the previous article, Burgon examines passage after passage. This time, he does it to highlight the inaccuracy of the Revised Version's translation. Burgon calls for applying the science of textual criticism, which he says has not yet been done. Such an endeavor would include thoroughly studying the manuscripts, versions, lectionaries, and the Fathers (Burgon, p. 125; see also p. 227). The Revised Version has a note on Revelation 13:19 about the 616 reading. Burgon points out that such a reading is only in one uncial, one cursive, and one Father, and Irenaeus (AD 170) rejected it. Irenaeus stated that 666 was found in all the best and oldest manuscripts (Burgon also mentioned others who accepted 666, pp. 135-136).

The third article, "Westcott and Hort's New Textual Theory," evaluates the application of textual criticism. In the process, Burgon makes statements concerning ℵ, B, the Traditional Text, and the proper method of textual criticism.

Burgon quotes Tischendorf's description of his discovery of ℵ. "I perceive a large and wide basket full of old parchment, and the librarian told me that two heaps like this had already been committed to the flames"

(Tischendorf, cited by Burgon, p. 343 fn.). Burgon claims B, ℵ, and D result from "arbitrary and reckless *recension*" (Burgon, p. 248, italics his). B and ℵ were "deliberately condemned" by the four Patriarchs of Eastern Christendom (Burgon, p. 286). In the Gospels, B has 589 readings particular to itself, affecting 850 words, and ℵ has 1460 such readings, affecting 2640 words (Burgon, p. 319). After observing that it took them 30 years of laborious research to develop only eight conflated readings, Burgon examines all eight in detail (Burgon, pp. 258-262).

Burgon contends, "A majority of extant documents is more likely to represent the majority of ancestral documents than *vice versa* (Burgon, p. 254, italics his). Assuming the Westcott and Hort view that the Traditional Text was fabricated at Antioch about AD 350, then for 1532 years (350 to 1882), the *Antiochian* standard has been faithfully retained and transmitted and "it will be impossible to assign any valid reason why the inspired Original itself the apostolic standard should not have been faithfully transmitted and obtained from the *Apostolic* age to the Antiochian" (Burgon, p. 296).

Burgon says again that the Traditional Text (TR) requires revision in many of its lesser details is "undeniable" (Burgon, p. 209). The only trustworthy method of textual criticism is to "ascertain WHICH FORM OF THE TEXT ENJOYS THE EARLIEST, THE FULLEST, THE WIDEST, THE MOST RESPECTABLE, AND—ABOVE ALL THINGS—THE MOST VARIED ATTESTATION" (Burgon, p. 339, all capitals his). "If several Fathers, living in different parts of ancient Christendom, all observed to recognize the words, or to quote them in the same way,—we have met all the additional confirmation we ordinarily require" (Burgon,

p. 340). "The method we plead for consists merely in a loyal recognition of the whole of the Evidence," setting off one authority against another, laboriously and impartially, and adjudicating fairly between them *all*. Even so hopelessly corrupt a document as Clement of Alexander's copy of the Gospels proves to have been—(described at pp. 326-331)—is by no means without critical value" (Burgon, p. 341, italics his). Burgon says that he "insists that the Truth of the Text of Scripture is to be elicited exclusively from the consistent testimony of the largest number of the best Copies, Fathers, and Versions" (Burgon, p. 518).

Burgon also responds to Ellicott's pamphlet regarding two of his articles. Burgon says, "You flout me; you scold me; you lecture me." But I do not find that you ever *answer* me" (Burgon, p. 370, italics his). Burgon says he spent 5½ years laboriously collating the five "old uncials" throughout the Gospels and that Ellicott only used secondhand information (Burgon, p. 376). Burgon insists he did not use the "Received Text" as his standard (Burgon, p. 388). While he esteems it good enough for all ordinary purposes, he makes his appeal to the threefold witness of copies, versions, and Fathers whenever he feels the testimony of the Received Text is challenged (Burgon, p. 392). Burgon goes into great detail discussing the textual problem of "God" versus "who" in 1 Timothy 3:16 (Burgon, pp. 429-503; that's right—74 pages!). Burgon says, "I hold (and surely so do you!), the right interpretation of God's Word may not be attained without the guidance of the Holy Spirit, whose aid must first be invoked by faithful prayer" (Burgon, p. 507).

The Traditional Text

During his lifetime, Burgon amassed an enormous amount of material that was never published. After his death, a friend named Miller published some of that material in two books. In 1990, Jay P. Green, Sr., published a volume containing the complete works of Burgon, titled "Unholy Hands on the Bible." The following material about those books was taken from that volume.

In *The Traditional Text of the Holy Gospels Vindicated and Established* (1896), Burgon and Miller vindicate the Traditional Text by covering such topics as the test of truth, the witness of the early Fathers, the witness of the Syriac versions, the witness of the Western, low Latin text, Alexandria and Caesarea, the influence of Origen on old uncials, the old uncials, and the late uncials and cursives. In the process, they examined verse after verse and passage after passage.

According to Burgon and Miller, the seven tests of truth are" 1) Antiquity or Primitiveness. 2) Consent of Witnesses, or Number. 3) Variety of evidence, or Catholicity. 4) Respectability of Witnesses or Weight. 5) Continuity or Unbroken Tradition. 6) Evidence of the Entire Passage or Context. 7) Internal Consideration, or Reasonableness. (Burgon and Miller, *Tradition Text*, pp. 15, 22-30).

Because the Textus Receptus was dethroned based on the discovery of two earlier manuscripts, it is interesting that Burgon argues that the first test of truth is antiquity. He defines antiquity as "the greater age of the earlier copies, Versions or Fathers. That which is older will possess more authority than that which is more recent, but age will not by itself confer any exclusive, or indeed paramount power of decision" (Burgon and Miller, *Tradition Text*, p. 23, capital letters theirs).

Burgon considers such Fathers as "Irenaeus and Hippolytus; Athanasius and Didymus; Epiphanius and Basil; the two Gregories and Chrysostom; Cyril and Theodoret, among the Greeks—and Tertullian and Cyprian; Hilary and Ambrose; Jerome and Augustine, among the Latins—are more respected witnesses by far than the same number of Greek or Latin Codexes. Origen, Clemens Alexandrinus, and Eusebius, though first-rate authors, were too much addicted to Textual Criticism themselves, or else employed such inconsistent copies, that their testimony is that of an indifferent witness or bad judges" (Burgon and Miller, *Tradition Text*, pp. 25-26).

Here is one example of their examination of a verse to demonstrate their point. John 1:42 records that Jesus said, "You are Simon, the son of Jonah." They point out that B, ℵ, L, 33 reads "son of John" [ιωνα (Jonah) vs. ιωαννου (John); see John in NASB, NIV, and ESV]. Burgon and Miller say Jonah is "sufficiently established by the fact that it is the reading of all codexes, uncials, and cursive, excepting the four vicious MSS noted above. Add to the main body of the codexes, the Vulgate, the Peshitta, the Harkleian Syriac, the Armenian, Ethiopic, Gregorian, and Slavonic versions—besides several of the Fathers, such as Serapion, Basil, Epipphanius, Chrysostom (four times), Asterius and another (unknown) writer of the fourth century, and with Cyril of the fifth—this is a body of evidence which in respect of its antiquity, its number, its variety, and its respectability cast the four dissenting witnesses into the shade. When it is further remembered that we have preserved to us in S. Matt. 16:17 our Savior's plane designation of Simon Peter's surname, "*Simon bar Jona*"

(Simon, son of Jona), what else but irrational is the contention of the modern school that in S. John 1:43 (sic) we are to read John instead of Jona? The plain fact is that some second-century critics supposed that Jona and John were identical, and out of his weak imagination, the only surviving witnesses at the end of 1700 years are three uncials and one cursive copy, a few copies of the old Latin, which fluctuates between *Johannis, Johanna, and John*; the Bohairic version, and Nonnus" (Burgon and Miller, *Tradition Text*, p. 39).

Burgon and Miller list citations from Fathers before AD 400. that support the Traditional Text in thirty passages, including Matthew 1:25, Matthew 5:44, Matthew 6:13, Matthew 7:13-14, Matthew 9:13 (Mark 2:17), Matthew 11:27, Matthew 17:21, Matthew 18:11, Matthew 23:38 (Luke 13:35), Matthew 27:34, Matthew 28:2, Matthew 28:19, Mark 1:2, Mark 16:9-20, Luke 1:28, Luke 2:14, Luke 10:41- 42, Luke 23:34, Luke 23:38, Luke 23:45, Luke 24:40, Luke 24:42, John 1:3-4, John 1:18, John 3:13, John 17:24, John 21:25. The Fathers cited to support the Traditional readings in these verses include the Didache, Polycarp, Justin Martyr, Tertullian, Clement of Alexandria, Origen, Cyprian, Irenaeus, Eusebius, Barnabas, Papias, Marcion, Arius, and many more (Burgon and Miller, *Tradition Text*, pp. 48-60).

Several statements of note include, "We fully admit that corruption prevailed from the very first" (Burgon and Miller, *Tradition Text*, p. 43; see also p. 61). "As there are no vellum MSS. dating from before AD 330, except the merest fragments, we are driven to infer that the material for the writing of the perishable nature was generally employed before that period (Burgon and Miller, *Tradition Text*, p. 83). "When quoting Scripture for a purpose, the ancient Fathers freely exercise the liberty of leaving out whatever was irrelevant to their team—and of retaining just as much of the text as was made for the argument—and this should never be allowed to slip out of sight" (Burgon and Miller, *Tradition Text*, p. 136).

Causes of Corruption

In *Causes of Corruption of the Traditional Text of the Holy Gospels* (1896), Burgon and Miller list 13 causes of corruption:" 1) General Corruption. 2) Accidental Causes. 3) Likeness of Endings. 4. Errors from Writing in Uncials. 5) Itacism. 6) Linguistic Influence. 7) Harmonistic Influence. 8) Assimilation. 9) Attraction. 10) Omission. 11) Transposition Errors. 12) Glosses. 13) Orthodox. (Burgon and Miller, pp. 1-103). Burgon and Miller give multiple New Testament examples of each of these "corruptions."

For example, concerning the ending of the Lord's prayer, which reads, "And do not lead us into temptation, But deliver us from the evil one. For Yours is the kingdom and the power and the glory forever. Amen" (Mt. 6:13), Burgon and Miller and Miller say, "Four uncial MSS (אBDZ), supported by five cursives of bad character (1, 17, which gives Amen, 118, 130, 209), and all the Latin copies except four, omit these words. Thus, it is assumed that these 15 words must have found their way surreptitiously into the text of all other existing copies. But let me ask: Is it at all likely, or rather is it in any way credible, that in a manner like this, all the MSS in the world but nine should have become corrupted? (Burgon and Miller, p. 39).

Burgon and Miller admit that these words are absent from most Latin copies except four, but these 15 words are in "Curetion's Syriac and the

Sahidic version; the Gothic, Ethiopic, Armenian, Gregorian, Slavonic, Harkleian, Palestinian, Erpenius' Arabic, and the Persian of Tawos versions. It is also testified to in the Didache (with variation), Apostolical Constitution (iii. 18-vii 25 with variation), in St. Ambrose and Caesarius. Chrysostom comments on the words without suspicion and often quotes them, as does Isidore of Pelussium. See also Opus Imperfectum" (Burgon and Miller, p. 39).

Burgon and Miller ask, since these 15 words can be traced back to the second century, since without appreciable variety, they are in all manuscripts, and since they are in all lectionaries, how will men pretend to explain the interpolation as universal as this one? Burgon and Miller go on to say the critics explain the addition by quoting the 1514 Complutensian Polyglot, which says, "in the Greek liturgy, after the choir has said *And deliver us from evil*, it is the priest who responds as above [i.e., with those 15 words]; and those words, according to the Greeks, the priest alone may pronounce. This makes it probable that the words in question are of no empirical part of the Lord's prayer; but that certain copyists inserted them in error, supposing from their use in the liturgy that they formed part of the text" (Burgon and Miller, p. 39).

Burgon and Miller say the explanation is simply that the choir never pronounced the doxology. Therefore, it was omitted in the archetype copy from which the nine extant MSS, Origen, and old Latin versions originally derived their text. They say, "There can be no simpler solution to the alleged difficulty. That Tertullian, Cyprian, and Ambrose recognized no more of the Lord's prayer than they found in their Latin copies cannot create surprise. The wonder would be if they did" (Burgon and Miller, p. 40).

Similarly, Burgon and Miller methodically explain each cause of corruption by showing how it operates in passage after passage.

Summary: Before he died, Burgon wrote two books, and after he died, Miller wrote two more, using Burgon's research to defend the Traditional Text type.

In his volume *Unholy Hands on the Bible*, which includes the complete works of Burgon, Green also includes other writings by Burgon, such as his explanations of 1 Timothy 3:16 and John 7:53-8:11, as well as Hort's eight examples of conflated readings.

Burgon's biographer listed over fifty unpublished works on a variety of subjects. Burgon's index of New Testament quotations by early Christian authors consists of 16 manuscript volumes containing 86,489 quotations, currently in the British Library (E. M. Goulburn, *Life of Dean Burgon*, London: John Murray, 1892, 2 vols. I, vii). He may be the only person collating the five great uncials (א, A, B, C, D). He also cataloged 374 MSS (Pickering and Freitas, p. iii).

Chapter 5

THE CRITICAL GREEK TEXTS

So, what happened after Westcott, Hort, and John Burgon? Martin said, "To the average student of the Greek New Testament today, it is unthinkable to question the [Westcott and Hort] theory, at least in its basic premises" (Martin, in Fuller, p. 260). Virtually the entire Christian community has adopted the Westcott-Hort theory with some slight revisions. Textual scholars have produced critical Greek texts based on the Westcott-Hort theory. Here is a brief explanation of that development.

The Nestle Text

In 1898, Eberhard Nestle, a German professor, published *Novum Testamentum Graece*. Later, Erwin Nestle, Eberhard's son, continued his father's work. Their editions of the Greek text generally contained the text of Westcott and Hort, with an apparatus at the bottom of each page listing the "variant readings" of different manuscripts.

Aland says the editions of Tischendorf and the Westcott and Hort "were sufficient to make the Textus Receptus obsolete for the scholarly world." Nevertheless, the British and Foreign Bible Society says, "Then the largest and most influential of all Bible societies, continued to distribute it officially for fully twenty years after the publication of Westcott-Hort's edition. It was not until 1904 that it adopted the Nestle text, which was then in its fifth edition. This marked the final defeat of the Textus Receptus, nearly 400 years after it was first published" (Aland, p. 19).

Nestle-Aland Text

In 1952, Kurt Aland became co-editor of the Nestle Greek text, now called the Nestle-Aland Text. New editions of the Nestle-Aland text are designated as NA with a number attached; for example, NA28 is the 28th edition (2012).

The United Bible Society Texts

William Wilberforce, who was instrumental in the abolition of slavery, founded the first Bible Society in 1804. By the 1940s, more than a dozen Bible societies had been established. In 1946, they created the Global Fellowship of United Bible Societies (UBS). In 1966, the United Bible Society produced its first critical Greek text for translators. Kurt Aland was one of the principal editors of Nestle-Aland—*Novum Testamentum Graece* and *The Greek New Testament* for the United Bible Societies. UBS5 is the 5th United Bible Society's edition based on the 28th Nestle-Aland edition. All editions remain close to Westcott-Hort's text. Epp points out that all critical editions contain a text that has never existed in any manuscript form (Epp in Black, p. 44).

Further Developments

Text types Since the discovery of $\mathfrak{P}^{66}$ (1952) and $\mathfrak{P}^{75}$ (1950s), the Westcott-Hort Neutral text and Alexandrian text have been combined into one called the Alexandrian. Aland declares, "There is no such thing as a 'neutral' text of the New Testament" (Aland, p. 14). That would leave three: Alexandrian, Byzantine, and Western.

The Western text type has also been called into question. Rather than calling it a "text type," current critics refer to it as "Codex D." This would leave two: Alexandrian and Byzantine.

Other text types that have been suggested have also been called into question. For example, some scholars have suggested there is a Caesarean text type. Carson says it "probably originated in Egypt and may have been brought to Caesarea by Origen. It boasts a unique mixture of Western ... and Alexandrian ... readings, prompting some scholars to question the value of calling it a text type" (Carson, p. 27). However, Aland says, "Whatever else may be proposed, especially with reference to the so-called Western, Caesarean, and Jerusalem text types, is theoretical, based on dubious foundations, and often built completely in the clouds. Particular caution is needed with any proposed textual group qualified by the prefix 'pre-' (such as the pre-Caesarean text).... [D's] actual role in the manuscript tradition of the New Testament has been minimal, quite in contrast to the amount of attention it has received in modern critical literature" (Aland, p. 67).

Aland puts text types into five categories, one of which is "uncategorized." He categorizes the papyri as normal, strict, free, and least normal. Metzger remarks, "But how can anyone know whether a scribe produced a 'strict' copy of an exemplar that is nonexistent today?" (Metzger, p. 290 fn.).

Today, New Testament Greek manuscripts can be divided into two text types. Aland concluded, "Only the Alexandrian text, the Koine text [a.k.a. Byzantine text], and the D text are incontestably verified" (Aland, p. 67). He still contends that the earliest is the best (Aland, p. 95).

Methods Textual criticism boils down to two issues: 1) An examination of the external evidence (date of text and text type) and 2) An examination of the internal evidence (the habit of the scribes and the style of the author). Older documents are preferred, but the date of the text type is more important than the date of a particular manuscript. Scribes were more prone to add than omit, so a shorter reading is preferred. Scribes are more prone to correct errors, so the more difficult reading is preferred. Scribes are more prone to harmonize, so the reading different from the parallel reading is preferred. The reading that explains the origin of the others, which involves the application of the three principles mentioned earlier, is preferred. The next Chapter explains the methods of criticism in more detail.

Summary: Since Westcott and Hort, 28 critical Greek text (NA) editions have been produced, none of which are in any manuscript.

The Westcott-Hort theory deposed the Syrian (Byzantine) text type and elevated the earlier manuscripts (א and B) as being the closest to the original manuscripts. Although the approach has been revised 28 times, it remains the prevailing view among textual critics.

Chapter 6

METHODS OF TEXTUAL CRITICISM

With this massive amount of information available, what method should be used to determine which words are the original words of the authors of the New Testament? As noted, that is the job of textual criticism. What methods do textual critics use? Over the last several hundred years, various methods have been employed. Currently, there are three main approaches.

Reasoned eclecticism is the method practiced by most textual critics and scholars. Simply put, it evaluates both the external (manuscripts) and internal (various possibilities) evidence to determine the preferred reading. Rigorous eclecticism considers the internal evidence (such things as the style of the author and the habits of scribes) and pays little or no attention to the number and alleged weight of manuscripts. This method stemmed largely from C. H. Turner and was popularized by George D. Kilpatrick. The manuscript method primarily focuses on the majority of manuscripts, specifically the Byzantine text type (also known as the Syrian text, the Traditional Text, and the Majority Text).

In essence, this amounts to either 1) weighing all the evidence, both external and internal, 2) determining the preferred reading based on internal evidence, or 3) taking whatever the external manuscript records.

Reasoned Eclecticism

Epp describes reasoned eclecticism as employing "a combination of external and internal arguments, applied evenly and without prejudice (though, admittedly, many lean toward the external when appropriate or even as often as they dare), with the goal of reaching a reasonable decision based on the relative probabilities among all applicable arguments for priority" (Epp in Black, p. 34).

Tregelles (1813-1875) emphasized "the authority of the ancient copies without allowing the 'received text' any prescriptive rights" and preferred both the harder reading and the shorter reading (Epp in Black, p. 23). According to Westcott and Hort (1882), methods of textual criticism include 1) Internal evidence of readings (Hort, pp. 19-30). 2) Internal evidence of documents, that is, determining the trustworthiness of the individual document (Hort, pp. 30-39). 3) Genealogical evidence, that is, determining the genealogical tree (historical relationships) of the manuscript (Hort, pp. 39-66).

Michael W. Holmes (Princeton Ph.D., where he studied under Metzger) briefly defines reasoned eclecticism as "by means of external evidence we identify the oldest surviving reading(s), which we then further evaluate by means of internal considerations" (Holmes, in Black, p. 78). He says the difference between reasoned eclecticism, rigorous eclecticism, and the documentary approaches is emphasis. Rigorous eclecticism emphasizes the internal criteria and generally allows only a minimal role for the documentary evidence. The documentary approach place all or nearly all the weight for textual decisions on external evidence. Reasoned eclecticism works with both external and internal evidence in a balanced manner (Holmes in Black, pp. 81-82).

Rigorous Eclecticism

Epp describes rigorous eclecticism (also known as thoroughgoing eclecticism) as utilizing internal arguments mainly to the exclusion of external ones (Epp in Black, p. 34).

Rigorous eclecticism includes the use of different principles. Bengel (1687-1752) utilized the principle that "the harder reading was to be preferred" (Epp in Black, p. 22). Wettstein (1693-1754) preferred the shorter reading and the one that conformed to the author's style (Epp in Black, p. 22). The shorter/shortest reading has priority because scribes tend to expand the text rather than shorten it (Epp in Black, pp. 27-28).

Colwell (1901-1974) favored the longer reading because scribes more frequently omitted rather than added material (Epp in Black, p. 27). George D. Kilpatrick (1910-1989) and his pupil Keith Elliott argued that, in general, the longer reading is more likely to be the original because, in the process of copying, scribes tended to accidentally shorten rather than deliberately lengthen the text (Epp in Black, pp. 27-28). Elliott says, in general, that the shorter reading preferred is improbable because scribes were more prone to omission than addition. "Omission was a frequent occurrence.... Addition demands conscious mental activity" (Elliott, in Black, p. 107 fn. 9).

Another principle is that reading has priority that best conforms to the author's style (Epp in Black, p. 31). Tregelles (1813-1875) wrote, "I am well aware that arguments on *style* are often very fallacious and that *by themselves* they prove very little" (Tregelles, italics his, cited by Burgon, p. 249). Origen (185-254) rejected the reading "Jesus" before "Barabbas" in Matthew 27:16-17 because the name "Jesus" would not be used for evildoers (Origen in his commentary on Matthew; Epp, p. 21).

Tischendorf (1815-1874) stressed that the "text should be sought solely from ancient witnesses," but he also gave preference to "the reading that appears to have occasioned the other reading" (Epp in Black, p. 23).

J. K. Elliott says that thoroughgoing eclecticism "is the consistent application of criteria and principles of assessing textual variants that are based *primarily* (but not, I should add, exclusively) on internal evidence (Elliott, in Black, p. 103, italics his). His principles include" 1) The more difficult reading is to be preferred (scribes would frequently bring divergent passages into harmony with one another and scribes would sometimes alter a less refined grammatical form in accord with contemporary preferences), and 2) The style and vocabulary of the author throughout the book are taken into account. Elliott comments that the editors of the UBS apply these principles only when א and B differ from each other. Thus, the principles are not applied consistently or used thoroughly (Elliott in Black, p. 106). Elliott insists that thoroughgoing eclecticism "is not a subjective exercise" (Elliott in Black, p. 109).

One of Elliott's illustrations of thoroughgoing eclecticism is the reading "Son of God" rather than "Son of Man" in Acts 7:56. Son of God is only in $\mathfrak{P}^{74}$, 491, 614. He argues that "stylistically conscientious scribes would have good reason to reduce the number of occurrences of θεος [God] in this passage, not altering θεος [God] to ανθρωπου [man], they created the only occurrence of the title *Son of Man* outside of the Gospels" (Elliott in Black, p. 112)

In another example, Elliott argues for χωρις θεου (apart from God) instead of χαριτι θεου (by the grace of God) in Hebrews 2:9. He argues, "Although we have very few witnesses favoring the reading χαριτι θεου, nevertheless Origen in his day claimed that this was a popular reading known in many manuscripts. χωρις θεου is the more difficult of the two readings. It seems to fit with the early first-century belief that at the point of his death, the incarnate Jesus was by definition separated from God" (Elliott and Black, pp. 112-113).

Then there is Matthew 21:28-32. As Elliott explains, "In ℵ, one child first refuses but later changes his mind. The second child then agreed to the man's request but reneged on the promise. The child who is said to have done the father's will is identified as ο πρωτος (the first). In the reading of B, the first child is the one who promises to work in the vineyard but disobeys; the second child refuses but later obeys. The child doing the will of the father is identified as ο usteros [the latter], ο deuteros [the second], or ο escatos [the last]. A third version is found in Codex Bezae, which agrees with the sequence in ℵ. However, in D, the child who does the will of the father is said to be the one who agrees with the request but then fails to fulfill it. Westcott and Hort took the reading of D ... and tried to make sense of it.... Jerome tried to make sense of the reading we know from D.... The Alands label [it] one of the most difficult in textual criticism but ... tried to make sense [of it]" (Elliott in Black, p. 114).

Documentary Approach

Irenaeus (AD 115?-202) preferred a reading in Revelation 13:18 because it was "found in all the good and ancient copies" (Irenaeus, *Ag. Her*. 5.30.1).

Robinson says the principles used in the practice of Byzantine priority are identical to those found in the eclectic methods except for the elimination of 1) the principle that the shorter reading is to be preferred (an examination of the early papyri demonstrates that scribes were more prone to omit than to add material) and 2) the anti-Byzantine bias that has prevailed for the last century and half (Robinson in Black, p. 129).

The principles of internal evidence are: 1) The reading most likely to have given rise to all others is to be preferred. 2) The reading is more difficult as a scribal creation is to be preferred. 3) Readings that conform to the original author's known style, vocabulary, and syntax are preferred. 4) Readings that harmonize the wording of another passage are to be rejected (harmonization is not widespread). 5) Readings reflecting religiously motivated expansion or alteration tend to be secondary. 6) The primary evaluation should be based on transcriptional probability. 7) Error rather than deliberate alteration is more likely to be the source of many sensible variants. 8) Neither the shorter nor the longer reading is to be preferred (accidental omission occurred more frequently than deliberate expansion). (Robinson in Black, pp. 130-132).

The principles of external evidence include: 1) The original text is presumed to have been preserved. 2) Readings that appear spasmodically are suspect. 3) Readings supported by various versions and Fathers are highly regarded. 4) Many manuscripts can be demonstrated to have descended from a single archetype. 5) Manuscripts need to be weighed, not merely counted. 6) Seek readings with demonstrable antiquity. (Two copying revolutions occurred when writing material shifted from papyrus to parchment in the fourth century and when handwriting switched from uncials to minuscules in the ninth century.) 7) A single best manuscript or a small group of manuscripts is unlikely to have evidence. 8) Following the oldest manuscripts is flawed. 9) External and internal evidence points to the Byzantine Textform as the leading force in the transmission history. (Robinson in Black, pp. 132-136).

Summary: Among textual critics, the three primary contemporary methods are reasoned eclecticism, rigorous eclecticism, and commitment to the Byzantine text type.

External evidence considers the number, age, and geographical distribution of manuscripts, ancient translations, and quotations from early Christian writers. Internal evidence is concerned with the author's style and the scribes' habits. Currently, textual critics are divided into three groups: rational eclecticism, rigorous eclecticism, and the documentary approach. The documentary approach is concerned with external evidence, especially the Greek manuscripts. Rigorous eclecticism concentrates on internal evidence. Rational eclecticism considers all the evidence. However, as Ellicott has observed, "The three methods represented by the three approaches ... have differences and nuances, but in practice, these methodologies cannot be confined in watertight containers. In many ways, the result of the three methods does not differ in all respects" (Elliott, in Black, p. 104).

Textual critics employ various methods and arrive at differing conclusions regarding the early centuries of manuscript history. The Alands claim that the text type did not form until the fourth century. They identify three text types, but only from the 3rd century AD: the Alexandrian, Koine, and D-text. They do not recognize a Caesarean text (Epp, in Black, pp. 38-39). Epp suggests that as of the 21st century, 1) B-text and $\mathfrak{P}^{75}$ are the chief representatives of the earliest text type with roots in the second century. 2) D-text represented by Codex D, the Old Latin, and the Old Syriac (in part), and some fragmentary papyri are perhaps equally early. 3) An abortive C-text in Mark is represented by $\mathfrak{P}^{45}$ and Codex W but continues no further. It is between B-text and D-text. 4) Codex A and most later minuscules represent the Byzantine text type (Epp in Black, p. 38 fn. 49). "There is also a difference of opinion among textual critics as to which fragmentary papyri can be placed in these groups with confidence, due to the small number of variant readings in many of them" (Epp in Black, p. 39).

Today, virtually all textual critics agree that, by AD 300, there were three text types: Alexandrian, D-text, and Byzantine, and that no pre-sixth-century papyri support the Byzantine text type. Papyri that represent or "were influenced by" the Byzantine text type are $\mathfrak{P}^{63}$ (*ca.* 500), $\mathfrak{P}^{54}$ (sixth century), $\mathfrak{P}^{66}$, perhaps $\mathfrak{P}^{79}$ and $\mathfrak{P}^{74}$ (seventh century), and $\mathfrak{P}^{42}$ (seventh/eighth century). Many accept that a C-text existed in the early fourth century, but no longer refer to it as Caesarean (Epp in Black, p. 39, fn. 54).

Jacobus Petzer summarizes the current situation by saying that the 19th century solved the riddle of the fourth century and settled the question of the Byzantine text. The 20th century solved the mystery of the third century. The 21st century needs to solve two remaining riddles: the second and first centuries (Epp, in Black, p. 43). Second-century papyri include 𝔓^{52} (John), 𝔓^{90} (John), 𝔓^{104} (Matthew), and 𝔓^{98} (Revelation). Three other papyri date around 200, 𝔓^{46}, 𝔓$^{64-67}$, 𝔓^{66} (Epp, in Black, pp. 43-44 fn. 65).

For an explanation and evaluation of Aland's 12 basic rules of textual criticism, see Appendix II.

Chapter 7

AN EVALUATION OF THE TEXT TYPES

Let's review. By one count, there are over 6000 New Testament Greek manuscripts (papyrus, uncials, minuscules, and lectionaries). Some say these manuscripts can be divided into three basic text types (Alexandrian, Byzantine, and Western).

Perhaps it would be possible to argue that each of those three could be the closest to the original text of the New Testament. That has happened. J. H. Ropes (1926) claimed the Alexandrian text type was the original text type and the Western text type was an intentional rewriting of the original text. A. C. Clark (1933) argued that the Western text type was the original and that the Alexandrian text type was formed from the Western text type during the third century by an abbreviator (Hills, Introduction, p. 22). John Burgon (1871) maintained that the Traditional text type (a.k.a. the Byzantine and Syrian Text) was closest to the original.

It is also possible to conclude that there is only one text type! The UBS no longer uses symbols for "text types" except for "*Byz*," which refers to the Byzantine manuscript tradition (Pickering, p. 37 fn. 3).

Of course, another possibility is that in a manuscript, one text type is the original reading in one passage, and, in the same manuscript, in another passage, another text type is the best reading. The Westcott-Hort/Critical Text theory does just that. It combines readings from all the text types but basically follows Vaticanus, Sinaiticus, and a few other manuscripts. It relies "heavily on a relatively small number of manuscripts derived mainly from Egypt" (Hodge and Farstad, p. ix).

Be all those possibilities as they may, virtually all of those who practice textual criticism today claim the Byzantine text (a.k.a. the Syrian Text and the Traditional Text) is an edited, late text and, therefore, is not as reliable as the Alexandrian text, which is earlier. The Western text type is sometimes given some consideration.

If it is that simple and settled, why, throughout the history of this debate, have there been such adamant critics of the Westcott-Hort/Critical Text? Are there problems with the arguments for the Westcott-Hort/Critical Text theory? To say the same thing another way, are there problems with the Alexandrian text type? Is there solid evidence to support the Byzantine text type?

The Alexandrian Text type

The Alexandrian text type has about 13 manuscripts (ℵ, B, A, C, L, 33, $\mathfrak{P}^{75}$, $\mathfrak{P}^{66}$, and maybe half a dozen others (Pickering and Freitas, pp. 60, 63). Colwell said that for MSS to be grouped as a family, they had to agree that at least 70% of the time, there is variation; however, the Alexandrian MSS do not reach that amount, except that B and $\mathfrak{P}^{75}$ agree 78% of the time (Pickering and Freitas, p. 63).

Alexandrian text type readings tend to use fewer words and have readings that are difficult. The best witnesses of the Alexandrian text type are Codices B and $\mathfrak{P}^{75}$. Codex B is dated in the fourth century, and $\mathfrak{P}^{75}$ is dated AD 175-225. "Now, thanks to $\mathfrak{P}^{75}$, there is proof that the kind of Greek text found in B was in circulation in the latter part of the second century AD and, no doubt, even earlier" (Hodges, *Bib. Sac.* 1968, p. 336). Primary Alexandrian readings are in $\mathfrak{P}^{66}$ and citations of Origen. Secondary witnesses are included in C, L, 33.

Since Hort articulated the arguments that dethroned the TR and enthroned the Alexandrian text type, an evaluation of the Alexandrian text type should begin with his arguments against the Byzantine text type and for the Alexandrian text type.

Against the Byzantine Text type In the first place, Hort was a biased critic. He began with a strong prejudice against the TR. In 1851, at the age of 23, "before he had studied the evidence, before he had worked through the text to evaluate variant readings one by one" (Pickering, p. 84), Hort wrote to a friend, "I had no idea till the last few weeks of the importance of text, and having read so little Greek Testament, and dragged on with the villainous Textus Receptus ... think of the vile Textus Receptus leaning entirely on late MSS, it is a blessing there are such early ones" (Pickering, p. 17). Colwell stated that Hort's goal of discrediting the Byzantine text influenced his view of the text's history (Colwell, "Hort's Redivivus," pp. 158-159; cited by Holmes in Black, p. 93, fn. 42).

Hort used four arguments to prove that the Byzantine text type was an edited, and therefore late, type of text: 1) genealogy, that is, determining the genealogical tree (historical relationships) of the manuscript (Hort, pp. 39-66), 2) quotations from Christian writers, 3) translations, and 4) internal evidence.

1. Genealogy. To begin with, M. M. Parvis stated, "Westcott and Hort never applied the genealogical method to the NT MSS and Colwell wrote, "That Westcott and Hort did not apply this method to the manuscripts of the New Testament is obvious. Where are the charts that start with the

majority of late manuscripts and trace back to the diminishing generations of ancestors, ultimately reaching the Neutral and Western texts? The answer is that they are nowhere" (Parvis and Colwell, cited by Pickering, p. 32; Fee agreed, see fn. 2). Pickering wrote, "Actually, Hort produced no 'demonstration' at all—just assumptions. Since the genealogical method has not been applied to the MSS of the New Testament, it may not honestly be used as an integral part of the theory of the NT criticism" (Pickering, p. 34).

Furthermore, there is no data to demonstrate a genealogy. Aland concluded, "It is practically impossible to distinguish their [NT MSS] sources and their mutual relationships. This is precisely the situation that textual critics find when attempting to analyze the history of the New Testament text" (Aland, p. 70). "Codex Claromontanus apparently has a 'child' three centuries younger than it (also, minuscule 205 may have been copied from 208)" (Pickering, p. 32 fn. 1), but not much more can be demonstrated.

Colwell tried to find an archetype and concluded, "The results show convincingly that any attempt to reconstruct the archetype of the beta text type (his name for the Byzantine text type) on a qualitative basis is doomed to failure. The text thus reconstructed is not reconstructed but constructed; it is an artificial entry that *never existed*" (Colwell, "The Significance of Grouping of the New Testament Manuscripts," *New Testament Studies*, IV (1957-1958), 86-87, cited by Pickering and Freitas, p. 59, italics added).

Obviously, genealogies exist. Manuscripts were copied from manuscripts, creating a family tree. The issue is having enough information to identify a genealogy. Textual scholars such as Aland, Colwell, Klijn, Parvis, Vaganay, Wikgren, and Zuntz have stated that such relationships have not been identified. Some of these scholars "go on to affirm that we cannot identify such relationships, at least by direct genealogy—almost all the links are missing" (Pickering, p. 37 fn. 3, who adds that UBS no longer uses symbols for "text types" except for "*Byz*," which refers to the Byzantine manuscript tradition).

Therefore, using a theoretical geological tree to prove that the Byzantine text type is edited and late is useless. Colwell pointed out that the genealogical diagram Hort printed did not have any mixture and added, "When there is a mixture, and Westcott and Hort stated that it is common, in fact almost universal in some degrees, then the genealogical method is useless" (Colwell, cited by Pickering, p. 33).

If Hort did not apply the genealogical method and if subsequent scholars have concluded that there is not enough data to construct a genealogy, how did Hort justify using it? He used "conflate" readings, that is, a combination of readings from two other manuscripts (Hort, p. 53), that is, he used conflated readings to prove that the genealogy of the Byzantine text type is an edited text and, therefore, late (Pickering, p. 30 fn. 2).

The notion of conflated readings has numerous problems. For example, Hort only gave a total of eight examples in two books of the New Testament. That is eight verses out of 7957 verses in 2 books out of 27. Hills says only a few more have been found. Kenyon candidly admitted that he did not think there were many more. Moreover, these alleged examples are not convincing. Even Bousset, a radical scholar, said so (Hills, *King James Version Defended*, p. 72). In *Causes of Corruption*, Miller and Burgon refute all eight (Miller and Burgon, pp. 269-282).

Pickering argues that it is not unreasonable to suspect that the original reading was the conflated reading and that the Alexandrian or Western reading omitted part of it. For example, the Byzantine text type of Luke 24:53 reads, "praising and blessing." The Western text type reads "praising and" and the Alexandrian text type reads "blessing God." Instead of "praising and blessing" being a conflated reading, the Alexandrian text type omitted "praising and" (Pickering, p. 51).

"From all sources," Pickering has listed 105 "conflated" readings and analyzed each one (Pickering, pp. 275-297). He demonstrates that Alexandrian and Western witnesses have "clear, undoubted conflations" and that 60% of the examples of the "Byzantine" readings are built upon and not vice versa. Furthermore, there are over 800 places where the Byzantine text could have conflated "Western" and "Alexandrian" readings, but did not. With this analysis, Pickering says the "specter of 'Syrian conflation' has been laid to rest" (Pickering, pp. 296-297). In his opinion, the whole matter of "conflation" is "a pseudo-issue, a tempest in a teapot. There simply are not enough putative examples to support generalizations" (Pickering, p. 51).

The conflated readings do not indicate that the Byzantine text type is late, as conflated readings date back to the second century. "The support of distinctive Byzantine readings by early Egyptian papyri has provided proof that WH was wrong at this point" [that there are no historical signs of the distinctively Syrian text before the middle of the third century] (Sturz, p. 61). For example, in John 10:19, Codex D reads σχισμα ουν (therefore division), ℵ and B read σχισμα παλιν (division again), and the Byzantine text type reads σχισμα ουν παλιν (division therefore again). The Alexandrian text type is supported by $\mathfrak{P}^{45}$ and $\mathfrak{P}^{75}$, but the Byzantine text type is supported by $\mathfrak{P}^{66}$ (the earliest papyri) (Sturz, pp. 83-84). Furthermore, Sturz says conflated readings are in B and quotes Colwell, who says, "Vaticanus lacks the conflated readings of the 'Syrian text,' but has conflated readings of its own" (Mk. 1:28; Sturz, pp. 85-86).

According to Hort, conflated readings resulted from a recension, probably by Lucian; however, there is no historical evidence to support this. Sturz says, "History is completely silent with regard to any recension of the Byzantine text" (Sturz, p. 122) and "There is not a shred of historical evidence that such recension was made" (Sturz, p. 126). Kenyon said, "We know the names of several revisers of the Septuagint and the Vulgate. It would be strange if historians and church writers had all omitted to record or mention such an event, as the deliberate revision of the New Testament and its original Greek" (Kenyon, cited by Hills, Introduction, p. 61). Hodges says the silence of history about such an event is like the publication of the R.S.V. going unnoticed by the adherents of the K.J.V. Had it happened, we would have known about it (Hodges, unpublished notes, p. 11).

Modern scholars have rejected the view of a definite revision in favor of a more gradual theory, but Hodges says that even a long, slow process spread out over many centuries and many lands and many copies could not achieve the widespread uniformity of the majority text (Hodges, *Bib Sac* 1968, p. 341). Later, he wrote, "It is virtually impossible to conceive of any kind of an unguided process which could have resulted in the Majority Text. The relative uniformity within the text shows clearly that its transnational history has been stable and regular to a very large degree" (Hodges, *The Greek New Testament*, p. xi). In other words, the gradual revision theory is refuted by the uniformity of the Majority Text. Chrysostom (347-407) used the Byzantine text *before it had centuries to be slowly revised.*

2. Hort's view that no Ante-Nicene Father quotes a distinct reading of the Syrian (Byzantine) text type is not accurate. For example, The Didache, a document many say was written before AD 100, contains Matthew 6:13, a Byzantine text type reading. It says, "For Yours is the power and the glory forever" (Didache 10:5).

Hort argued there were no Syrian text type readings in Origen. In response, Hills says, "In the first 14 chapters of the Gospel of John (that is, in the area covered by Papyrus Bodmer II) out of 52 instances in which the Byzantine text stands alone, Origen agrees with the Byzantine text 20 times and disagrees with it 32 times.... These statistics suggest that Origen was familiar with the main families of manuscripts that modern scholars have isolated" (Metzger, cited by Pickering, p. 53). Miller found that Origen sided with the Byzantine text type 460 times, and Irenaeus did so 63 times (Pickering, pp. 53-54).

"According to von Soden (1907), Byzantine readings are found in the writings of Athanasius (293-373), Didymus (313-398), and Cyril (d. 444), all of whom lived at Alexandria. This would indicate that the Byzantine text was known in Egypt in the days of these illustrious Fathers" (Hills, Introduction, p. 48). The Byzantine text was used in Antioch and its vicinity by Diodorus (died *ca.* 394), Chrysostom (347-407), Theodore of Mopsuestia (*ca.* 350-428), and Theodoret (397-457). And this same text is also found in the writings of the three great Cappadocian Fathers (natives of the province of Cappadocia in Asia Minor), namely, Basil (330-379), Gregory Nazianzen (329-390), and Gregory of Nysa (d. 394)" (Hills, Introduction, p. 61).

Pickering concludes, "'Byzantine' readings are recognized (most notably) by the Didache, Diognetus, and Justin Martyr in the first half of the second century, the Gospel of Peter, Athenagotus, Hegesippus, and Irenaeus (heavily) in the second half; by Clement of Alexandria, Tertullian, Clementines, Hippolyus, and Origen (all heavily) in the first half of the third century; by Gregory of Thaumaturgus, Novatian, Cyprian (heavily), Dionysius of Alexandria and Archelaus in the second half by Eusebius, Athanasius,, Macarius Magnus, Hillary, Didymus, Basil, Titus of Bostra, Cyril of Jerusalem, Gregory of Nyssa, Apostolic Canons and Constitutions, Epiphanius and Ambrose (all heavily) in the fourth century" (Pickering, pp. 67-68). Miller listed "2630 citations from 76 Fathers or sources, ranging over a span of 300 years (AD 100-400), supporting readings of the 'Byzantine' text as opposed to those of the critical text of the English Revisers (which received 1753 citations)" (Pickering, p. 66).

Carson explains away ante-Nicene Byzantine readings with such arguments as "early Byzantine readings do not necessarily argue for the presence of an early Byzantine text type" (Carson, p. 117) and "many Byzantine readings in the late manuscripts of the fathers may well be due to assimilation of the Byzantine text type in the post-Nicene period" (Carson, p. 110). He speaks of "the Byzantine tradition in its mature conflated form" (Carson, p. 112). He concludes, "There is still no hard evidence that the Byzantine text type was known in the ante-Nicene Byzantine Period" (Carson, p. 113). Yet he admits, "Pickering rightly points out that the Ante-Nicene fathers also contain some uniquely Byzantine readings," that is, readings that are found in no text type other than Byzantine. There are not many of them, but there are a few" (Carson, p. 111).

3. Hort's notion that no version supports the Syrian (Byzantine) text type is not true. "Until the latter part of the nineteenth century, the Peshitta

was generally regarded as the oldest translation of the New Testament into Syriac, a second-century date being assigned to it" (Hills, Introduction, p. 55). Burkitt (1904) argued for the fifth-century date, but Hills rebutted that hypothesis. Although there have been some modifications concerning its text type, "all scholars still seem to agree that the Peshitta frequently supports the Byzantine text. If, therefore, the Peshitta actually does date from the second century, it remains an outstanding witness to the antiquity of the Byzantine text and, consequently, to the falsity of Hort's theory; this text is a late text" (Hills, Introduction, p. 56).

4. Hort's internal evidence argument does not demonstrate that the Syrian text type was a late, edited text. The problem with that notion is that evaluating variant readings is subjective. Hodges explains, "Personal opinion—and even personal bias—can easily determine one's decision. This has recently been acknowledged by a leading textual critic who, himself, has in the past endorsed this reading through his own methodological approach. Speaking of the two criteria primarily relied on by modern critics in deciding on a reading (namely, 'choose the reading which fits the context' and 'choose the reading which explains the origin of the other reading'), E. C. Colwell has confessed, 'as a matter of fact, these two standard criteria for the appraisal of the inner evidence for readings can easily cancel each other out and leave the scholar free to choose in terms of his own prejudgment.' Indeed, it was Colwell who has most effectively pointed out that the generalizations which scholars have been making for so long about scribal habits are based upon a quite inadequate induction of the evidence." Hodges adds, "The knowledge possessed by modern textual critics about scribes and manuscripts is so

ambiguous that it can, without difficulty, be used to reach almost any conclusion (Hodges, 1968, pp. 342-344).

To sum up, Hort's four arguments that the Byzantine text type was edited and, therefore, late are not valid. Moreover, the proof that the Byzantine text type is not a late, edited text is the discovery of the papyrus manuscripts. For example, while there are other text type readings in the Bodmer papyri, there are 26 Byzantine readings in the Gospels, 8 in Acts, and 31 in Paul's epistles. Some scholars have argued that these are Caesarea in readings, but that is not true in Acts or Paul's epistles. In commenting on the Bodmer papyri, Britannica says, "These and other papyri witness to the state of the early text of the New Testament in Egypt, indicating that no *one* text dominated and that text types of different origin flourished side by side" (see the complete article at the website https://www.britannicacom/topic/biblical-literature/Minuscules#ref598026).

For the Alexandrian Text Type Hort's theory that the Alexandrian text type is earlier and, therefore, closer to the autographs is also weighed and found wanting.

1. Hort placed great weight on genealogical evidence (historical relationships of the manuscript). He emphatically declares, "ALL TRUSTWORTHY RESTORATION OF CORRUPTED TEXT IS FOUNDED ON THE STUDY OF THEIR HISTORY" (Hort, p. 40; the all-caps are his). However, he never used it to support the Alexandrian text type. Gordon Fee said, "It must be remembered that Hort did not use genealogy in order to discover the original NT text. Whether justified or not, Hort used genealogy *solely* to dispense with the Syrian (Byzantine) text. Once he has [sic] eliminated the Byzantines from serious

consideration, his preference for the Neutral (Egyptian) MSS. was based *strictly* on intrinsic and transcriptional probability" (Gordon Fee, in an article for *Society of Biblical Literature*, italics his, cited by Green, p. 11).

Colwell concluded, "The genealogical method is not of primary importance" and Leon Vaganay, another textual critic, asserted that "applied to the New Testament text, the system is useless" (both quotations are cited by Metzger, p. 160). Sturz says, "Colwell deals a devastating blow to the genealogical method as applied (or rather, as it was not applied) by WH" (Sturz, p. 30).

2. Westcott and Hort argued that because Vaticanus and Sinaiticus were the oldest manuscripts, they represented the autographs best. Aland states, "The oldest manuscript does not necessarily have the best text. $\mathfrak{P}^{47}$ is, for example, by far the oldest of the manuscripts containing the full or almost full text of the Apocalypse, but it is certainly not the best" (Kurt Aland, "The Significance of the Papyri for Progress in New Testament Research," *The Bible in Modern Scholarship*, ed. J. Philip Hyatt, p. 333). Blindly preferring the "oldest" manuscripts does not ensure arriving at the correct readings. $\mathfrak{P}^{115}$ date between 225 and 275 According to $\mathfrak{P}^{115}$, Revelation 13:18 reads "or 616," which can be proven wrong. Besides, Aland concludes, "Westcott and Hort had no direct witness to the New Testament earlier than the fourth century" (Aland, p. 14).

3. Westcott and Hort's Neutral text type (the Alexandrian text type) came from Egypt. But as Farstad points out, "As far as we know, not a single original autograph of a Gospel or Epistle was ever sent to Egypt, the country of origin of Codex Vaticanus and Codex Sinaiticus" (Farstad, p. 110). Metzger says, "It is widely agreed that the Alexandrian text was prepared by skillful editors, trained in the scholarly traditions of

Alexandria" (Metzger, p. 215). Sinaiticus and Vaticanus "represent a local text which never had any significant currency except in that part of the ancient world. By contrast, the majority of manuscripts were widely diffuse, and their ancestral roots must reach back to the autographs themselves" (Hodges and Farstad, p. x).

Hodges says the Nestle-Aland and the United Bible Society texts rely heavily on manuscripts mainly from Egypt, including Vaticanus and Sinaiticus, along with $\mathfrak{P}^{45}$, $\mathfrak{P}^{46}$, $\mathfrak{P}^{47}$, $\mathfrak{P}^{66}$, and $\mathfrak{P}^{75}$. He adds, "The text which results from dependence on such manuscripts as these may fairly be described as Egyptian. Its evidence in earlier times outside Egypt is unproven" (Hodges, *The Greek New Testament*, p. ix).

Egypt is known for corrupting Greek manuscripts of the New Testament. "Clement of Alexandria (fl. 194) complained of those who tampered with (or metaphase) the Gospel for their own sinister ends (Stromata, IV.6)" (Sturz, p. 117). Tertullian (160-220), from Carthage in the Roman province of Africa, was known as the "Father of Latin Christianity" and the "Founder of Western theology." "He discouraged the use of Scripture with heretics because they do not use, but only abuse Scripture.... He said they abuse Scripture by the rejection of parts or through changing by diminishing or adding and also by false interpretation.... He charged ... the Valentinians with using perverse interpretation, though 'they also have added and taken away'" (Sturz, p. 117). Origen (185-254) became a teacher at Alexandria while still in his teens. He wrote, "The differences among the manuscripts [of the Gospels] have become great, either through the negligence of some copyists or through the perverse audacity of others; they either neglect to check over what they have transcribed, or, in the process of checking, they lengthen or shorten, as they please" (Metzger, p. 152).

In response to Aland's article entitled "The Text of the Church," Pickering wrote, "By way of background, I will start with some observations that Aland makes about the early Egyptian church. 'The earliest form of the New Testament text in Egypt obviously had its origins outside Egypt' (p. 138). It was necessary since Egypt did not possess any autographs. This means that the textual tradition in Egypt was second-hand from the start. Then Aland informs us that 'At the close of the 2nd century' the Egyptian church was 'dominantly gnostic' and goes on to state: 'The copies existing in the gnostic communities could not be used [by bishop Demetrius] because they were under suspicion of being corrupt' (p. 138). Now, this is all very instructive—what Aland is telling us, in other words, is that up to AD 200, the textual tradition in Egypt could not be trusted. Aland's assessment here is most probably correct. Notice what Bruce Metzger says about the early church in Egypt: Among Christian documents that originated in Egypt or circulated there during the second century among both Orthodox and Gnostic groups are numerous apocryphal gospels, Acts, epistles, and apocalypses. There are also fragments of exegetical and dogmatic works composed by Alexandrian Christians, chiefly Gnostics, during the second century…. In fact, to judge by the comments made by Clement of Alexandria, almost every deviant Christian sect was represented in Egypt during the second century; Clement mentions the Valentinians, the Basilidians, the Marcionites, the Peratae, the Encratites, the Docetists, the Haimetites, the Cainites, the Ophites, the Simonians, and the Eutychites. What proportion of Christians in Egypt during the second century were orthodox is not known. So, the situation in

Egypt at the end of the second century (A.D. 200) appears to have been this: Both the Christian church and her Scriptures were in a bad way. In the year 200 (the approximate date of 𝔓⁴⁶, 𝔓⁶⁶, 𝔓⁷⁵), Egypt would be one of the last places in the Mediterranean world where one would go to find 'the Text of the Church'" (Pickering p. 1; see the article at https://www.prunch.com.br/wp-content/uploads/2018/09/ALAND-Biblicapdf).

Additionally, the Alexandrian text type is marred by mistakes, including some factual errors. Compared to the Traditional Text, B omitted 2877 words from the four Gospels alone, and ℵ eliminated 3455 words (Burgon, p. 75). In the Gospels, B has 589 readings particular to itself, affecting 850 words, and ℵ has 1460 such readings, affecting 2640 words (Burgon, p. 319). For a sample list, see Appendix III. Also, the UBS no longer recognizes the Alexandrian text type (Pickering, p. 37 fn. 3).

The Western Text type

Contents The main witness of the "Western" text type is the fifth-century uncial Codex Bezae (D), which only has the four Gospels and Acts. It is also in the sixth-century Codex Claromontanus, which only has Paul's epistles, and in two ninth-century uncials, F and G. In Codex Sinaiticus, the first eight chapters of John have Western readings. Some of the papyri from Egypt have Western readings (𝔓²⁹, 𝔓³⁸, 𝔓⁴⁸). It is the predominant text type in the old Latin versions.

Aland wrote Codex D, which "has been the most controversial of the New Testament uncials, the principal witness of the text called "Western," although it was written in either Egypt or North Africa, probably by a scribe whose mother tongue was Latin. The Latin text is related to the accompanying Greek text, standing independent of the main Latin tradition and probably representing a secondary product. When and how the Greek exemplar of D originated is unknown" (Aland, p. 109).

Today, the academic community prefers to refer to Codex D and Codex θ (theta) instead of the Western text. "Paleography has demonstrated that Codex Bezae Cantabrigiensis was not written in the West (despite its Greek-Latin text), but either in North Africa or Egypt. Of course, the provenance [origin] of the exemplar used by the scribe of D (05) is another matter" (Aland, p. 52). Aland wrote, "The text found in the Codex Bezae (D) of the fifth century, however, represents (in its exemplar) the achievement of an outstanding early theologian of the third/fourth century. In its day, it achieved only a limited following" (Aland p. 69). Codex D is roughly 50% Byzantine (Pickering and Freitas, p. 61).

Circulation Metzger says, "The Western type of text can be traced back to a very early date, where it was used by Marcion (and probably Tatian), Irenaeus, Tertullian, and Cyprian" (Metzger, p. 213). In other words, it has quotations by Irenaeus from *Gaul* (modern-day France), Tertullian from Carthage in *Africa*, and Cyprian also from Carthage. Metzger adds that it "circulated widely, not only in North Africa, Italy, and Gaul (which are geographically 'Western') but also in Egypt and (in somewhat different text forms) in the East" (Metzger, pp. 213-214).

Characteristics Metzger says the "so-called Western" text type is "characterized by longer or shorter additions and by certain striking omissions" (Metzger, p. 213). As Hort pointed out, the Western text type is characterized by *changes* in words, clauses, and even sentences "with astonishing freedom" (Hort, p. 122) and *additions* (Hort, p. 123). Burgon says, "No text is more thoroughly disfigured by corruption and interpolations than that of Codex D. He speaks of its invertible … practice of expanding the narrative by means of interpolation which seldom recommend themselves as genuine by a semblance of internal probability" (Burgon, *The Last Twelve Verses*, p. 155).

In Luke 3:22, instead of "You are my beloved Son in whom I am well pleased," certain Old Latin manuscripts, including D, Justin Martyr, and Clement of Alexandria, read, "You are my beloved Son, this day I have begotten You." If that reading is true, Luke was inclined to the adoptionist view that Jesus became the Son of God at His baptism (Hills, Introduction, p. 36).

In Luke 18:19, Jesus said, "No one is good except one, God the Father." The same reading is found in Justin Martyr, Clement of Alexandria, Origen, and in certain manuscripts of the Armenian version and Old Latin manuscripts. Hills says, "According to this reasoning, Jesus actually does disclaim deity, attributing essential goodness only to God the Father…. Randall Harris may have been right in attributing this reading to Marcion (c. 144)…. Or it may be that Burgon was correct in crediting the great gnostic leader Valentinus (c. 140) with the invention of it, seeing that it appears to have been advocated by him and by his disciple Ptolemaeus and to have been much in vogue among the Marcosians, the Naasenes and other gnostic sects (Hills, Introduction, pp. 35-36).

Pickering points out that the 25th edition of the Nestlé text denies the existence of a "Western" text. Klijn contends that a Western text does not exist, and Aland speaks of the "phantom Western text," referring to it as the "D text," which is Bezae. Kenyon says it is not so much a text "as a congeries of various readings, not descending from any one archetype, but possessing an infinitely complicated and intricate parentage. No one manuscript can even approximately represent the *d*-text" (Pickering, p. 38). Pickering adds, "No one has ever reconstructed a 'Western' archetype, and there is general agreement among scholars that there never was one. That is why critical editions of the Greek NT do not include a cover symbol for the 'Western' text. In their recent textbook, the Alands now speak of the 'B' text, referring to Codex Bezae" (Pickering, p. 153).

The Byzantine Text type

As much as 80 to 95% of all Greek manuscripts comprise one family of Greek manuscripts (Farstad, p. 109). That family of manuscripts has been referred to as the Textus Receptus, the Syrian Text, the Traditional Text, the Majority Text, and the Byzantine Text (hereafter, this family of manuscripts will be collectively referred to as the Byzantine text type). Here is the case for the Byzantine text type.

The Area of Origin: The Byzantine text type originates from the area where almost all of the autographs were originally written or where they were sent, and therefore, were first copied. Sixteen books of the New Testament were either written from or to Asia Minor: Matthew, John, Galatians, Ephesians, Colossians, 1 and 2 Timothy, Philemon, 1 and 2 Peter, 1, 2, 3 John, Revelation, and probably James and Jude. Revelation was written to seven churches in Asia Minor, including Ephesus, Smyrna, Pergamum, Thyatira, Sardis, Philadelphia, and Laodicea. Six books of the New Testament were written to the Greeks: 1 and 2 Corinthians, Philippians, 1 and 2 Thessalonians, and Titus, in Crete. Five books of the New Testament were connected with Rome, including Mark, Romans, probably Luke, Acts, and possibly Hebrews. In other words, 22 of the 27 books of the New Testament were either written from or to Asia Minor or Greece. The other five pertain to Rome.

Borland puts it like this: "Practically the entire corpus of NT autographs was sent originally to Asia Minor and Europe—e.g., Rome, Corinth, Thessalonica, Philippi, Ephesus, Colossae, Crete, Asia, Cappadocia, Pontius, Galatia, etc. The earliest generations of copies would have been made in the same areas. It is perhaps fortunate that the great majority of our extant MSS come to us from these very areas" (Borland, The *Journal of the Evangelical Theological Society*, vol. 25, p. 506).

Today, historians refer to that area as the Byzantine Empire. Here is how it got that name. Byzantium was an ancient Greek city. In AD 330, Constantine moved the capital of the Roman Empire to Byzantium and renamed it Constantinople (Istanbul today). After the fall of the Western Roman Empire in AD 476, the eastern part of the Roman Empire was called the Byzantine Empire, with its capital in Constantinople. The people considered themselves Romans, but their language was Greek, and their religion was the Orthodox Church. The Byzantine Empire existed until it fell to the Ottoman Empire in 1453, when Constantinople was captured.

Early Existence: The Byzantine text type was present in early Greek manuscripts, translations, and Christian writings. Consider the manuscript evidence. The second-century Chester Beatty Papyri contain "many Byzantine readings which previously had been regarded as late. Twenty-six Byzantine readings occur in the Gospels, eight in Acts, and 31 in the Pauline epistles (Hills, Introduction, p. 50). The Bodmer II Papyri contain 22 papyrus manuscripts discovered in Egypt in 1952. These manuscripts have been dated as early as about AD 200, although some date them later.

While the text type has been identified as Alexandrian, there are Byzantine text type readings. Hills says, "To be precise, Papyrus Bodmer II contains thirteen percent of all the alleged readings of the Byzantine text in the area it covers (18 out of 138). Thirteen percent of the Byzantine readings, which most critics have regarded as late, have been proven by Papyrus Bodmer II to be early readings" (Hills, Introduction, p. 54).

Sturz lists 150 distinctively Byzantine readings that have early Egyptian papyri support (Sturz, pp. 61, 145-159) and lists corrections in papyri from a Byzantine text type to an Alexandrian text type (Sturz, p. 63).

Mark 6-9 of $\mathfrak{P}^{45}$ (where extant), there is 38% agreement with Codex D, 40% with the TR, 42% with B, 59% with f^{13}, and 68% with W^3. In Mark 5-16 of codex W, there is 34% agreement with B, 36% agreement with D, 38% with the TR and 40% with ℵ (Pickering, p. 43). Pickering lists more on page 44.

> $\mathfrak{P}^{45}$ agrees with ℵ 19 times, with B 24 times, and with TR 32 times
> $\mathfrak{P}^{66}$ agrees with ℵ 14 times, with B 29 times, and with TR 33 times
> $\mathfrak{P}^{75}$ agrees with ℵ 9 times, with B 33 times, and with TR 29 times
> $\mathfrak{P}^{45,66,75}$ agree with ℵ 4 times, with B 18 times, and with TR 20 times
> $\mathfrak{P}^{45,66}$ agree with ℵ 7 times, with B 3 times, and with TR 8 times
> $\mathfrak{P}^{45,75}$ agree with ℵ 1 time, with B 2 times, and with TR 2 times
> $\mathfrak{P}^{66,75}$ agree with ℵ 0 times, with B 8 times, and with TR 455 times

An early translation has Byzantine text type readings. The Peshitta is the Syriac version of the New Testament. Syria was part of what became known as the Byzantine Empire. The date of the Peshitta is a matter of debate. Most critics today date it from the fifth century, but there is evidence that it's probably from the second century (for details, see the chapter "Conclusion").

Metzger says a debate took place at Oxford on May 6, 1897. Edward Miller and several others were on one side, holding up Burgon's position, and William Sandy and A. C. Headlam were on the other. As Metzger explains, "One of the chief points of contention was the date of the Peshitta Syriac version of the New Testament. Miller maintained that this version, which is a witness to the Syrian type of text, dates back to the second century, and that, therefore, the Syrian type of text did not originate with Lucian and his contemporaries at the beginning of the fourth century. Sandy acknowledged that the date of the Peshitta was the 'sheet anchor' of Miller's position but was unable to produce convincing evidence for its late origin" (Metzger, pp. 136-137 fn., who cites *The Oxford Debate on The Textual Criticism of the New Testament*, 1897, p. 28).

Early Christian authors have Byzantine text type readings. Most scholars believe the Didache was written in Palestine before AD 100 (see article: https://www.earlychurch.org.uk/article_didache.html#gsc.tab=0). It claims to be the teaching of the 12 apostles. It quotes the Lord's Prayer, including the ending, which is in the Byzantine text type and not in the Alexandrian text type (8:2-7). Papias (AD 95-110; see below) from Hierapolis near Colossae refers to the story of the woman taken in adultery, which is found in the Byzantine text type but not in the Alexandrian text type. Two of the earliest Christian authors include passages with the Byzantine text type.

Sturz says Byzantine readings have early church Father support" 1) Luke 10:21, Clement; 2) Luke 12:5, Tertullian; 3) Luke 12:22, Clement;

4) Luke 12:31, Clement and Marcion; 5) John 2:24, Origen; 6) John 4:31, Origen; 7) John 13:26, Origen; 8) Romans 10:14, Clement; 9) 1 Corinthians 4:11, Clement and Origen; 10) 1 Corinthians 5:10, Origen; 11) 1 Corinthians 7:5, Origen; 12) 1 Corinthians 7:7, Origen; 13) 1 Corinthians 9:7, Origen; 14) 1 Corinthians 9:21, Origen; 15) Ephesians 2:12 (Origen) and Tertullian; 16) Philippians 1:14, Maricon 17) Hebrews 11:32, Clement; 18) 1 Peter 2:5, Clement and Origen (Sturz, p. 79).

The quotation from a church Father indicates the type of Text he used in his time and in his area. Irenaeus, who lived in Gaul (France), used a Western text type. Origen, one of the chief supporters of the Alexandrian and Caesarea texts, lived in both areas. Granted, Chrysostom was the earliest Father to use the Byzantine text type, but there are no earlier Antiochian Fathers whose literary remains are extensive enough to allow for the analysis of New Testament quotations in terms of the type of text they used. Besides, consider this. "While Irenaeus is a second-century father and Origen a third, the fact that Irenaeus' quotations do not support the form of text used later by Origen in Egypt cannot be used as proof that the Alexandrian text type did not exist earlier than Origen" (Sturz, p. 80).

The conclusion is clear. Byzantine text readings existed earlier than the fourth century. As mentioned before, the Didache, which was written before AD 100, quotes the Lord's prayer, including the ending omitted by the Alexandrian text types. Papias, who wrote between AD 95 and 110, refers to the story of the woman taken in adultery, which is omitted by the Alexandrian text types.

Furthermore, the autograph remained in existence until late into the second century. Daniel Wallace, an authority on textual criticism, points out that Tertullian, who wrote about AD 180, said, "Come now, you who would indulge a better curiosity if you would apply it to the business of your salvation, run over [to] the apostolic churches, in which the very thrones of the apostles are still pre-eminent in their places, in which their own authentic writings are read, uttering the voice and representing the face of each of them severally." Wallace adds that "Tertullian goes on to discuss each of these 'authentic writings' as being found in the very churches to which they were written. He mentions Corinth, Philippi, Thessalonica, Ephesus, and Rome. He urges his readers to visit these sites to check out these authentic writings. This seems to suggest that he believed that these documents were autographs. At the least, it suggests that by his day, carefully done copies of the originals were considered important for verifying what the apostles meant, and such copies had a strong connection to the churches to which they were originally written. One still has to wonder why Tertullian focuses on the very churches that received the originals if he didn't mean by the comment that these churches still preserved the autographs." Wallace concludes, "From the context and from lexical usage, Tertullian meant the autographs" (see Wallace, "Did the Original New Testament Manuscripts still exist in the Second Century?" See the article at https://bible.org/article/did-original-new-testament-manuscripts-still-exist-second-century-0).

Wallace also says that Peter, Bishop of Alexandria, who died the last year of the Diocletian persecution in AD 311, "speaks of the autograph of the Gospel of John as still existing in his day. The copy itself that was written by the hand of the evangelist, which, by the divine grace, has been preserved in the most holy church of Ephesus, and is there adored by the faithful" (see the article at https://bible.org/article/did-original-new-testament-manuscripts-still-exist-second-century-0). Galen (AD 129-216), a Greek physician and philosopher, spoke of papyrus manuscripts lasting 300 years (see the article by Pearse, "Galen on a 300-year-old papyrus roll," at https://www.roger-pearse.com/weblog/2011/02/02/galen-on-a-300-year-old-papyrus-roll/).

The significance of this information from Tertullian and Peter, Bishop of Alexandria, lies in the fact that the original autographs were still in the churches to which they were written—the very area that produced the Byzantine text.

Byzantine text type readings existed not only earlier than 350, but there is no question that the Byzantine text type was in existence in the fourth century. Even Hort agreed that John Chrysostom (347-407) used the Byzantine text type. He wrote, "An overwhelming proportion of the variants common to the great mass of cursive and late uncial Greek MSS are identical with the readings followed by Chrysostom" (Hort, *Introduction and Appendix*, p. 91).

So, although the existing Byzantine text type manuscripts are dated from 900 to 1500, there is evidence that this type of manuscript not only existed by the fourth century (Chrysostom) but also goes as far back as the first century (the Byzantine text type readings in the Didache and Papias).

The Attitude of the Copyist From the beginning, those who received the Scriptures were warned not to mishandle them. Moses cautioned, "You shall not add to the word which I command you, nor take from it, that you may keep the commandments of the LORD your God which I command you" (Deut. 4:2). Later, he repeated the caution, "Whatever I command you, be careful to observe it; you shall not add to it nor take away from it" (Deut. 12:32). Proverbs echoes the admonition, "Every word of God *is* pure; He *is* a shield to those who put their trust in Him. Do not add to His words, Lest He rebuke you, and you be found a liar" (Prov. 30:5-6). The Old Testament saints were taught not to change the Scriptures,

"Josephus confirms that the Old Testament principle ... continued to be recognized in the first century" (Kruger, *The Early Text of the New Testament*, p. 72). Josephus wrote, "We have given practical proof of our reverence for our own Scripture. Therefore, although such long ages have now passed, no one has ventured either to add or to remove, or to alter a syllable" (*Ag. Ap.* 1.42).

Until the mid-20th century, the oldest known copy of the Hebrew Old Testament was a Masoretic Text dated to approximately AD 900. Then, the Dead Sea Scrolls were discovered. Among the Dead Sea Scrolls was a copy of Isaiah, dated between 100 and 200 BC. In other words, with the discovery of the Isaiah scroll, we have jumped 1000 years closer to the time when the original Hebrew manuscripts were written.

The differences between the Isaiah manuscript of the Masoretic Text and the Isaiah manuscript of the Dead Sea Scrolls are few and minor. In a few places, there are differences, such as the presence or absence of an article or the distinction between singular and plural forms. That's incredible! If that is true for the Isaiah manuscript, it is no doubt true of the remainder of the Masoretic Text of the Old Testament. There is little doubt that we have an accurate copy of the Hebrew Old Testament.

As far as the New Testament is concerned, Paul claimed he wrote Scripture. He said, "If anyone thinks himself to be a prophet or spiritual, let him acknowledge that the things which I write to you are the commandments of the Lord" (1 Cor. 14:37). "For this we say to you by the word of the Lord, that we which are alive and remain until the coming of the Lord will by no means precede those who are asleep" (1 Thess. 4:15).

"Not only do Pauline letters regularly make claims that they had been written with divinely given authority (Gal. 1:1; 1 Thess. 2:13; 1 Cor. 7:12, 14:37), but they also include commands that they be read publicly at the gathering of the church (Col. 4:16; 1 Thess. 5:27; 2 Cor. 10:9). This practice of reading Scripture in worship can be traced back to the Jewish synagogue, where portions from the Old Testament were routinely read aloud to the congregations (Lk. 4:17-20; Acts 13:15, 15:21). Indeed, 1 Timothy makes this connection clear when Timothy is exhorted to 'devote yourself to the public reading of Scripture' (1 Tim. 4:13:6)" (Kruger, p. 67).

Peter recognized Paul's epistles as Scripture. He wrote, "As also our beloved brother Paul, according to the wisdom given to him, has written to you, as also in all his epistles, speaking in them of these things, in which are some things hard to understand, which untaught and unstable *people* twist to their own destruction, as *they do* also the rest of the Scriptures" (2 Pet. 3:15-16). "This passage does not refer to just one letter of Paul, but to a *collection* of Paul's letters (how many is unclear) that had already begun to circulate throughout the churches—so much so that the author could refer to 'all his [Paul's] letters' and expected his audience will understand that to which he was referring…. He mentions it quite casually, offering no introduction, defense, or explanation of this idea" (Kruger, p. 66). "Meade even argues that the author of 2 Peter includes Petrine text within the category of Christian scripture by referring to Paul as 'our beloved brother' (3:15), a likely reference to the 'college' of apostles in which Peter certainly participated (cf. Pet. 1:16)" (Kruger, p. 67).

Paul called Luke Scripture. He wrote, "For the Scripture says, 'You shall not muzzle an ox while it treads out the grain,' and, 'The laborer is worthy of his wages' (1 Tim. 5:18). The first quotation is from Deuteronomy 25:4 and the second is from Luke 10:7. Paul calls Luke Scripture. Meade considers this evidence of an early "Cameron consciousness" (Meade, cited by Kruger, p. 68). John Meier notes, "The only interpretation that avoids contorted intellectual acrobatics or special pleading is the plain, obvious one. [1 Timothy] is citing Luke's Gospel alongside Deuteronomy as normative Scripture for the ordering of the church's ministry" (Meier, cited by Kruger, p. 69).

The point is that many of the books of the New Testament are referred to as Scripture in the New Testament. "Furthermore, the apostles and other early Jewish members of the Antioch church had the tradition of Israel's careful copying of the Scriptures as an example for their care" (Sturz, pp. 104-105).

Kruger argues Paul's statement that when it comes to covenants, "no one holds it adds to it once it has been ratified" (Gal. 3:15) echoes Deuteronomy 4:2 and "therefore, for Paul— and no doubt early Christians influenced by Paul or who shared Paul's Jewish background—covenant documents were not to be altered." He concludes, "The overall attitude for the reproduction of the Old Testament Scriptures—particularly the language of 'not adding or taking away'—is not abandoned when we reach the New Testament era but is reaffirmed and applied (implicitly or explicitly) by early Christians to the New Testament writings" (Kruger, p. 73).

Kruger is right. The Apostle John wrote, "For I testify to everyone who hears the words of the prophecy of this book: If anyone adds to these things, God will add to him the plagues that are written in this book, and if anyone takes away from the words of the book of this prophecy, God shall take away his part from the Book of Life, from the holy city, and *from* the things which are written in this book" (Rev. 22:18-19).

This concern for correctly copying Scripture extended beyond the New Testament. "One area that has been largely overlooked is the *attitude* toward that text that is actually expressed by Christians in the earliest literary sources, that is, statements about how they would have viewed their sacred writings, they would have understood the transmission and preservation of the text, and how they would have responded to the changes and alterations of the text. In other words, how much attention has been given to the literary products of early Christians (the text itself), less has been given to the literary culture of early Christians (their expressed attitude to the text)" (Kruger, pp. 63-64, italics added).

Shortly after the New Testament was written, in the early second century and throughout the century, authors recognized the New Testament books as Scripture, which influenced their attitude toward it.

1. Didache. The Didache is the popular name for The *Teaching of the Apostles* (Eusebius, *Ecclesiastical History 3:25*). It is called the Didache because the Greek word translated as "teaching" is didache. Ehrman says it appears to have been written "at the same time as or possibly even earlier than some of the books of the New Testament" (Ehrman, vol. 1, p. 165). Zdziarski dates it between 49-79 (www.zdziarski.com/papers/didache). The dating of the Didache at 49 is probably too early; however, dating it before 100, or even between 80 and 90, is reasonable.

The Didache contains quotations and numerous allusions to Matthew. The author says, "Neither pray like the hypocrites, but as the Lord has commanded in His Gospel, in this way pray" (8:2). He also states, "The meek will inherit the land" (3:7). Several times, he mentions being double-minded (2:4; 4:4), reminiscent of James 1:8. There are allusions to other New Testament books, including slaves told to be subject to their masters (4:11; Eph. 6:5; Col. 3:22), believers being told not to eat meat sacrificed to idols (6:3; Acts 15:29), believers being instructed that if people do not work, do not let them live with you idle (12:4; 2 Thess. 3:11-12), and prophets are worthy of their food as workmen are worthy of theirs (13:1-2; 1 Tim. 5:17). Thiessen says, "It uses Matthew a good deal and Luke some" and "it knows most of our New Treatment books" (Thiessen, p. 13).

Kruger observes that the Didache declares, "Do not abandon the commandments of the Lord, that guard what you have received, neither adding to them or taking away' (4:13).... "The 'commandments of the Lord' in the Didache are no longer a reference to the Old Testament commandments as in Deuteronomy 4:2, but now refer to the teachings of Jesus. Therefore, the teachings of Jesus, whatever they may be, not only have equal (if not superior) authority to the Old Testament, but now they have a new 'inscriptural curse' attached to them—the people must be careful that they are 'neither adding to them nor taking away.' ... Such a written text is suggested in Didache 8:2, 'nor should you pray like the hypocrites, but as the *Lord commanded in his gospel*, you should pray as follows, 'our Father in heaven ...' Here we have a reference to what Jesus 'commanded' Anatole that is contained in the gospel and that when the Text proceeds to cite the Lord's prayer in a manner very close to Matthew 6:9-13" (Kryger, p. 74, italics his).

The Didache recognized the New Testament as Scripture and instructed scribes to be careful in their transmission of it. It quotes the Lord's Prayer, including the ending, which is in the Byzantine text type and not in the Alexandrian text type (8:2-7).

2. Papias. Papias, who wrote between AD 95 and 110, was the author of five books entitled The *Interpretations of the Sayings of the Lord*, which, unfortunately, have disappeared, except for a few fragments that are recorded in the writings of Irenaeus (*Against Heresies*, 5:33.4, 5:36.1-2) and Eusebius (*Ecclesiastical History*, 3:39.3-5, 15-16; see 3:24 for Eusebius' view). The Eusebius section says Matthew wrote in Hebrew, and Mark was Peter's interpreter (Cairns, p. 76). Papias mentions Matthew and Mark, quotes 1 John and 1 Peter, and knows John's Gospel (Thiessen, p. 13). Papias refers to the story of the woman taken in adultery (Morris, in his commentary on the Gospel of John, p. 883; he cites Eusebius, Eccl.. *Hist.*, 3:39, 17).

"Mark was the interpreter of Peter; he wrote down accurately everything that he recalled of the Lord's words and deeds.... For he was intent on just one purpose: *to leave nothing that he heard or to include any falsehood among them* (Eusebius, *H.E.* three. 39. 15). The italicized portion of this statement is a clear echo of the 'neither add nor take away' principle of Deuteronomy 4:2 and is here being applied specifically to the New Testament books (Mark).... This passage provides critically early testimony—especially given that Papias received his tradition from an even earlier source (the Elder)—that Christians were concerned that their stories of Jesus were accurately preserved in written form and (if need be) accurately translated" (Kruger, p. 75).

The Papias recognized the New Testament as Scripture and the attitude of scribes to be careful how they transmitted it. It refers to the story of the woman taken in adultery, which is in the Byzantine text type and not in the Alexandrian text type.

3. Polycarp. Polycarp wrote an epistle to the Philippians in 110 (Cairns, p.75). There are about sixty quotations from the New Testament, of which thirty-four are from Paul's writings (Cairns, p. 75). To be more specific, he quotes 14 books of the New Testament, including Matthew, Luke, Acts, Romans, 1 Corinthians, Galatians, Ephesians, Philippians, 1 Timothy, 2 Timothy, 1 Thessalonians, 2 Thessalonians, 1 Peter, and 1 John (Thiel claims that Polycarp alludes to all 27 books of the NT; for his proof see www.COGwriter.com). He says, "Only, as it is said in these Scriptures, Be angry and sin not, and Let not the sun set on your wrath" (Chapter 12). The word "Scriptures" is in the plural. In other words, he is citing two passages of Scripture. The first, "Be angry and sin not," is from Psalm 4:4, and the second, "Let not the sun go down on your wrath," is from Ephesians 4:26. Polycarp referred to Ephesians 4:26 as Scripture. "Polycarp's knowledge of Paul's writings is well-established, and he has demonstrated a 'very good memory' regarding Pauline citations" (Kruger, p. 70).

While describing those who engaged in wicked behavior, Polycarp made sure to include "whoever perverts the oracles of the Lord to his own lust." ... In the very next verse, Polycarp refers to the λογονη [translated "oracles" in the previous sentence] and then appears to quote from Matthew 26:41 (Kruger, p. 77), indicating he is referring to Scripture.

Polycarp (XIII) answered a request from the Philippi church to send them a collection of Ignatius' letters. This was probably within five years after Ignatius wrote, and it indicates that it was normal to make copies and collections of the writings so that each assembly could get a set (Pickering, video).

Polycarp recognized the New Testament as Scripture and the attitude of scribes to be careful how they transmitted it.

4. The Epistle of Barnabas. This Epistle (AD 130) says, "As it is written, 'Many are called, but few were chosen'" (Mt. 20:16 or 22:14). This statement is introduced by a formula that is common for the quotation of Old Testament Scripture—'as it stands written' (*The Epistle of Barnabas*, 4:14)" (Everett Harrison, p. 93; see also McDonald, p. 275). In Chapter 5, he says, "He came not to call the righteous, but sinners to repentance" (Mt. 9:13; Mk. 2:17; Lk. 5:32). In Chapter 7, he writes, "The Lord says, 'Behold, I will make the last like the first'" (Mt. 20:16). "The author of *Barnabas* regarded Matthew as scriptural" (Paget, cited by Kruger, p. 70). There is a possible allusion to Colossians 1:16 (Barnabas 11). Thiessen says, "It quotes Matthew and there are echoes of Romans, 1 and 2 Corinthians, and Ephesians. The writer perhaps knew 1 Peter and certain passages reminded us of John" (Thiessen, p. 17).

"While exerting Christians in the 'path of light,' *Barnabas* 19.11 declares, 'guard the injunctions you have received, *neither adding to them nor taking away.*' The author—again drawing clear parallels to Deuteronomy 4:2—continues to affirm that early Christians were concerned to pass along their tradition with care, not to make alterations or changes" (Kruger, 75, italics his).

The Epistle of Barnabas recognized the New Testament as Scripture and advised scribes to be careful in their transmission of it. It quotes Matthew 20:16, which is found in the Byzantine text type but not in the Alexandrian text type, as well as in the NASB, NIV, and ESV.

5. Justin Martyr. In his *Dialogue*, Justin Martyr (*ca.* 150) "complains that some Jews were altering the Scriptures, 'and from the sayings of

Jeremiah that have cut out the following: 'I [was] like a lamb that is brought to the slaughter' ... [and] this passage from the sayings of Jeremiah is still written in some copies in the synagogue of the Jews (with only a short time since they were cut out." ... Kruger points out that Justin Martyr "bases his argument on a principle accepted by both himself and his audience: the Scriptures are not to be altered or changed" (Kruger, p. 78).

6. Dionysius of Corinth. In Dionysius of Corinth (*ca.* 170), "Frustrated with the alternations to his own writings, Dionysius says, 'the apostles of the devil have filled them with tears, *by leaving out some things and putting in others.* The world awaits them. Therefore, it is no wonder that some have gone about to falsify even the scriptures of the Lord" (Kruger, pp. 75-76).

7. Irenaeus. Irenaeus (*ca.* 180) "complains about copyists who have changed the number 666 in Revelation 13:18 to 616. After stating that 666 stood in 'all the most approved and ancient copies,' he reminds the reader, 'there shall be no light punishment [inflicted] upon him who either adds or subtracts anything from the Scripture'" (*Haer.* 5.5.13.1). Such harsh language is particularly noteworthy given the relatively minor nature of the Text will change in Revelation 13:18. Elsewhere, Irenaeus affirms a similar attitude of care for the reproduction of Christian Scripture when he claims that the church's doctrine is 'being guarded and preserved without any forging of Scripture ... Neither receiving additions nor [suffering] curtailment" (Kruger, 76).

At the end of one of his letters, Irenaeus said, "I adjure thee, who shalt copy out of this book ... that thou compare what thou shalt transcribe and correct it with this copy whence thou art transcribing, with all care.' Kruger comments, "If Irenaeus was so concerned about changes to his own writings, then, no doubt, his concern about changes in the scriptures would be equal, if not greater. This concern is borne out by his severe criticism of the Valentinians for how they take the Scriptures and 'dismember and destroy the truths' which are in them 'by transferring passages' and 'adapting oracles of the Lord to their own opinions.' And, of course, the same attitude is evident when Irenaeus condemns the actions of Marcion because he 'mutilated the gospel which is according to Luke ... [and] dismembered the epistles of Paul'" (Kruger, p. 78).

An anonymous author cited by Eusebius "critiques the heretics of his day because they 'lay hands on the divine Scriptures, saying that they had corrected them ... their disciples have diligently written out copies corrected as if they say, but really corrupted by each one of them." Kruger said, "Note his *attitude* to the Text (Kruger, p. 78).

To summarize, several key observations need to be noted. First, New Testament books were recognized as Scripture early. "By the early second century, some New Testament books ...were not only functioning as Scripture but were regarded as Scripture by early Christians. [Several recent studies] have argued that the fourfold gospel was established by the early or middle second century. Likewise, John Barton has argued in an insightful study that the court books of the New Testament, mainly the Gospels and core epistles, were the authoritative sources for Christians 'amazingly early.' He concludes that it would be 'mistaken to say that [by the early second century] there was no Christian Scripture other than the Old Testament' for much of the core already had a high status as it would ever have'" (Kruger, p. 71).

Second, some changed the Scripture. "It seems evident two historical realities *coexisted* within early Christianity: early Christians, as a whole, valued the text of Scripture and did not view unbridled textual changes as acceptable, and, at the same time, some Christians changed the New Testament text and altered its wording (and sometimes in substantive ways)" (Kruger, p. 79, italics his).

Notice how many of these authors came from what later became known as the Byzantine Empire. Only one was from Egypt. Papias, who wrote between AD 95 and 110, was from Hierapolis near Colossae. Polycarp (AD 110) was from Smyrna. The Epistle of Barnabas was written from Alexandria. Justin Martyr (*ca.* AD 150) was from Palestine and later Ephesus. Dionysius of Corinth (*ca.* AD 170) was from Corinth. Irenaeus (*ca.* AD 180) was from Antioch. In other words, the people from the area that produced the Byzantine Text were aware that Scripture should be copied correctly.

However, Egypt, which produced the Alexandrian text type, is known for corrupting the Greek manuscripts of the New Testament. For one thing, Egypt was renowned for its expertise in textual criticism. In an article on textual criticism in general, rather than the textual criticism of New Testament manuscripts, the *Encyclopedia Britannica* provides an overview of the history of textual criticism. (see the article at https://www.britannicacom/topic/textual-criticism/History-of-textual-criticism). Here are some of the highlights gleaned from that article.

"The systematic study and practice of the subject [of textual criticism] originated in the 3rd century BCE with the Greek scholars of Alexandria.... The aim of the librarians ... was to collect and catalogue every extant Greek book and to produce critical editions of the most important ones together with textual and interpretative commentaries.... The copyist was expected to reproduce his exemplar [the MS being copied] as exactly as he could, and corrections were based on comparison with other copies, not on the unaided conjectural sagacity of the scribe. Such was the practice of the best monastic scriptoria." In other words, textual criticism *changes the text*.

No wonder Egypt had a problem with changing the text. Pickering points out, "To copy a text by hand in a language you do not understand is a tedious exercise—it is almost impossible to produce a perfect copy .... You virtually have to copy letter by letter and constantly check your place. (It is even more difficult if there is no space between words and no punctuation, as was the case in the NT text in the early centuries.) But if you cannot understand the text, it's very difficult to remain alert. Consider the case of $\mathfrak{P}^{66}$, [an Egyptian manuscript]. This papyrus manuscript is perhaps the oldest (c. 200) extant NT manuscript of any size (it contains most of John). It is one of the worst copies we have. It has an average of roughly two mistakes per verse, many being obvious, stupid, and nonsensical. From the pattern of mistakes, it is clear that the scribe copied syllable by syllable. I have no qualms in affirming that the person who produced $\mathfrak{P}^{66}$ did not know Greek. Had he understood the text, he would not have made the number and sort of mistakes that he did" (Pickering, "Preservation of the New Testament: who is best qualified?" https://www.youtube.com/watch?v=8o35ftvTfwk).

"E. C. Colwell analyzed $\mathfrak{P}$ and found about 145 itacisms plus 257 other singular readings, 25% of which were nonsensical. From the pattern of mistakes, it is clear that the copyist who did $\mathfrak{P}^{75}$ copied letter by letter! This means he did not know Greek" (from Pickering video).

K. Aland argued that before 200, the tide had begun to turn against the use of Greek in the areas that spoke Latin, Syriac, or Coptic (Egyptian), and 50 years later, the changeover to local languages was well advanced" (Aland, cited by Pickering, video). Pickering says, "Even if Egypt had started with a good text, already by the end of the second century, its competence to transmit the text was steadily deteriorating" (Pickering, video).

Additionally, Egyptian Christians complained that people were *corrupting* the copies of the New Testament text. "Clement of Alexandria (fl. 194) complained of those who tampered with (or paraphrased) the Gospel for their own sinister ends (Stromata, IV.6)" (Sturz, p. 117). Tertullian (160-220) was from Carthage in the Roman province of Africa. "He discouraged the use of Scripture with heretics because they do not use, but only abuse Scripture.... He said they abuse Scripture by the rejection of parts or through changing by diminishing or adding and also by false interpretation.... He charged ... the Valentinians with using perverse interpretation, though 'they also have added and taken away'" (Sturz, p. 117). Origen (185-254) became a teacher at Alexandria while still in his teens. He wrote, "The differences among the manuscripts [of the Gospels] have become great, either through the negligence of some copyists or through the perverse audacity of others; they either neglect to check over what they have transcribed, or, in the process of checking, they lengthen or shorten, as they please" (Metzger, p. 152).

Aland said, "Egypt was distinguished from other provinces of the church, so far as we can judge, by the early dominance of Gnosticism." He adds, "At the close of the second century," the Egyptian church was "dominantly gnostic." He also states, "Our knowledge of the church in

Egypt begins at the close of the second century with bishop Demetrius, who reorganized the dominantly gnostic Egyptian church by founding new communities, concentrating bishops, and above all by establishing relationships with the other provinces of the church fellowship. Every church needed manuscripts of the New Testament—how was Demetrius to provide them? Even if there were a scriptorium in his own see, he would have had to procure 'orthodox' exemplars for the scribes. The copies existing in the gnostic communities could not be used because they were under the superstition of being corrupt. There is no way of knowing where the bishop turned for squabble exemplars or for the large number of papyrus manuscripts he could give directly to the communities" ("The Text of the church?" Kurt Aland, *Trinity Journal*, Vol. 8, No. 92, Fall, 1987, p. 138).

To sum up, in Egypt, the text of the New Testament changed, even corrupted, due to textual criticism, the challenges of copying a foreign language, and deliberate tampering by false teachers. Remember, the Alexandrian text type originated in Egypt, and all modern English translations are based on it.

To put this in perspective, remember Christianity began in Jerusalem (Acts 1-7). When it was scattered (Acts 8:1), the epicenter of Christianity became Antioch in Asia Minor (Acts 13-20). In AD 95, John sent the book of Revelation to seven churches in Asia Minor, indicating that Christianity was still flourishing in Asia Minor. "Kurt Aland agreed with Adolf Harnack that "about 180 the greatest concentration of churches was in Asia Minor and along the Aegean coast of Greece.... Even around AD 325, the scene was largely unchanged. Asia Minor continued to be the heartland of the church" (from the Pickering video). The Byzantine Text type originated from an area where Greek was spoken and a tradition of accurate text copying prevailed, as Scripture was considered to be of utmost importance.

By the way, another indication of the attitude of the Christians in the Byzantine Empire concerning the Scriptures is their method of interpretation. The Syrian School of Antioch practiced literal interpretation. The earliest known author is Theophilus of Antioch (d. *ca.* 185). He claimed that Genesis 2:6-7 is "plainly related." He took the story of man's creation as he did the rest of Scripture in their plain and historical sense. Other members of the Syrian School include Dorotheus (d. *ca.* 300), Lucian (d. *ca.* 312), and Diodore of Tarsus (379-394), Bishop of Antioch, is said to have written commentaries on the epistles and a treatise on the principles of interpretation (Gilbert, cited by Ferguson, pp. 10-11). He also started a class to train young men in the principles of sacred exegesis (Macgilvray, cited by Ferguson, p. 10).

Chrysostom is a notable example of the Syrian School of Antioch. In contrast to the allegorical School of Alexandria, which denied the historicity of Old Testament events, Chrysostom believed the genuine historical character of the Old Testament must be recognized, or its spiritual significance would be marred. The superstructure of doctrine must be built on the rock of historical interpretation (Chase, cited by Ferguson, p. 23). Chrysostom recognized the importance of historical context in interpreting Scripture (Ferguson, pp. 24-25). He was also mindful that the Scripture must be interpreted in context (Ferguson, pp. 25-26). In his expositions, Chrysostom also took notice of grammatical details (Chase, cited by Ferguson, p. 28).

Eventually, the Syrian School ceased to exist in Antioch, but its interpretive principles had an immediate and long-range impact. For example, in his early days, Jerome was a convinced allegorist. His commentary on Obadiah was thoroughly allegorical. Although he was inconsistent, the Syrian School influenced him to more literal exegesis (Buttrick, cited by Ferguson, p. 37).

The Majority of the Manuscripts The Byzantine Text is the text type of 80 to 95 percent of all Greek manuscripts (Farstad, p. 109). How does one explain that the vast majority of manuscripts support the majority text type? Westcott and Hort explained away the majority by claiming it was a late, edited edition. Later theories suggest that the Byzantine text type evolved gradually over a prolonged period. Is there not a better explanation that this text type was closer to the original and, therefore, there was more time to produce more copies?

The Declaration of Independence was written in 1776. Suppose there was no printing press at that time, and people began to copy the Declaration of Independence by hand. Then, imagine that somewhere around 1820, someone made a copy that contained changes, and it began to be copied. All things being equal, which document would produce the most manuscripts today, the original 1776 document or the copy that was changed in 1820? Adam Boyd puts it this way: Imagine that 20 people make a copy of a document, and each of them asks 20 people to copy their copy. If 95% read one way and 5% read another way, common sense says that 95% is almost certainly the correct copy (see article at https://www.youtube.com/watch?v=rz2DfD_ej14).

Unity The Byzantine text type contains remarkable unity. Hort said, "An overwhelming proportion of the text in all known cursive MSS, except a few, is as a matter of fact identical, most especially in the Gospels and Pauline epistles; however, we may account for the identity. Further, the identity of readings implies identity of origin" (Hort, p. 143). The Byzantine text "has maintained a high degree of homogeneity. It has not undergone an extensive cross-fertilization from other text types" (Sturz, p. 125).

Furthermore, the majority of Greek manuscripts consist of a smooth Greek text with no grammatical, historical, or geographical errors. Hort says it has "completeness" and removes "all stumbling blocks out of the way of the ordinary reader.... New omissions, accordingly, are rare, and where they occur, are usually found to contribute to the apparent simplicity. Both in manner and diction, the Syrian text is conspicuously a full text. It delights in pronouns, conjunctions, and expletives and supplies links of all kinds, as well as in more steerable additions. It presents the New Testament in the form smooth and attractive." It is "Entirely blameless on either literary or religious grounds as regards vulgarised or unworthy diction" (Hort, p. 135). "In themselves, Syrian readings hardly ever offend at first. With rare exceptions, they run smoothly and easily in form and yield at once to even a careless reader a passable sense, free of surprises and seemingly transparent" (Hort, pp. 115-116). Yet, "The very smoothness and completeness of the text led these scholars [Westcott and Hort] to believe it [Byzantine text type] was late, edited, and hence corrupt" (Farstad, p. 108).

Metzger states that scribes corrupted the Vulgate and that, in an attempt to purify it, several recensions were produced during the Middle Ages. "Unfortunately, however, each of these attempts to restore Jerome's original version resulted evidently in still further textual corruption through a mixture of several types of Vulgate text, which had come to be associated with various new European centers of scholarship. As a result, the more than 8000 Vulgate manuscripts that are extant exhibit the greatest amount of cross-contamination of textual types" (Metzger, p. 76). The majority of Greek manuscripts display more uniformity than the Vulgate, an official fourth-century edition of the Latin manuscripts by Jerome. That's incredible!

Used throughout the Centuries The Byzantine text type has been used throughout the centuries. That's why it's called the Traditional Text. Everyone agrees it was used in the fourth century (Chrysostom) and throughout the Middle Ages. It was the text of the Protestant Reformation. Luther used it to translate the New Testament into German. Tyndale used it to translate the New Testament into English. It was the text used to translate the King James Version. It was the text used during the Wesleyan Revivals, the Great Awakening, and the modern missions movement. Is it not interesting and impressive that throughout history, until the latter part of the nineteenth century, the church used the Byzantine Text? It is the only family of the New Testament manuscripts that has had continuous use throughout church history, at least from about 500 (some argue even earlier). Hills asks, "How did it (the Byzantine text) become the text of the whole Greek-speaking church, in all nations, in all the Christian communities, during the greater part of the Byzantine Period (312-1453)?" (Hills, Green, p. 35).

Preservation The Byzantine text type is the only text type that has been *continually* preserved. Several verses appear to indicate that God will preserve His Word (Mt. 5:18; 24:35; Mk. 13:31; Lk. 16:17; 21:33; 1 Pet. 1:24-25). Perhaps God preserved His Word in a manuscript such as the

Codex Vaticanus or Codex Sinaiticus. That would be like God putting His Word in a safety deposit box to be opened centuries later. Hills argues "that it was through the usage of the Church that Christ has fulfilled His promise always to preserve the true New Testament and that therefore the Byzantine text found in the vast majority of Greek Testament manuscripts is the true text" (Hills, Introduction, pp. 65-66). That only appeals to people who believe in the inspiration and preservation of the Word of God, but as has been said, "To what better kind of person would you want to appeal?"

Summary: Neither the Alexandrian nor Western text types are considered text types, but the geographical origin, early existence, care of the copyist of Scripture, majority, unity, and use throughout the centuries, as well as divine preservation, support the claim that the Byzantine text type is the best representation of the autographs.

Pickering concludes, "The point is, although different manuscripts exhibit varying affinities, share certain peculiarities, they each differ substantially from all the others (especially the earlier ones) and therefore should not be lumped together. There is no such thing as the testimony of a "Western" or "Alexandrian" text type (as an entity)—there is only the testimony of individual MSS, Fathers, versions (or MSS of versions)" (Pickering, p. 43).

For a more detailed explanation of the case for the Byzantine text, see the Conclusion.

Chapter 8

THE MAJORITY TEXT

As has been pointed out, the vast majority of New Testament Greek manuscripts are so similar that they form a single family of manuscripts compared to other manuscripts. That, however, does not mean that all the manuscripts within that family (the Byzantine text type) are in perfect agreement. There are differences among the manuscripts that comprise the Byzantine text type.

Several attempts have been made to produce a "better" version of the Byzantine text type. One such attempt is *The Greek New Testament According to the Majority Text*, edited by Zane C. Hodges and Arthur L. Farstad. Both Hodges and Farstad are graduates of Dallas Seminary. Hodges taught Greek there for 27 years.

The Majority Text type

Later Manuscripts Hodges concedes that the Majority Text type manuscripts "on the whole [are] substantially later than the earliest Egyptian witnesses" (Hodges, *The Greek New Testament*, p. ix), but just because the surviving manuscripts are later does not mean that the content of those manuscripts is later. Hodges presents several arguments to demonstrate that the Majority text type represents the earliest textual form.

Majority of Manuscripts For one thing, the vast majority of extant Greek manuscripts of the New Testament are of the Majority text type. Hodges explains, "It is also well known among students of textual criticism that a large majority of this huge mass of manuscripts—somewhere between 80-90%—contains a Greek text which in most respects closely resembles the kind of text which was the basis of our King James Version" (Hodges, *Bib. Sac.* 1968, p. 335). The point is "the manuscript tradition of an ancient book will, under any but the most exceptional conditions, multiply in a reasonably regular fashion with the result that the copies nearest the autograph will normally have the largest number of descendants" (Hodges, *Bib. Sac.* 1968, p. 344). Hort even conceded this. He wrote, "A theoretical presumption indeed remains that a majority of extant documents is more likely to represent a majority of ancestral documents at each stage of transmission than vice versa" (Hort, p. 45, cited by Hodges, *Bib. Sac.* 1968, p. 344 fn.).

Wide Distribution Furthermore, "The witnesses to the Majority Text come from all over the ancient world. Their very number suggests that they represent a long and widespread chain of the manuscript tradition. It is necessary, therefore, to postulate that the surviving documents are descended from not extant ancestral documents of the highest antiquity. These must have been in their own time as old or older than the surviving witnesses from Egypt" (Hodges, *The Greek New Testament*, pp. ix-x).

Early Evidence There is evidence before the 4th century for the Majority Text. Burgon and Miller have charts listing the Majority Text readings in the Fathers (Burgon and Miller, *Traditional Text*, pp. 98-117). They also argue for an early date for the Syriac Peshitta, which supports the Majority Text (Burgon and Miller, *Traditional Text*, Appendix VI).

Burgon has a chapter on the early evidence (Burgon, *The Last Twelve Verses of Mark*). Hodges says, "The versions and the fathers contain a veritable host of Majority readings and it is a form of question-begging to pass them off as western or Caesarean (Hodges, p. 6). In John, there are no less than 13 places where the United Bible Society Text has changed the readings of the Nestle text back to the TR because readings agree with $\mathfrak{P}^{75}$ (Hodges, paper p. 5). Hodges also says, "There are times when the majority text has the best reading (even the critics agree) and therefore must be earliest." (Hodges, Jn 5:2, *Bib Sac* 1968, p. 337).

Internal Evidence Hodges says there is not a majority reading (including so-called conflated ones) that cannot be strongly defended on internal or transcriptional grounds or both (source unknown).

Divine Preservation God promised to preserve His Word providentially. This doctrine is taught concerning the Old Testament (Ps. 12:5-7; Mt. 5:18; 24:25; Mk. 13:31; Lk. 16:17; 21:33) and concerning the New Testament (implied in Mt. 28:19-20; 1 Pet. 1:23, 25) and demonstrated in church history (The Majority Text is the only text that has had a continuous use by the church throughout history). The Critical Text has more problems than the doctrine of preservation can bear.

The Majority Text

The Greek New Testament According to the Majority Text, which was published in 1982, was edited by Zane C. Hodges and Arthur L. Farstad. The consulting editors were Jacob Van Bruggen (Professor of New Testament Exegesis at the Reform Theological College in Kampen, the Netherlands), Alfred Martin (Vice-President and Dean of Education

Emeritus of Moody Bible Institute in Chicago, Illinois), Wilbur N. Pickering (Linguist-translator and Director of Public Relations for Wycliffe in Brasília, Brazil) and Harry A. Sturz (chairman of the Greek Department at BIOLA University). Maurice Robinson was one of the proofreaders (from the "Acknowledgments" section of *The New Testament According to the Majority Text*).

In the introduction to their *The Greek Text According to the Majority Text*, Hodges and Farstad state that the NA and UBS critical texts rely heavily on a relatively small number of manuscripts, including ℵ, B, 𝔓45, 𝔓46, 𝔓66, and 𝔓75, primarily from Egypt. That this text type existed "in earlier times outside of Egypt is unproved.... [The Majority Text] on the whole [is] substantially later than the earlier Egyptian witnesses [but] come from all over the ancient world. Their very number suggests that they represent a long and widespread chain of manuscript tradition" (Hodges, *The Greek Text*, p. ix).

The Majority Text is "often viewed as the result of a long-continued scribal process.... It is virtually impossible to conceive of any kind of an unguided process that could have resulted in the Majority Text. The relative uniformity within the text shows clearly that its transmission history has been stable and regular to a very large degree." The suggestion that the "intrinsic character of the Majority Text is inferior to the Egyptian ... usually partakes of an unduly large element of subjectivity" (Hodges, *The Greek Text*, p. xi).

The editors say that their method of the Majority Text is based on two premises.

1. "Any reading overwhelmingly attested by the manuscript tradition is more likely to be the original than its rival(s).... In any tradition where

there are not major disruptions in the transmission of history, the individual reading which has the earliest beginning is the one most likely to survive in a majority of documents. And the earliest reading of all is the original one. Unless an error is made in the very first stages of copying, the chances of survival of the error in extant copies in large numbers are sufficiently reduced. The later a reading originates, the less likely it is to be widely copied" (Hodges, *The Greek Text*, pp. xi-xii).

2. The final decision about the reading should be made based on a reconstruction of their history in the manuscript tradition. This means that a genealogy of the manuscripts ought to be constructed for each New Testament book. The data available in standard sources is inadequate, except for the Apocalypse. This method remains the only logical one. If Westcott and Hort employed it poorly, it is not for that reason to be abandoned" (Hodges, *The Greek Text*, p. xii).

That last point is important. Although they called it the Majority Text and argued that the majority of manuscripts support their theory, the Majority Text theory of Hodges and Farstad is more than just counting the number of manuscripts. It is much more complicated than that. It involves a transmission theory of text that develops a family tree of textual transmission. A more detailed explanation of this is provided in Chapter 35, Family.

Summary: One version of the Byzantine text type is the Majority Text, edited by Zane Hodges and Arthur Farstad.

Although the Textus Receptus and the Majority Text are from the Byzantine text type, they are not identical. Wallace says there are 1838 differences between the two; 300 are listed in Appendix V.

The Majority Text theory has been challenged. One example is Gordon D. Fee: "Modern Textual Criticism and the Revival of the Textus Receptus," *Journal of the Evangelical Theological Society (JETS)*, 1978, 21:19-33. Hodges answered. See Zane C. Hodges: "Modern Textual Criticism and the Majority Text: A Response," *JETS*, 1978, 21:143-55. Fee answered the answer in Gordon D. Fee: "Modern Textual Criticism of the Majority Text: A Rejoinder," *JETS,* 1978, 21:157-60. Hodges responded a final time in "Modern Textual Criticism and the Majority Text: a Surrejoinder," *JETS*, 1978, 21:161-64.

Wallace has also written a critique. Here are several of his statements, along with a summary of his entire article.

"Hodges has constructed a family tree of the extant Greek manuscripts using von Soden's data. He sees the manuscripts as belonging to seven subgroups according to their distinctive readings. A group of approximately 250 manuscripts, given the label M6, is viewed as the original form of the pericope from which all other groups are descended.'"

"A look at the textual apparatus here reveals a startling fact. Of the 30 textual problems listed, the editors, on the basis of their stemmatic reconstruction, have adopted at least 15 readings supported by a *minority* of manuscripts. In other words, for the Pericope Adulterae, the *Majority Text* in half its readings is a minority text."

Here is Wallace's summary of his article. "Three major points were made in this article: (1) The *Majority Text* differs from the Textus Receptus in almost 2,000 places, suggesting that the Byzantine text type has been seen only through a glass darkly in the printed editions of the Textus Receptus. (2) The *Majority Text,* differing from the critical text in over 6,500 places, has over 650 readings shorter than the critical text; such readings call out for an exhaustive evaluation. (3) In 'Hodges versus Hodges,' five points were noted: (a) The statistical demonstration of majority rule for the New Testament transmissional history, though ingenious, seemed to be irrelevant, for it did not deal with the phenomenon of a literary document. (b) Hodges's second principle of stemmatics, as applied in the Pericope Adulterae and Revelation, overturned, in large measure, his principle of 'majority rule' (thus rendering *The Greek New Testament according to the Majority Text* something of a misnomer). (c) Hodges's reconstructed family tree also contradicts the 'normal rate of copying' canon, for it seems to imply abnormal (i.e., heavy) copying in particular places and at particular times. (d) The 'majority rule' principle does not consider the majority of Greek manuscripts in the first eight centuries, the versions, or any future cache of manuscripts. (e) The genealogical method (Hodges's final vindication of 'majority rule') ultimately depends on internal criteria and as such vitiates any statements about an objective method."

Chapter 9

THE BYZANTINE TEXT

Maurice A. Robinson and William G. Pierpont have edited another version of the Byzantine text type. Their first edition was *The New Testament in the Original Greek: According to the Byzantine-Majority Textform* (1991). Their second edition was *The New Testament in the Original Greek: Byzantine Textform*, edited by Maurice A. Robinson and William G. Pierpont (2005, rereleased in 2018).

The Editors

Robinson Maurice Arthur Robinson (b. 1947) was born in Quincy, Massachusetts, but grew up in Bradenton, Florida. He earned his B.A. in English and secondary education from the University of South Florida (1969), a M.Div. (1973), a Th.M. (1975) from Southeastern Baptist Theological Seminary, and a Ph.D. (1982) from Southwestern Baptist Theological Seminary (dissertation: "Scribal Habits among Manuscripts of the Apocalypse"). He was a professor of New Testament and Greek (now retired).

Pierpont William Grover Pierpont (1915-2003) was reared in a Christian home. The family belonged to a Baptist church affiliated with the Southern Baptist Convention. He attended Friends University in Wichita for two years and later in life was active in an Evangelical Free

Church. He wrote a training manual for ham operators, *The Art and Skill of Radio-Telegraphy*. He was mostly self-taught, learning ancient, biblical, and modern Greek, as well as biblical and Rabbinic Hebrew and Aramaic, from a local Rabbi.

As a freshman in college, he was introduced to the Westcott-Hort theory and became an ardent student of the Greek New Testament for the remainder of his life. As a result of intense study, working through all the variants cited in von Soden's 4-volume Prolegomena and Text, he moved away from the Westcott-Hort theory toward a Byzantine Textform (text type). In 1976, Robinson became a research partner with Pierpont, a collaboration that lasted until Pierpont's death in 2003. Together, they developed the "Byzantine-priority theory" of textual criticism. By 1986, a Byzantine text became available online. In 1991, *the Greek New Testament, According to the Byzantine/Majority Text form,* was published. Robinson and Pierpont were co-editors of *The Greek New Testament Byzantine Textform.*

When Robinson wrote Pierpont's obituary, he said, "The order of the editors' names (Robinson-Pierpont) was chosen by Pierpont, arranged more for euphony than for any other factor. Over 95% of the Byzantine Textform edition remains that Pierpont had initially prepared in note form, long before Robinson's association with him."

The Theory

The Byzantine text type is called Byzantine "because all modern critics acknowledge that this was the Greek New Testament text in general use throughout the greater part of the Byzantine Period (312-1453)" (Hills, Introduction, p. 20).

Robinson explains the principles behind the Byzantine text in the "New Testament Textual Criticism: The Case for the Byzantine Priority." Here is an edited summary.

In the introduction, he says, "Even though the numerical base of the Byzantine Textform rests primarily among the late minuscules and uncials of the ninth century and later, the antiquity of that text reaches at least as far back as its predecessor exemplars of the late fourth and early fifth century." The Byzantine Textform is not the Textus Receptus; it "is the form of text which is known to have predominated in the Greek-speaking world from at least the fourth century until the invention of printing in the sixteenth century." He says he intends to demonstrate "the weaknesses of current theories and methodologies" and establish "the case for the Byzantine Textform."

Modern Eclecticism

"The best modern eclectic texts simply have *no* proven existence within transmissional history, and their claim to represent the autograph or the closest approximation thereunto cannot be substantiated from the extant MS, versional or patristic data…. Not only is the original text *no longer extant* in any known MS or text type but no MS or group of MSS reflects such in its overall pattern of readings. There thus remains *no* transmissional guide to suggest how such an 'original' text would appear when found. One should not be surprised to find that the only certain conclusions of modern eclecticism seem to be that the original form of the NT text (a) will *not* resemble the Byzantine Textform, but (b) *will* resemble the Alexandrian text type."

"Colwell noted that 'Westcott and Hort's genealogical method slew the Textus Receptus.' ... [They] appealed to a purely hypothetical stemma of descent which they 'did not apply ... to the manuscripts of the New Testament'; yet they claimed thereby to 'show clearly that a majority of manuscripts is not *necessarily* to be preferred as correct.' *Possibility* (which is all that was claimed) does *not* amount to *probability;* the latter requires evidence which the former does not.... Hort's reader of the stemmatic chart was left uninformed that the diagrammed possibility which discredited the Byzantine Textform was not only *unprovable*, but highly *improbable* in light of transmissional considerations."

"The problem with the resultant sequential aspect of modern eclectic theory is that its preferred text *repeatedly* can be shown to have no known MS support over even *short* stretches of text—and at times even within a single verse. The problem increases geometrically as a sequence of variants extends over two, three, five, or more verses. This raises serious questions about the supposed transmissional history required by eclectic choice."

"One of the complaints against the Byzantine Textform has been that such could not have existed at an early date due to the lack of a single pre-fourth-century MS reflecting the specific *pattern of agreement* characteristic of that Textform, even though the Byzantine Textform *can* demonstrate its specific pattern within the vast majority of witnesses from at least the fourth century onward. Yet those who use the modern eclectic texts are expected to accept a proffered 'original' which similarly lacks any pattern of agreement over even a short stretch of text that would link it with what is found in *any* MS, group of MSS, version, or patristic witness in the *entire* manuscript tradition…... If a legitimate critique can be made against the Byzantine Textform because early witnesses fail to reflect its specific pattern of readings, the current eclectic models (regardless of edition) can be criticized more severely since their resultant texts demonstrate a pattern of readings even *less* attested among the extant witnesses.... The cautious scholar seriously must ask which theory possesses the fewest speculative or questionable points when considered from all angles."

Byzantine-priority Method

In "modern reasoned eclecticism, … preferred readings are all too often defended as primary simply because they are non-Byzantine…. The real issue facing NT textual criticism is the need to offer a transmissional explanation of the history of the text, which includes an accurate view of scribal habits and normal transmissional considerations…. This is not a new procedure or a departure from a previous consensus that can be seen by the expression of an essential Byzantine-priority hypothesis in the theory of Westcott and Hort (quite differently applied, of course). The resultant methodology of the Byzantine-priority school is, in fact, more closely aligned with that of Westcott and Hort than any other. Despite his myriad of qualifying remarks, Hort stated quite clearly in his *Introduction* the principles which, if applied directly, would legitimately support the Byzantine-priority position: 'As soon as the numbers of a minority exceed what can be explained by accidental coincidence, … their agreement … can only be explained on genealogical grounds. [W]e have thereby passed beyond purely numerical relations, and the necessity of examining the genealogy of both minority and majority has become apparent. *A theoretical presumption indeed remains that a majority of extant documents is more likely to represent a majority of ancestral documents at each stage of transmission* than *vice versa.*"

"There is nothing inherently wrong with Hort's 'theoretical presumption.' Apart from the various anti-Byzantine qualifications made throughout the entire *Introduction*, the Westcott-Hort theory would revert to an implicit acceptance and following of this initial principle in accord with other good and solid principles which they elsewhere state. Thus, a 'proper' Westcott-Hort theory which did not initially exclude the Byzantine Textform would reflect what might be expected to occur under 'normal' textual transmission."

"Had all things been equal, the more likely scenario which favored a predominantly Byzantine text, would have been played out. In that sense, the present Byzantine-priority theory reflects a return to Hort, with the intent to explore the matter of textual transmission when a presumed formal Byzantine recension is no longer a factor."

"The Alexandrian text of the NT is clearly shorter, has apparent Alexandrian connections, and may well reflect recensional activity. The NT Western text is generally considered the 'uncontrolled popular text' of the second century with similar characteristics. Between these extremes, a 'medium' or 'vulgate' text exists, which resisted both the popular expansions and the critical revisions; this text continued in much the same form from the early period into the minuscule era. The NT Byzantine Textform reflects a similar continuance from at least the fourth century onward."

Principles Applied

"The Byzantine-priority position (or especially the so-called 'majority text' position) is often caricatured as only interested in the weight of numbers and simple 'nose-counting' of MSS when attempting to restore the original form of the NT text. Aside from the fact that such a mechanical and simplistic method would offer no solution in the many places where the Byzantine Textform is divided among its mass of witnesses, such a caricature leads one to infer that no serious application of principles of NT textual criticism exists within such a theory. This, of course, is not correct. There are external and internal criteria that characterize a Byzantine-priority praxis, and many of these closely resemble or are identical to the principles espoused within other schools of textual restoration. Of course, the principles of Byzantine-priority necessarily differ in application from those found elsewhere."

"The Byzantine-priority principles reflect a 'reasoned transmissionalism' which evaluates internal and external evidence in the light of transmissional probabilities. This approach emphasizes the effect of scribal habits in preserving, altering, or otherwise corrupting the text, the recognition of transmissional development leading to family and texttype groupings, and the ongoing maintenance of the text in its general integrity as demonstrated within our critical apparatuses. The overriding principle is that *textual criticism without a history of transmission is impossible*. To achieve this end, *all* readings *in sequence* need to be accounted for within a transmissional history, and no reading can be considered in isolation as a 'variant unit' unrelated to the rest of the text."

"In this system, final judgment on readings requires the strong application of internal evidence *after* an initial evaluation of the external data has been made. Being primarily transmissionally-based, the Byzantine-priority theory continually links its internal criteria to external considerations. This methodology always asks the prior question: does the reading which may appear 'best' on internal grounds (no matter how plausible such might appear) *really* accord with known transmissional factors regarding the perpetuation and preservation of texts? Such an approach parallels Westcott and Hort but with the added *caveat* against dismissing the Byzantine Textform as a significant transmissional factor. Indeed, the present theory in many respects remains quite close to that of Westcott and Hort; the primary variance is reflected in certain key assumptions and a few less obvious principles. Because of these initial considerations, the conclusions regarding the original form of the NT text will necessarily differ significantly from those of Westcott and Hort."

Principles of Internal Evidence

"The basic principles of internal and external evidence utilized by Byzantine-priority advocates are quite familiar to those who practice either rigorous or reasoned eclecticism. At least one popular principle (that of favoring the shorter reading) is omitted; other principles are cautiously applied within a transmissional-based framework in which external evidence retains significant weight. The primary principles of internal evidence include the following:" [Here are his principles, in his words, minus his explanations.]

1. Prefer the reading that is most likely to have given rise to all others within a variant unit. [This is the] "guiding principle of the Nestle-Aland 'local-genealogical' method."

2. The reading, which would be more difficult as a scribal creation, is to be preferred.
3. Readings that conform to the original author's known style, vocabulary, and syntax are to be preferred.
4. Readings that clearly harmonize or assimilate the wording of one passage to another are to be rejected.
5. Readings reflecting common scribal piety or religiously motivated expansion and alteration are secondary.
6. The primary evaluation of readings should be based on transcriptional probability. This principle goes back to Westcott and Hort and has no inherent weaknesses. Scribes did make errors and deliberate alterations, and readings need to be categorized and assessed according to their conformity to such scribal tendencies.
7. Transcriptional error is more likely to be the ultimate source of many sensible variants rather than deliberate alteration.
8. Neither the shorter nor longer reading is to be preferred.

Principles of External Evidence

"The Byzantine-priority method looks at external evidence as a primary consideration within a transmissional-historical framework. The key issue in any unit of variation is not the mere number, but how each reading may have arisen and developed in the course of transmission to reflect whatever quantitative alignments and textual groupings might exist."

1. The quantity of preserved evidence for the text of the NT precludes conjectural emendation. The NT text has been preserved to an

extent far exceeding that of any other hand-transmitted literature of antiquity. Thus, the likelihood that conjectural emendation might restore the original form of the text is virtually nil.

2. Readings that appear sporadically within transmissional history are suspect.

   a. Reading preserved in only a single MS, version, or father is suspect.
   b. Readings preserved in a small group of witnesses are suspect.
   c. A variety of testimony is highly regarded. This principle addresses two areas, neither of which is sufficient to establish the text, but neither of which lends support to a given reading. A reading supported by various versions and fathers demonstrates a wider range of support than a reading lacking such support. Among Greek MSS, a reading shared among differing texttypes is more strongly supported than that which is localized to a single texttype or family group.
   d. Wherever possible, the raw number of MSS should be intelligently reduced. "Genealogical method" is accepted whenever such can be firmly established. "Family" groups such as f^1 and f^{13} have long been cited under one siglum, and a few MSS have known copies of earlier extant witnesses. In many other cases, a close genealogical connection can be established, and thus, mere numbers can be reduced in a proper manner. At times, a group of MSS can be shown to stem from a single scribe with one exemplar.
   e. Manuscripts still need to be weighed and not merely counted.
   f. It is important to seek out readings with demonstrable antiquity.

g. The concept of a single 'best' MS or small group of MSS is unlikely to have transmissional evidence in its favor.

h. An exclusive following of the oldest MSS or witnesses is transmissionally flawed.

i. Transmissional considerations coupled with internal principles point to the Byzantine Textform as a leading force in the history of transmission.

Selected Objections

1. No early Byzantine manuscripts prior to the fourth century.
    a. The limited and localized nature of the extant early MSS suggests that presumptions regarding text-critical antiquity may be flawed.
    b. The 'copying revolutions' previously noted seriously affected the continuity of the transmissional stream.
    c. The local text of Egypt is unlikely to reflect that which permeated the primary Greek-speaking portion of the Empire (Southern Italy through modern Greece and Turkey to Antioch on the Orontes), from which we have no manuscript, versional, or patristic data before the mid-fourth century. After that point, one finds a highly pervasive and dominant Byzantine stream in that region. It is far more reasonable to assume that the predecessors of that stream simply retained the same textual complexion that earlier had permeated that region.
    d. The silence of early testimony from the primary Greek-speaking region of the Empire gives rise to two opposing views.

Modern eclectics assume an early dominance of a non-Byzantine text in those areas, which became the stronghold of Byzantine support, despite the historical unlikelihood of such an occurrence. The Byzantine-priority advocates suggest that the later existence and dominance of the Byzantine Textform in that region provides presumptive evidence favoring a similar dominance in earlier times.

e. The early existence of the Byzantine Textform rests on a stronger basis than the Synoptic Q.

f. Until the discovery of $\mathfrak{P}^{75}$ in 1955, there was no proof that a text similar to that of Codex Vaticanus existed before the fourth century.

2. Major disruptions in transmissional history eliminated non-Byzantine predecessors. To assume that during the Diocletian, the Alexandrian text alone was overwhelmingly surrendered is to assume too much. Persecutions, however, were not selective in their textual targets. The Islamic Conquest was not as totally destructive to NT MSS as has been claimed. Monasteries and churches in both Palestine and Egypt continued literary activity following the conquest and maintained communication with the Eastern and Western Empires, even while facing pressure to abandon Christianity and convert to Islam.

3. Chrysostom's influence made the Byzantine the preferred text of Constantinople. A 'new' or localized text, even if used by a popular Greek Father, would not become transmissionally popular merely due to his reputation.

4. The Byzantine Textform is the result of a process that, over the centuries, steadily moved away from the text's original form in the interest of smoothness, harmonization, grammatical, and other 'improvements.' For the most part, scribes were generally careful and reasonably accurate in their copying endeavors.

Inaccuracies and Misleading Claims

1. Gordon Fee makes an outstandingly inaccurate claim when opposing the Byzantine inclusion of Jn 5:3^b-4. He speaks dogmatically regarding the enclosed (or "embedded") genitive construction, την του υδατος κινησιν, which appears at the end of Jn 5:3 in the Byzantine Textform.... Yet a simple electronic scan of the Johannine writings reveals that the embedded genitive construction not only appears three times elsewhere in John (Jn 6:51; 14:30; 18:10) but, with one exception (Mt 13:55, ο του τεκτονος υιος), this construction is otherwise exclusive to John among the gospels. The embedded genitive in John 5:3b is actually more characteristic of Johannine style than of any other Gospel, and its presence in John 5:3b argues more for Johannine authenticity than for inauthenticity.

2. On the same page, Fee claims inauthenticity in Jn 5:4 because of the phrase ἄγγελο καριὸυ, which is claimed to be in "almost all of the early uncials." Since this phrase does not tally with Johannine usage, it must have been a Byzantine 'creation.' Fee admits that καριὸυ is 'lacking in the later majority' of MSS (the bulk of the Byzantine Textform), but he directs his attention to the "early uncials" (which are not listed). But *contra* Fee, the "Byzantine"

reading is simply ἄγγελο standing alone, in accord with the minuscule data.

3. Daniel Wallace creates "revisionist history" in asserting that the Byzantine Textform was neither dominant nor in the "majority" until the ninth century. Not only does such a claim run counter to what has been acknowledged since Westcott and Hort, but it simply does not accord with the known facts. Sufficient manuscript and patristic evidence exist from the mid-fourth century onward to establish this point. Wallace not only ignores a previous scholarly consensus but also fails to consider the transmissional factors that have limited all evidence from the pre-ninth-century period. His current claim is little more than "eclectic nose-counting" of extant witnesses on the faulty presumption that such might accurately depict the total NT transmissional situation in the pre-ninth-century era. There is *no* reason to engage in nose-counting against a previous scholarly consensus, let alone to ignore contrary versional and patristic evidence that is strongly supportive of Byzantine dominance from the mid-fourth century onward.

Concluding Observations

Every variant unit can be evaluated favorably from a Byzantine-priority perspective, and all units should be carefully examined when attempting to restore the original text.

The Byzantine-priority hypothesis is far more complex than it may appear; it does not encourage a simplistic eclectic approach nor a narrow theological outlook toward a predetermined result. The final determination of that text remains problematic in many situations, despite a primarily externally based methodology. Given the evidence as preserved, absolute certainty regarding the entire NT text cannot be expected. Under all theories, *ca.* 90% of the original text of the NT *is* considered established. Byzantine-priority attempts to extend that quantity, following reasonable internal and external evidence principles, balanced by historical and transmissional factors.

Byzantine-priority provides no domain or shelter for those unwilling to labor diligently or unscholarly individuals whose goal is merely a biased theological perspective or advocacy of a particular translation.

Byzantine-priority has a methodological consistency that cannot be demonstrated among the modern eclectic alternatives.

The problem within modern eclecticism has long been recognized. Colwell declared in 1955, "The great task of textual criticism for the generation of scholars who are now beginning their work is the rewriting of the history of the text and the recreation of theory'.... For the past century, eclecticism has functioned without an integrated history of textual transmission. That its resultant text has no root in any single document, group of documents, or text type is an unfortunate by-product of its self-imposed methodology."

"Despite modern eclectic expressions regarding what NT textual criticism 'really' needs, modern text-critical thought steadily moves away from the highest ideals and goals. Current eclectic speculation involves heterodox scribes who are claimed to have preserved a more genuine text than the orthodox, as well as a general uncertainty of whether the original text can be recovered or whether any concept of an 'original' text can be maintained. The Byzantine-priority position offers a clear theoretical and practical alternative to the pessimistic suppositions of postmodern eclectic subjectivity."

The Differences

Textus Receptus The Byzantine Text omits four verses in the Textus Receptus: Luke 17:36, Acts 8:37, 15:34, 24:7. It also takes out "they" in Luke 2:22.

The Majority Text Robert Truelove says the differences in philosophy between the Hodges-Farstad and Robertson Pierpont is that Hodges-Farstad relied on Western and Alexandrian texts to decide what reading to follow when the Byzantine manuscripts were evenly divided, while Robinson-Pierpont applied the methods of textual criticism to the Byzantine manuscripts themselves. Here are some of the differences. As compared to the Majority Text, the Byzantine Text omits Luke 17:36, Acts 9:5-6, Colossians 1:13-14 (through his blood), and Revelation 16:5.

Family 35 Robinson-Pierpont lists the difference between their Byzantine Text and Pickering's Family 35 Text. They say, "This collation lists all differences between the Robinson-Pierpont Byzantine Textform 2005 Greek NT and Wilbur Pickering's f^{35} Greek NT, except differences in diacritical markings, punctuation, capitalization, and verse division. The verse numbering corresponds to the Robinson-Pierpont text. The collation lists 1183 places of variation between the two texts." For all 1183 of them, see www.https://byzantinetext.com/wp-content/uploads/2016/11/editions-pickering-rp-collated.pdf.

Summary: Robinson and Pierpont produced a Greek text based on the Byzantine text type.

The Robinson-Pierpont Byzantine Text can be found free at https://byzantinetext.com/study/editions/robinson-pierpont/. For a review, see https://www.youtube.com/watch?v=2KZCO_N7li4.

Chapter 10

FAMILY 35

Wilbur N. Pickering (Th.M., Dallas Seminary; Ph.D. in Linguistics, University of Toronto) joined Wycliffe Bible Translators in 1958 and went to Brazil in 1961 to conduct translation work with the Apurinã, an indigenous people living in western Brazil. He resigned from Wycliffe in 1996 to pursue other interests. He is the editor of *The Greek New Testament According to Family 35*.

Pickering's Discovery

His Book In 1977, Pickering wrote *The Identity of the New Testament Text*. Zane C. Hodges wrote the foreword. Pickering critiqued Westcott and Hort and the eclectic text and argued for the Majority or Byzantine text. [A free copy of the 2nd edition (2003) is available at http://www.revisedstandard.net/text/WNP/. The 3rd edition appeared in 2012, and the 4th edition in 2014.]

Ultimately, Pickering concluded that the text of the New Testament has never been lost. It has been preserved in the Byzantine manuscripts known as Family 35, which he claimed to be able to trace to the third century (Pickering, *The Identity of the NT IV*, pp. 131-132). Pickering has written other books. This one is mentioned because its various versions indicate a change in his approach concerning the Greek New Testament, from the Byzantine text type to Family 35.

His Discovery Pickering calls his view the "Original Text Theory" because he believes that God has preserved the original wording of the New Testament to the present day. His presuppositions include: the criteria must be biblical, objective, and reasonable, 90% attestation is unassailable and 80% virtually so, groupings and relationships supersede the counting of manuscripts, and both God and Satan have an ongoing interest in the fate of the New Testament text (Pickering pp. 159-160).

How did Pickering reach his conclusion? As he studied the Hodges-Farstad Majority Text of the *Periscope Adulterae* (John 7:53-8:11), which is based on von Soden's collation (compared text to see their similarities and differences) of 900 manuscripts, he noticed there were three main streams (von Soden's M^5, M^6, and M^7) and M^7 was always in the majority (except for one five-way split where there was no majority).

Then, Pickering studied the Hodges-Farstad Majority Text of Revelation, based on Hoskier's collation of approximately 200 manuscripts of Revelation, which identified nine groups (Hodges and Farstad used five of his nine groups). Pickering noticed again that there were three main streams (Ma-b, Mc., Md-e), and $M^{c.}$ was the best of the three (Pickering, pp. 160-161).

What happened next is a bit complicated, but in simple terms, Pickering noticed that M^7 in John 7:53-8:11 and $M^{c.}$ in Revelation were equal to von Soden's $K^{r.}$ and he wondered if it might not be the best elsewhere in the New Testament. He discovered that it was and that Minuscule 35, which contains the whole NT, reflects K^r, so he called that group of manuscripts Family 35 (f^{35}). (Pickering, p. 161).

Pickering lists examples from the Gospels (Lk., Jn.), Acts, Paul (Rom., 2 Cor.), and the General epistles (Jas., 1 Pet., 2 Pet., 3 Jn.) to demonstrate that K^r, is independent and ancient, dating to the third century. Maurice Robinson states that it dates back to the second century (Pickering, pp. 161-167; see also pp. 171-172).

According to Pickering, the F35 is by far the largest family of New Testament manuscripts, with at least 250 manuscripts in the Gospels. The second family doesn't have more than 100 MSS (in the Gospels) and is less cohesive. f^{35} is the only family so far identified that extends to the whole NT (Matthew-Revelation). The other families have a few books—like the Gospels: f^1 and f^{13}. "f^{35} represents about 16-18% of the total of extant (known) Greek MSS, but it is almost never entirely alone (there are f^{35} readings in other MSS that do not belong to the family). The percentage depends on the book. This is the average for the entire New Testament. It is the core of the NT stream of transmission. It is the core of the Byzantine Tradition. In a few cases (0.5%), f^{35} is distinct from the majority of the MSS. Therefore, we can't say it is a majority text" (Pickering and Freitas, p. 57).

The best manuscripts for family 35 are GA 2554, GA 2723, GA 35, GA 1072, GA 1652, GA 2382, GA 586, GA 789, GA 713, and GA 2253 (Pickering and Freitas, p. 121). Pickering claims, "I have a perfect copy of the family 35 archetypal text from most NT books (22); I have copies made from a perfect exemplar (presumed) for another four (4); as I have continued to correlate MSS I hope to add the last one (Acts), but even for it the archetypal form is demonstrable" (Pickering, p. 199). He also says he found one almost-perfect manuscript (GA 2554) (Pickering and Freitas, p. 106).

Pickering also points out, "There are f³⁵ all over the place—Jerusalem, Sinai, Athens, Constantinople, Trikala, Kalavryle, Lesbos, and most monasteries on Mt. Athos (that represent different denominations), etc. [if there were six monasteries on Cyprus—one Anglican, one Assembly of God, one Baptist, one church of Christ, one Methodist and one Presbyterian—to what extent what they compare notes?]" (Pickering, p. 172).

Pickering's View

His View The Foreword to Pickering's *The Sovereign Creator Has Spoken* says, "For some time, Dr. Pickering has felt that among the many hundreds of Greek manuscripts known to exist today, surely God would have preserved the original wording. After years of searching and comparing Greek NT manuscripts, he has concluded that God used a certain line of transmission to preserve that wording. That line is by far the largest and most cohesive of all manuscript groups or families. It is distinguished from all other groups by the high level of care with which it was copied (Dr. Pickering holds copies of perfect manuscripts for 22 of the 27 books). A comprehensive comparison of family representatives has empirically and objectively identified that the archetypal form *is* indeed error-free. As he expected, this error-free text is not seriously different from some of the other 'good' Greek texts. Nevertheless, he has done an English translation based on it."

In the Preface to *The Greek New Testament According to Family 35* (second edition), Pickering also details his view. He once believed that Hermann von Soden's Greek New Testament [1911-1913] was reliable. It is the work that underlies the Hodges-Farstad and Robertson-Pierpont editions of the Byzantine text type, but the *Text and Textwert* collations, edited by Kurt Alman and Walter de Gruyter (more than 12 volumes, covering the entire New Testament except for Revelation and the second half of John), "demonstrate that not infrequently Soden is seriously off the mark. Maurice Robinson's collations of the Pericope Adulterae [Jn. 7:53-8:11] demonstrate objectively that Soden is very seriously wrong there" [an unpublished study that Robinson allowed Pickering to study]. "With reference to Soden's treatment of Codex 223, K. W. Clark stated, 'Furthermore, our collation has revealed sixty-two errors in 229 readings treated by von Soden. 27% in error (62÷229) is altogether too much, and what is true of MS 223 may be true of other MSS as well.... I had to reconsider the evidence of the whole New Testament and that exercise led me to the conclusion that the most important segment of the relevant evidence has been overlooked (more precisely, it has been despised, and therefore ignored).'"

Pickering explains that his *Greek New Testament According to Family 35* is "based on that important segment." He calls it Family 35 "because cursive 35 is the complete New Testament, faithful to the family archetype." He says for a thorough explanation, see his book *The Identity of the New Testament Text IV*, where he argues, "God has preserved the *precise original wording* of the NT, and that we can, and do, know what it is based on an empirical procedure (Pickering, italics added). He states, "I claim to have demonstrated the superiority of Family 35 based on size, independence, age, distribution, profile, and care.... He adds, "for those who believe in an errant text, as I do, every word is important (and even the spelling may prove to be significant)." In a footnote, he continues, "I venture to affirm to the reader that all original wording of the New Testament is preserved in this edition, if not in the text, at least in the apparatus. 'Diminished not a word' Jeremiah 26:2 (see Deuteronomy 4:2 and Luke 4:4, 'every word' [as in 99.6% of the MSS]."

His Edition In the apparatus of his Greek New Testament, Pickering includes six editions of the Greek text. In brackets ([...]), he gives the percentage of manuscript support and evidence from a variety of sources. Here are his symbols for the six editions of the Greek text.

>RP: Robinson-Pierpont (2005)
>HF: Hodges-Farstad
>OC: Text of the Orthodox Church
>TR: Textus Receptus
>CP: Complutension Polyglot
>NU: Nestle-Aland 26/UBS 3

Pickering says that his Greek text differs from the Hodges-Farstad text and the Robinson-Pierpont text in over a thousand places. (https://www.amazon.com/gp/profile/amzn1.account.AH3DG7ITUSM2UXLC3SVMXHPHIWZA/ref=cm_cr_arp_d_gw_btm?ie=UTF8)

An interesting feature of his edition is that he includes dates, for example, the birthdate of Jesus is put at 4 BC (Mt. 2:1), His ministry at Capernaum at 27 AD (Mt. 4:12), His ministry in Perea at 29/30 AD (Mt. 19:1), and His triumphal entry on Sunday, March 31, 30 AD (Mt. 21:1). For an article by Pickering entitled "What Difference Does it Make?" see the article at https://www.cob-net.org/compare/docs/what-difference-pickering.pdf.

Summary: Pickering claims that the very words of the autographs are preserved in a group of manuscripts represented by cursive 35.

Pickering claims that he has "demonstrated the superiority of family 35 based on <u>size</u>, <u>independence</u>, <u>age</u>, <u>distribution</u>, <u>profile</u>, and <u>care</u>" (Pickering, p, 200, underlining his). To be more specific, in another book, it is said that he has demonstrated the superiority of Family 35 based on size (393 MSS), independence (not subordinate to any other text types), age (even though the earliest extant MSS are dated from the XI century, the text is older and goes back to at least the third century), geographical distribution (widespread in the Mediterranean area), profile (demonstrated for all books), care (the scribes made fewer mistakes per book, range (all 27 books). (Pickering and Freitas, pp. 177-178).

Pickering's English translation of his Greek text is entitled *The Sovereign Creator Has Spoken, and it is a New Testament Translation with Commentary, Offering Objective Authority for Living*. Publisher: Brasília (Brazil): Project Underground Church, 2016 (Prunch.org).

To purchase a copy, go to https://www.amazon.com/Greek-New-Testament-According-Family/dp/0989827372/ref=cm_cr_arp_d_pb_opt?ie=UTF8.

For a free online copy, see https://studybible.info/version/WPNT (search for "f^{35} group of Byzantine manuscripts").

For an online free copy collated with Robinson-Pierpont's text, see https://byzantinetext.com/wp-content/uploads/2016/11/editions-pickering-rp-collated.pdf.

Daniel B. Wallace, "Some Second Thoughts on the Majority Text," *Bibliotheca Sacra* 146 (1989): 270. Wilbur N. Pickering, "More "Second Thoughts on the Majority Text," A response to Wallace."

Chapter 11

WHAT DIFFERENCE DOES IT MAKE?

In the final analysis, the question is, "What difference does it make?" How many differences are there between the various printed Greek texts, that is, between the Textus Receptus (TR) and the Westcott-Hort Text (WH) and between the various versions of the Byzantine text type manuscripts, the Textus Receptus (TR), the Majority Text (MT), the Byzantine Text (BT), the Family 35 Text (f^{35})? More specifically, what difference does all of this make in the verses of the New Testament?

The differences are massive, numbering in the thousands, but the vast majority are inconsequential, such as a missing word, a misspelled word, or word order. For example, some Greek manuscripts read, "For this you know" at the beginning of Ephesians 5:5, and others have the words "For know this." None of the differences affects any major doctrine of biblical Christianity.

Nevertheless, all Scripture, every word of Scripture, was inspired by God (called verbal inspiration). So, in the careful study of the Word of God, every word needs to be considered. Here is a list of some of the differences. The list is not exhaustive.

Between Printed Greek Texts

TR and WH Using Scrivener's Greek New Testament, a version of the TR, David Cloud says there are 5,604 differences between the WH text and the TR. He says 1,952 are omissions (35%), 467 are additions (8%), and 3,185 are changes (57%) (see the complete article at https://www.wayoflife.org/database/how_many_differences_are_there.html).

Jack A. Moorman counted the words in the Received Text and the words in the Nestle/Aland Greek Text and said the Nestle/Aland text is shorter than the Received Text by 2,886 words. That is 934 words more than were omitted from the Westcott and Hort text (1,952 vs. 2,886; the edition of Nestle/Aland Greek Text is not given. See David Cloud at https://www.wayoflife.org/database/how_many_differences_are_there.html.

TR and MT Wallace says there are 1838 differences between the TR and the MT. See Appendix V for 300 of them. (1005 are "translatable" differences. See https://www.christianpublishinghouse.co/2020/07/26/the-byzantine-kr-family-35-text-form-1261-1453-c-e/).

TR and BT Robinson-Pierpont state that there are 1,818 differences between the Stephens 1550 TR and their text (see their article at https://www.byzantinetext.com/wp-content/uploads/2022/04/collation-stephanus-rp-2018.pdf).

TR and f^{35} To my knowledge, the differences have not been determined.

MT and CT According to Wallace, there are 6577 differences between the MT and the CT. "But of the 6,577 differences between the *Majority*

Text and the critical texts, in only 1,589 places is the *Majority Text longer* than the critical. This is less than one-fourth of the total differences.... In this writer's count, there are 657 places where the *Majority Text* is shorter than the critical" text (see article at https://www.bible.org/article/some-second-thoughts-majority-text).

MT and f³⁵ "In the General epistles, **f³⁵** does not differ from the H-F Majority Text all that much. For instance, in James, **f³⁵** differs from H-F nineteen times, only two of which affect the meaning (not seriously)" (Pickering, p. 173).

BT and f³⁵ Robinson-Pierpont say, "This collation lists all differences between the Robinson-Pierpont Byzantine Textform 2005 Greek NT and Wilbur Pickering's f³⁵ Greek NT, except differences in diacritical markings, punctuation, capitalization, and verse division. The verse numbering corresponds to the Robinson-Pierpont text. The collation lists 1183 places of variation between the two texts." The list can be found at https://www.byzantinetext.com/wp-content/uploads/2016/11/editions-pickering-rp-collated.pdf.

In Verses in the New Testament

Abbreviations are used for the Textus Receptus (TR), the Majority Text, edited by Hodges and Farstad (HF), the Byzantine Text, edited by Robinson and Pierpont (RP), and Family 35 (f³⁵). Underlying New Testament references indicate that either Vaticanus, Sinaiticus, or both are demonstrably defective in that verse.

Matthew 1:7 "Solomon begot Rehoboam, Rehoboam begot Abijah, and Abijah begot Asa." ασα (Asa) is in [98%], W, TR, HF, RP, NKJV,

NASB, NIV // ασαφ (Asaph) is in ℵ, B, C, $\mathfrak{P}^{1v}$, NU, ESV. Asaph was from the tribe of Levi, not the tribe of Judah. See the comments on Matthew 1:8. Wallace contends that Asaph is another way of spelling Asa, "since other ancient documents have variant spellings on the king's name (such as 'Asab,' 'Asanos,' and 'Asaph')" (See the complete article at https://www.bible.org/article/errors-greek-text-behind-modern-translations-cases-matthew-17-10-and-luke-2345).

Matthew 1:8 "Asa begot Jehoshaphat, Jehoshaphat begot Joram, and Joram begot Uzziah." ασα (Asa) is in [98%], W, TR, HF, RP, NKJV, NASB, NIV // ασαφ (Asaph) is in ℵ, B, C, $\mathfrak{P}^{1v}$, NU, ESV. Again, Asaph was from the tribe of Levi, not the tribe of Judah. Pickering says, "Metzger writes, 'Since, however, the evangelist may have derived material for the genealogy, not from the Old Testament directly, subsequent genealogical list, in which the erroneous spelling occurred, the committee saw no reason to adopt what appears to be a scribal emendation.' Metzger frankly declares that the spelling they have adopted is erroneous.' The NU editors have deliberately imported an error into their text, which is faithfully reproduced in the NAB (New American Bible) and NRSV. RSV and NASB offer a footnote to the effect that the Greek reads 'Asaph'—it would be less misleading if they had said that a tiny fraction of the Greek manuscripts so read" (Metzger, p. 323).

Matthew 1:10 "Hezekiah begot Manasseh, Manasseh begot Amon, and Amon begot Josiah." αμμων (Amon) is in [98%], W, TR, HF, RP, NKJV, NASB, NIV // αμως (Amos) is in ℵ, C, NU, and αμνων is in B, ESV. "Metzger says that 'Amos' is 'an error for Amon' and the NU editors have duly placed the error in their text" (Metzger p. 323). Wallace says,

"The reading 'Amos' in v. 10 in the Greek text is similar [to 1:7 & 8]: It is most likely the original reading, but it is a variation of the more common spelling 'Amon' (from the article by Wallace listed in the comments on Matthew 1:7 above).

Matthew 1:18 "Now the birth of Jesus Christ was as follows." γεννησις (birth) is in 96.5% TR, HF, RP, f³⁵, NASB, NIV, ESV // γενεσις (genesis, source) is in ℵ, B, 𝔓¹, NU. This is a case of a misspelled word. Pickering says, "Not counting Asa and Amon (see v. 10), Codex B misspells 13 names in this chapter; Aleph misspells 10" (Pickering p. 323).

Matthew 5:22 "Whoever is angry with his brother without a cause shall be in danger of the judgment." εικη (without a cause) is in 96.2%, D, W, TR, HF, RP, f³⁵ // It is not in ℵ, B, 𝔓⁶⁴, NU. If the omission is correct, Jesus says it is always wrong to get angry. If that is true, Jesus was a sinner (Mk. 3:5), and Paul contradicted Jesus (Eph. 4:26). On the other hand, if the inclusion is correct, there is a "righteous indignation."

Matthew 5:44 "But I say to you, love your enemies, bless those who curse you, do good to those who hate you, and pray for those who spitefully use you and persecute you." ευλογειτε τους καταρωμενους υμας καλως ποιειτε τοις μισουνσιν (bless those who curse you, do good to those who hate you) is in the TR and with a slight change [τους (accusative instead of dative) μισουντας (dative instead of accusative)] 91.2%, W, HF, RP have this sentence. There are other slight variations within the Byzantine text type. // ℵ, B, NU, NASB, NIV, ESV omit it.

Aland says, "This is nothing more than an adaptation from the parallel text of Luke 6:27-28. The variety of forms in which this occurs in the manuscript tradition only underscores the secondary character of that the expansion is undoubtedly made for a more edifying text, but it is not in the original Gospel of Matthew. Admittedly, the section of Greek manuscripts preserving the original text is not very large (ℵ, B, f¹, and a few others), but they are supported by representatives of all the early versions. As in the ending of Mark and frequently elsewhere as well, the expanded text is more impressive and 'better' than the original form, and few manuscripts have been able to withstand the momentum. Furthermore, the conclusive argument here (as in so many similar instances) is that if the expanded form were actually the original text, what would have been the motive for altering it? Accidental omission is hardly a possible cause (although a scribe could certainly have omitted a phrase by sheer chance as described above, and his manuscript could have been copied by another scribe because the shorter text is found in all parts of the early church. Further, an important point for all similar examples is the variety of forms assumed by the expansion, which is an irrefutable argument for it secondary character" (Aland, p. 306).

Matthew 6:1a "Take heed lest you do your alms before men." ελεημοσυνην (alms) is in 99%, W, TR, HF, RP, f^{35} // δικαιοσυνην (righteousness) is in ℵ, B, D, and NU. Some who take "righteousness" say that, in this passage, "righteousness" is another word for almsgiving, which was common among the Jews (Gill; Adam Clarke). Others who take "righteousness" say it is a "general heading" for what follows, namely, almsgiving, prayer, and fasting (JFB; et al.).

Matthew 6:13b "For Yours is the kingdom and the power and the glory forever. Amen." The doxology at the end of the Lord's prayer is in 97.6%, with variations TR, HF, RP // It is not in ℵ, B, D, or NU. It is also found in Luke, the Didache —a document that many believe was written before AD 100 —and in translations of the New Testament, which were much earlier than the fourth century.

Aland says, "Its [the doxology] supplemental character is obvious from the variety of forms it has taken, and the witness for its original absence is far stronger than Matt. 5:44. The reason for the addition is quite clear. Whether the Lord's prayer is used in public worship or for private devotions, the text needs an ending. The expansion must have been supplied quite early because it is found in the Didache, a writing composed shortly after AD 100" (Aland, pp. 306-307).

Farstad suggests that when this prayer fell from the lips of the Lord, it was "perfectly complete—and completely perfect" (Farstad, pp. 115-116). Without the doxology, the prayer concludes with the words "evil" or "evil one," which seems odd, especially in light of the fact that it is traditional to end a Jewish prayer with praise to God (Farstad, p. 115). Farstad asks, "Since most manuscripts do contain the ending, isn't it easier for Christians to believe that some manuscripts dropped off the ending simply by careless copying?" (Farstad, pp. 115-117).

Matthew 10:10 "nor bag for *your* journey, nor two tunics, nor sandals, nor staffs; for a worker is worthy of his food." ραβδους (staffs) is in 95%, C, N, W, HF, RP, f^{35}, KJV, NKJV // ραβδον (staff) is in ℵ, B, D, TR, NU, NASB, NIV, ESV. Matthew 10:10 and Luke 9:3 read "staffs" (plural), but Mark 6:8 says "a staff (singular) only.

Various solutions have been suggested. The Greek word translated "staff" in Mark 6:8 means "staff, rod." It was used of the staff carried on a journey, a ruler's scepter, and a rod of chastisement (1 Cor. 4:21; see A-S). Therefore, some suggest they were not to take a rod but were allowed to take a walking stick (Power, cited by Lane in a fn.). Others see the difference in the verbs used, concluding that Matthew forbids the *acquisition* of the staff, while Mark allows them to "take" the one they already possess (see France's commentary on Matthew; he adds that Luke indicates there were at least two injunctions, Lk. 9:3; 10:4; 22:35-36). Another possibility is that they were not to take anything that was not necessary, which might sometimes involve carrying a stick and sometimes not (Tasker on Mt. 10:10). Then, there is the explanation that they were not to take additional articles of this kind (Alexander on Mt. 10:10).

The best solution is relatively simple. Jesus said do not *provide* (Mt. 10:9) *extra* tunics, sandals, and staffs. Matthew's account says, "provide neither ... nor *two* tunics, nor sandals, nor staffs; *for* a worker is worthy of his food" (Mt. 10:9-10). He certainly did not mean they were to go barefoot. The point is that they were to take the sandals they had on and not provide for extras because a worker is worthy of provisions. The same applies to the staff. They were to take one, but not two.

Matthew 13:35 "This was to fulfill what was spoken by the prophet." δια του προφητου (by the prophet) is in ℵ^b, B, C, D, K, L, W, X, TR, HF, RP // ℵ^a has Ησαιου (Isaiah). (ℵ^a means the reading of the original scribe.) This verse quotes Psalm 78:2, which Asaph, not Isaiah, wrote; however, some manuscripts attribute the quotation to Isaiah. "Several MSS have Ησαιου (Isaiah), but this is a manifest error. Jerome supposes that Asaph was first in the text and that some ignorant transcriber, not knowing who this Asaph was, inserted the word Isaiah; and thus, by attempting to remove an imaginary error, made a real one" (Adam Clarke).

Matthew 16:2b-3 "He answered and said to them, 'When it is evening you say, *'It will be* fair weather, for the sky is red'; (16:3) and in the morning, *'It will be* foul weather today, for the sky is red and threatening.' Hypocrites! You know how to discern the face of the sky, but you cannot *discern* the signs of the times." ο δε αποκριθεις ειπεν αυτοις οψιας γενομενης λεγετε ευδια πυρραζει γαρ ο ουρανος (16:2) και πρωι σημερον χειμων πυρραζει γαρ στυγναζων ο ουρανος υποκριται το μεν προσωπον του ουρανου γινωσκετε διακρινειν τα δε σημεια των καιρων ου δυνασθε (16:3). ["When it is evening you say, *'It will be* fair weather, for the sky is red'" (16:2) "and in the morning, *'It will be* foul weather today, for the sky is red and threatening.' Hypocrites! You know how to discern the face of the sky, but you cannot *discern* the signs of the times'"(16:3)] is in 97%, C, D, N, W, TR, HF, RP, NKJV, NASB, NIV (with a note that says "Some early manuscripts do not have..."), ESV // א and B omit from "when" in verse 2 to the end of verse 3.

Aland says the omitted portion "represents a very early tradition.... In view of the support for the omission in the Greek manuscript tradition, the versions, and the Church Fathers, there can hardly be any doubt that both these passages [Jon 7:53- 8:11] were lacking in the original text of the Gospel. Matt. 16:2b-3 may have been suggested by Luke 12:54-56, but it is not a parallel in the strict sense. In any event, both texts must have been admitted in part of the Greek Gospel tradition at some time in the second century—a period when there was greater freedom with the text. Only then were such extensive insertions possible, and considering the amount of opposition apparently encountered by the Pericope Adulterae, it must have been quite strongly rooted in the evangelical tradition" (Aland, p. 307).

Matthew 19:17 "So He said to him, 'Why do you call Me good? No one *is* good but One, *that is,* God. But if you want to enter into life, keep the commandments." τι με λεγεις αγαθον ουδεις αγαθος ει μη εις ο θεος (Why do you call Me good? No one *is* good but One, *that is,* God) is in 99%, C, W, TR, HF, RP // τι με ερωτας περι του αγαθου εις εστιν ο αγαθος ει δε θελεις (why do you ask me about the good? One is good) is in א, (B, D), NU, NASB, NIV; ESV. Pickering explains, "NU in Matthew 19:17 contradicts NU in Mark 10:18 and Luke 18:19…. That the Latin versions offer a conflation suggests that both variants must have existed in the second century—indeed, the Diatessaron overtly places the majority reading in the first half of that century. Gnosticism dominated the church in Egypt during the second century. That such a 'nice' Gnostic variant came into being is no surprise, but why do modern editors embrace it? Because it is the 'more obscure' one (Metzger, p. 49)" (Pickering, p. 322).

Matthew 20:16 "For many are called, but few are chosen." γαρ εισιν κλητοι ολιγοι δε εκλεκτοι (and for many are called but few are chosen) is in 98.5%, C, B, N, W, TR, HF, RP, NKJV // א, B, NU, NASB, NIV, ESV Omit it. Aland says, "The argument for the secondary character of the addition, which is derived from Matt. 22:14 is the same as in all these examples: the attestation for the omission (which is relatively strong in this instance), together with the objection that no reason can be found for deleting such a pertinent statement if it had originally been a part of the Gospel of Matthew" (Aland, p. 307).

Matthew 20:22 and 23 "But Jesus answered and said, 'You do not know what you ask. Are you able to drink the cup that I am about to drink and be baptized with the baptism that I am baptized with?' They said to Him, 'We are able.' (20:23) So He said to them, 'You will indeed drink My cup, and be baptized with the baptism that I am baptized with; but to sit on My right hand and on My left is not Mine to give, but *it is for those* for whom it is prepared by My Father.'" In verse 22, το βαπτισμα ο εγω βαπτιζομαι βαπτισθηναι (be baptized with the baptism that I am baptized with) is in 99%, C, N, W, TR, HF, RP, NKJV // ℵ, B, D, NU, NASB, NIV, ESV omit it. In verse 23, και το βαπτισμα ο εγω βαπτιζομαι βαπτισθησεσθε (and be baptized with the baptism that I am baptized with) is in 99%, C, N, W, TR, HF, RP, NKJV // ℵ, B, D, NU, NASB, NIV, ESV omit it.

Aland says, "Matt. 20:22 and 23 are obvious examples of influence from parallel text. In both places, the words of Jesus to the sons of Zebedee have been expanded to the fuller form found in Mark 10:38-39. The impressive manuscript evidence against it needs no comment" (Aland, p. 307). In other words, A and B settle the issue.

Matthew 25:13 "Watch therefore, for you know neither the day nor the hour in which the Son of Man is coming." εν η ο υιος του ανθρωπου ερχεται (in which the Son of Man is coming) is in 89.3% TR, HF, RP, NKJV // ℵ, A, B, C, D, W, $\mathfrak{P}^{35}$, NU, in NASB, NIV, ESV omit these words. Aland says this insertion "belongs to the category of imperative explanatory addition so dear to the Byzantine Imperial text (in the score or more examples thus far 𝔐 [symbol for the Majority Text] has been prominent among the witnesses supporting such expansions, and this trait will remain characteristic of it!). The attestation for the addition is weak, and the source is Matt. 24:44" (Aland, p. 307).

Matthew 27:35 "Then they crucified Him, and divided His garments, casting lots, that it might be fulfilled which was spoken by the prophet: 'THEY DIVIDED MY GARMENTS AMONG THEM, AND FOR MY CLOTHING THEY CAST LOTS.'" ινα πληρωθη το ρηθεν υπο του προφητου διεμερισαντο τα ιματια μου εαυτοις και επι τον ιματισμον μου εβαλον κληρον (that it might be fulfilled which was spoken by the prophet: '

THEY DIVIDED MY GARMENTS AMONG THEM, AND FOR MY CLOTHING THEY CAST LOTS.') is in 5%, TR, NKJV. It is not in the NASB, NIV, or ESV. Aland says, "In Matt. 27:35, the supplementary quotation from the Psalms is derived from John 19:24. Besides the obvious presence of the devotional motive, support in the manuscript tradition is so weak that no discussion is necessary (in the Nestlé apparatus, the evidence for the omission is not even given)" (Aland, p. 307).

Mark 1:1 "The beginning of the gospel of Jesus Christ, the Son of God. υιου του θεου (the Son of God) is in 98.4%, A, TR, HF, RP. KJV, NKJV, NASB, NIV, ESV // υιου θεου (Son of God) is in B, D, W (.4%). The phrase is not in ℵ (.8%). WH" [υιου θεου]. NIV: [some manuscripts do not have *the* Son of God]. ESV: [some manuscripts omit *the* Son of God]. Burgon points out, "Irenaeus (AD 170) unquestionably read υιου του θεου in this place. He devotes a chapter of his great work to the proof that Jesus is the Christ, very God, and very man" (Burgon, p. 279; cited by Fuller, p. 78).

Mark 1:2 "As it is written in the Prophets" 'Behold, I send My messenger before Your face, who will prepare Your way before You.' the voice of one crying in the wilderness" 'prepare the way of the lord; make his paths straight.'" εν τοις προφηταις (in the prophets) is in 96.7%, A, W, TR, HF, RP // εν τω ησαια τω προφητη (in Isaiah the prophet) is in ℵ, B, NU, NASB, NIV, ESV. Mark quotes two prophets. The first quote is from Malachi (Mal. 3:1; Mk. 1:2). The second quote is from Isaiah (Isa. 41:3;

Mk. 1:3). "The former reading seems to be the better reading since two prophets are cited, and Isaiah is the last; to which agree the Arabic and Ethiopic versions and the greater number of Greek copies" (source unknown). Pickering makes several pertinent observations, including 1) in effect, Metzger uses the harder reading argument and 2) Malachi is quoted or alluded to a number of times in the New Testament but is never named and Mark quotes Isaiah and alludes to him about ten other places without naming him except when he is quoting Jesus (Pickering, p. 324).

Mark 2:26 "He went into the house of God *in the days* of Abiathar the high priest." Αβιαθαρ (Abiathar) is in 83.7%, א, B, TR. HF. RP, NU; it is omitted in D, W. The incident mentioned here occurred when Ahimelech was high priest, not Abiathar, the son and successor of Ahimelech (2 Sam. 8:17; 1 Chron. 24:6, 3, 31).

Various solutions have been suggested. 1) A copyist made an error because Abiathar was better known than his father. 2) The words "*in the days*" are in italics, indicating they are not in the original text. So the point could be "in the time of Abiathar, who was afterward the high priest" (Wesley; ATR). 3) In the Greek text, the word translated "of" is the particle επι, which may be rendered "about" or it is "before" Abiathar was high priest. 4) Ahimelech was the intended meaning. "That both father and son had two names, the father is also called Abiathar, appears almost certain from 2 Sam. 8:17; 1 Chron. 18:16, where Ahimelech seems evidently termed Abiathar, while Abiathar is called Ahimelech or Abimelech. (see 1 Kings 2:26-27). A. T. Robertson says, "It is possible that both father and son bore both names (1 Sam. 22:20; 2 Sam. 8:17; 1 Chron. 18:16)." This solution is possible. 5) Abiathar was present (Hort). Abiathar was the son of a high priest, and he succeeded his father in the office. He could have acted as his father's deputy, according to Jewish law (Gill). He is called a high priest because he was later a high priest. "As we say, 'General' Washington was present at the defeat of Braddock and saved his army, though the title of 'General' did not belong to him until many years afterward (Barnes). This satisfies the presence of the word "Abiathar." Jesus points out that David ate the showbread in the Temple with a priest, who later became a high priest.

Pickering says, "This verse has destroyed the faith of at least one scholar in our day, although he was reared in an evangelical home. He understood Jesus to be saying that Abiathar was the priest with whom David dealt when, in fact, it was his father, Abimelech. If Jesus stated a historical error is fact, then he could not be God. So he turned his back on Jesus" (Pickering, p. 216).

Mark 6:20 "For Herod feared John, knowing that he *was* a just and holy man, and he protected him. And when he heard him, he did many things, and heard him gladly." πολλα εποιει (he did many things) is in 98.4% A, C, D, N, TR, HF, RP // πολλα ηπορει (greatly puzzled) is in ℵ, B, NU, NASB: "he was very perplexed;" NIV: "he was greatly puzzled;" ESV: "he was greatly perplexed."

Herod did "many good things under the influence of the Baptist on his conscience" (JFB). "Not once or twice but many times Herod sent for his lonely prisoner … and listened to him as he reasoned with him of righteousness, temperance, and judgment to come, and not only listened, but *listened gladly;* nay more, he 'did many things;' many things, but not '*the thing.*' He would not put away his unlawful wife" (*Cambridge Bible for Schools and Colleges*, italics theirs). "He *did many of those things* which John in his preaching taught him. He was not only a *hearer of the word* but, in part, a *doer of the work*. Some sins which John in his preaching reproved, he forsook, and some duties he bound himself to; but it will not suffice to do *many* things unless we have *respect to all* the commandments" (Henry, italics his).

Mark 6:22 "when Herodias' daughter herself came in." αυτης της ηρωδιαδος (the daughter herself) is in 96.5% A, C, N, TR, HF, RP, in NASB; NIV; ESV // Αυτου ηρωδιαδος [his (daughter) Herodias] is in א, B, D, NU. Matthew 14:6 states that the girl was the daughter of Herodias, who had been the wife of Philip, Herod's brother, but was now living with Herod. In other words, she was not. Herod's daughter. She was his stepdaughter, but א, B, D, NU make her Herod's daughter. This is a case where modern translations part company with the NU.

Mark 6:33 "But the multitudes saw them departing, and many knew Him and ran there on foot from all the cities. They arrived before them and came together to Him." προηλθον αυτους (they arrived before them) και συνηλθον προςαυτον (and came together to Him) is in 96%, A, N, TR, HF, RP // Συνηλθον προς αυτον (and came together to Him) is omitted in א, B, (D), W, NU. Westcott and Hort consider this a conflated reading; they say the Byzantine text type combines the readings of א, B (προηλθον αυτους), and D (συνηλθον αυτον). Burgon reasoned that the TR was not derived from B, א, and the Western text but that B, ,א and the Western text have been derived from the TR, which is explained by the besetting fault of transcribers to admit part of the text (Burgon, cited by Miller in Green, p. H-5). Is it more likely that the scribe omitted something or added something?

Mark 8:26 "Neither go into the town nor tell anyone in the town." μηδε ειπης τινι εν τη κωμμη ("nor tell anyone in the town') is in 97.3%, A, C, N, TR, HF, RP. It is omitted in ℵ, B, W, and NU. But μηδει εις την κωμην εισελθης is in D, 56. There are other variant readings (see UBS). Simply put, the Alexandrian text type has "Do not enter the village," and the Western text type adds, "Do not speak to anyone in the village."

Westcott and Hort used Mark 8:26 as an example of a conflated reading demonstrating, in their opinion, the superiority of their "Neutral Text." The conflated is made up of μηδε εις την κωμνη εισλθης (ℵ, B, L, W) and μηδεί ειπης εν την κωμην (D, c, q, k). In his commentary on the Gospel of Mark, Swete says, "Further investigation has shown that the reading μηδεί ειπης μηδε εν την κωμνη was more widely current than they suppose and that its various forms give further support to the Western reading. Pointing to the Markan use of εις for εν, Turner claims that the case for its originality is unanswerable."

Miller responded, "The traditional reading is attested by ACNS and 13 other Uncials, all Cursives except eight, by several versions, and by Theophylact (i 210) who is the only Father found to quote the place.... Burgon remarks: ... Lachmann and for Tregelles abide by the Received Text; Tishendorf (sic), alone of Editors, adopts the reading of ℵ, while Westcott and Hort alone of Editors, adopts the reading of B (Miller in Green, p. H-6, capital letters his).

Mark 9:38 "Now John answered Him, saying, 'Teacher, we saw someone who does not follow us casting out demons in Your name, and we forbade him because he does not follow us.'" "απεκριθη δε αυτω ο ιωαννης λεγων διδασκαλε ειδομεν τινα εν τω ονοματι σου εκβαλλοντα δαιμονια ουκ ακολουθει ημιν (who does not follow us) και εκωλυσαμεν αυτον οτι ουκ ακολουθει ημιν (we forbade him because he does not follow us) is in A, C, N, E, F, G, K, S, U, V, TR, HF, RP.

Westcott and Hort claim this is a conflate; the Byzantine text type combined the readings of D, ος ουκ ακολουθει ημιν (who does not follow us we forbade him) [εκωλυσαμεν αυτον] and ℵ, B, και εκωλυσαμεν αυτον οτι ουκ ακολουθει ημιν (we forbade him because he does not follow us). Burgon reacted, "Why should the pretense be set up that there had been 'conflation' here? Two Omissions do not make one conflation!" (Burgon, cited by Miller in Green, p. H-6).

Mark 9:49 "For everyone will be seasoned with fire, and every sacrifice will be seasoned with salt." πας γαρ πυρι αλισθησεται και πασα θυσια αλι αλισθησεται (the whole verse) is in A, C, (D), N (88.5%), TR, HF, RP // (ℵ) B, (W) omit και πασα θυσια αλι αλισθησεται (and every sacrifice will be seasoned with salt). Westcott and Hort claim this is a conflate; the Byzantine text type combined the readings of (ℵ), B πας γαρ πυρι αλισθησεται (for everyone will be seasoned with fire), and D θυσια αλι αλισθησεται (and every sacrifice will be seasoned with salt).

"In the Gospel of Mark, the text of 9:49 presents exegetical difficulties which have given rise to a variety of improvements in the tradition.... The most radical change is found in the D tradition (as usual), which replaces the text with Lev. 2:13. The new text and the reading of the earlier exemplar were then combined to form conflated readings in the Majority text and numerous other manuscripts. Not only does the manuscript evidence require the original text, but so do the internal criteria. It is the ... [most difficult reading] which alone can account for the development of the other forms of the text (including the misconstruction) in a genealogical pattern" (Aland, pp. 307-308).

Burgon replied, "Such an ordinary circumstance as the omission of half a dozen words by Cod. D is so nearly without textual significance as scarcely to merit commemoration. And do Drs. Westcott and Hort really propose to build their huge and unwieldy hypothesis on so flimsy a circumstance as the concurrence in an error of A, B, L, D??" (Burgon, cited by Miller in Green, p. H-7).

Mark 10:7 "FOR THIS REASON A MAN SHALL LEAVE HIS FATHER AND MOTHER AND BE JOINED TO HIS WIFE." και προσκολληθησεται προς την γυναικα αυτου (and be joined to his wife) is in 98%, D, W, TR, HF, RP, NKJV // ℵ, B, NU, NASB, NIV, ESV omit it.

Aland says, "In Mark 10:7, the decision is difficult, and the reading has been retained in simple brackets. The manuscript [ℵ and B] supporting the omission are of considerable authority. Furthermore, the addition makes very good sense: by omitting the familiar words from Gen. 2:24, the text of Mark seems incomplete and probably misleading (*cf.* the sequel). Besides, as we have seen in a number of instances, it is the Gospel of Mark that tends to borrow from the Gospel of Matthew rather than the reverse. All this would argue for the omission. Against this possibility, homoioarcton [the scribe's eye skipped down the page to a similar word] should be considered…. And yet it is incredible that the identical omission could occur accidentally in all the manuscripts (A, B, Ψ, 892*, 2427, and others) testing the omission?" (Aland, p. 208).

Mark 10:21 "Then Jesus, looking at him, loved him, and said to him, 'One thing you lack: Go your way, sell whatever you have and give to the poor, and you will have treasure in heaven; and come, take up the cross, and follow Me.'" αρας τον σταυρον (take up the cross) is in 96.1% A, N, TR, HF, RP, NKJV // ℵ, B, C, D, NU, NASB, NIV, ESV omit this phrase. Aland says, "An accommodation interest is clear in addition to Mark 10:24: it is only those who put their trust in riches that find the kingdom of God difficult to enter. This softens the statement in 10:23, making its secondary character obvious (cf. the severity of verse 25), especially in view of its variations in manuscript tradition" (Aland, p. 308).

Mark 10:24 "And the disciples were astonished at His words. But Jesus answered again and said to them, "Children, how hard it is for those who trust in riches to enter the kingdom of God!" τους πεποιθοτας επι τοις χρημασιν (who trust in riches) is in 99.5%, A, C, N, (TR) HF, RP, NKJV. NASB: "those who are wealthy." // ℵ, B, NIV, and ESV omit this phrase. Aland says the addition is probably suggested by Mark 8:34. "The evidence for the omission is incomparably strong" (Aland, p. 308). Pickering says, "Within the context, the Majority reading is clearly correct.... The Latin and Syriac versions take the Majority reading back to the 2nd century" (Pickering, p. 332).

Mark 14:68 "But he denied it, saying, 'I neither know nor understand what you are saying.' And he went out on the porch, and a rooster crowed." και αλεκτωρ εφωνησεν (and a rooster crowed) is in 98.5%, A, C, D, TR, HF, RP, NU, NKJV // ℵ, B, W, NASB, NIV, ESV omits this phrase.

Aland says, "In Mark 14:68, the final word words of the verse ... are placed in single brackets because the evidence for their omission is of considerable spring, and for their inclusion it is distinctly superior. The internal criteria, however, are ambivalent. It can be argued that the omission occurred because of the occurrence in the other gospels mentioned only a single cockcrow, and the text directly parallel to Mark 14:68 does not refer to it. Yet, on the other hand, it can be argued that at the end of the periscope, where Matt. 26:74 and Luke 22:60 mentioned a cock's crow. Mark 14:72 [immediately the rooster crowed the second time]" (Aland, p. 308).

Mark 14:52 "and he left the linen cloth and fled from them naked. απ αυτων ("from them," which is at the end of the sentence) is in 98.8%, AD, N, W, TR, HF, RP, f^{35} // Omitted in ℵ, B, C, NU, NASB, NIV, ESV. Elliott criticizes the NA/USB for omitting these words based only on A, B, and C (Elliott in Black, p. 108).

Mark 16:9-20 Concerning these verses, Metzger says they "are lacking in the two earliest parchment codices, B and ℵ, in the Old Latin manuscript k [in a number of ancient versions]. Clement of Alexander, Origen, and Ammonius show no knowledge of the existence of these verses; other Church Fathers state that the section is absent from Greek copies of Mark known to them (e.g., Jerome, Epist. cxx. 3, *ad Hedibiam*, 'almost all the Greek copies do not have this concluding portion')." ... The ending in the KJV is "in the vast number of witnesses, (including several which also contain the immediate ending), namely A, C, B, L, W, θ, most of the late uncials, the great majority of the minuscules, most of the Old Latin witnesses, the Vulgate, Syr[c, p], and Coptic[pt]. It is possible that Justin Martyr, at the middle of the second century, knew this ending; in any case, Tatian, his disciple, included it in his Diatessaron" (Metzger, pp. 226-227).

Pickering gives the manuscript evidence for this passage. "It is contained in every extant Greek MS (about 1700) except three (really only two, B and 304—Aleph is not properly extant because it is a forgery at this point). [In a footnote, Pickering points out, "Tischendorf ... warned that the folded sheets containing the end of Mark and beginning of Luke appeared to be written by a different hand with different ink than the rest of the manuscript."] Every extant Greek lectionary (about 2000?) contains them (one of them, 185, doing so only in the Menologion). Every extant Syriac MS except one (Sinaitic) contains them. Every extant of the Latin MS (8000?) except one (k) contains them. Every extant Coptic MS except one contains them" (Pickering, pp. 327-328).

In Vaticanus, there is a blank space for it, the only blank space in the whole manuscript! (Burgon, who adds, "Never was blank more intelligible! Never was silence more eloquent!" (Burgon, *The Last Twelve Verses*, p. 165). The scribe who was copying Vaticanus knew about the passage. Perhaps the manuscript he was copying did not have the last page of Mark (Farstad, p. 112).

The Vulgate contains the last twelve verses of Mark. About 382, Jerome (*ca.* 345-420) was commissioned by Damascus in Rome to improve the "old Latin" translation of the Bible. As a result, he produced the Vulgate Bible, which became "the standard Bible of the Roman Catholic Church." He finished the New Testament before 391 and the Old Testament around 404 or 405. "Apparently, those two copies which lack this passage (Vaticanus and Sinaiticus) were not representative in their own time" (Farstad, p. 113).

Pickering says, "The Diatessaron (according to the Arabic, Italian, and Old Dutch translations) and Irenaeus clearly attest the last twelve verses in the second century! As does Hippolytus, a few years later. Then comes Vincentius, the Gospel of Nicodemus, and Apostolic Constitutions in the third century, Eusebius, Aphraates, Ambrose, and Chrysostom in the fourth century, followed by Jerome, Augustine, Cyril of Alexandria, Victor of Antioch, etc. Clement of Alexandria and Origen are usually cited as being against these verses, but it is an argument from silence. Clement's surviving works do not seem to refer to Mark's last chapter but instead to Matthew's last chapter" (Pickering, p. 307).

Irenaeus (115?-202) cites Mark 16:9 and Justin (100-165) echoes Mark 16:20. Lane, who does not accept the passage as genuine, concedes, "The evidence is sufficient to assert that the longer ending was in circulation by the middle of the second century, while its composition should be assigned to the first half of the second century. In *The Last Twelve Verses of Mark*, John Burgon demonstrates that the arguments about vocabulary and style do not prove that Mark did not write Mark 16:9-20."

If the Gospel of Mark ends with Mark 16:8, it concludes with the Greek word "gar" (meaning "for"), which would be abrupt and abnormal. "To end a book on this word seems most unlikely" (Farstad, p. 113). It is usually the second word in the sentence. Metzger says, "To terminate a Greek sentence with the word **gar** is most unusual and exceedingly rare— only a relative few examples have been found in all of the vast range of Greek literary works, and no instances have been found where **gar** stands at the end of the book. Moreover, it is possible that in verse 8, Mark uses the verb εφοβουντο to mean 'they were afraid of' (as he does in four of the other occurrences of this verb in his gospel). In that case, obviously, something is needed to finish the sentence" (Metzger, p. 228). Even Hort, who believes the book ends with verse 8, observes that it ends with "singular abruptness," adding that the sentence is not even complete.

Taylor says that Lightfoot cites examples of sentences ending with "for," but none of them stand at the end of a book. He points out that there is no parallel in the conclusion of any Markan pericope, John, Jewish, or Hellenistic literature. He adds, "It is incredible that Mark intended such a conclusion." Cole says ending Mark in verse 8 is abrupt linguistically and theologically. If Mark ends with Mark 16:8, it ends with the disciples being afraid (16:8). Can you imagine Mark doing that?

In his commentary on Mark, Hort says, "It cannot have been meant to conclude thus" either some accident may have prevented its completion, or a leaf of the original copy may have been lost." Alexander, the famous Princeton Theological Seminary professor of the 19th century, said that to suppose that Mark ends with verse 8 is "folly."

Luke 1:26 Nazareth is called "a city of Judea" εις πολιν της ιουδαιας (Judea) η ονομα ναζαρεθ in ℵ, instead of a city of Galilee (γαλιλαιας).

Luke 2:14 "Peace, goodwill toward men." ειρηνη εν ανθρωποις ευδοκια (goodwill toward men; goodwill is normative) is in 99.4%, TR, HF, RP // ειρηνη εν ανθρωποις ευδοκιας (to men of goodwill; goodwill is genitive) is in ℵ, A, B, D, W, NU. NASB: "Peace among men with whom He is pleased." NIV: "Peace to those on whom his favor rests." ESV: "Peace among those with whom He is pleased!

Aland points out the significant difference in meaning between ευδοκια and ευδοκιας, which adds an ς (s) at the end of the word. He claims, "It is certain that ευδοκια [goodwill toward men] is the secondary form and ευδοκιας [to men of goodwill] is the more difficult reading.... The external evidence for ευδοκιας [to men of goodwill] is indubitably far more extensive, but the force of internal criteria favoring ευδοκιας [to men of goodwill] is irrefutable" (Aland, pp. 288-289).

Godet says, "The gen. εὐδοκίας, *of goodwill*, may refer to the pious dispositions towards God with which a part of mankind are animated. But this interpretation is hardly natural.:εὐδοκία, from εὐδοκεῖν, *to delight in*, א, denotes an entirely gracious goodwill, the initiative of which is in the subject who feels it. This term does not suit the relation of man to God, but only that of God to man. Therefore, with this reading, we must explain the words thus: Peace on earth *to the men who are the objects of divine goodwill*. But this use of the genitive is singularly rude and almost barbarous; the *men of goodwill*, meaning those on whom goodwill rests..., is a mode of expression without any example. We are thus brought back to the reading of the TR, which is also present in 14 Mjj. [codex], among which are L. and Z., which generally agree with the Alex., the Coptic translation, of which the same may be said, and the *Peshitta*." (See also Burgon, *The Last Twelve Verses of Mark 16:9-20*, pp. 337-344.)

Luke 3:33 "the son of Amminadab, *the son* of Ram." του αμιναδαβ του αραμ του (Amminadab .... Ram) is in 95%, K, (D), TR, HF, RP, NIV // Pickering explains, "The fictitious Admin and Arni are introduced into Christ genealogy." He lists ten readings from various manuscripts, including א and B (Pickering, p. 321). NASB: "Amminadab ... Admin ... Ram; ESV: "Amminadab ... Admin ... Arni.

Luke 2:33 "and Joseph and his mother marveled at these things which were spoken of him." ιωσηφ και η μητηρ αυτου (Joseph and his mother) is in 98.8%. (B), TR, HF, RP // ο πατηρ αυτου και η μητηρ (his father and the mother) is in (א), B, D, W, Vulgate, Origen, Jerome, Augustine, NU,

NIV: "the child's father and mother marveled at what was said about him."
ESV: "and his father and his mother marveled at what was said about him."

ATR wrote, "Luke had already used 'parents' in Luke 2:27. He by no means intends to deny the Virgin Birth of Jesus so plainly stated in Luke 1:34-38. He merely employs here the language of ordinary custom. The late MSS. wrongly read 'and Joseph' instead of 'his father.'" Bullinger says, "Most of the texts (not the Syriac) read 'His father.'" *The Cambridge Bible for Schools and Colleges* says, "The undoubted reading is '*His father*,' ℵ, B, D, L, &c." Baker says, "'The *parents* brought in the child.' This is no denial of the virgin birth (Luke 1:34-35). In the legal sense, Joseph and Mary were Jesus' parents. See also Luke 2:48, '"Your father and I."'"

Gill says, "The Vulgate Latin reads, 'and his father and mother.' The Ethiopic version retains both his name and his relation and reads, 'and Joseph his father, and his mother,' but all the ancient copies read only 'Joseph,' without the addition, his father; and so the Syriac, Arabic, and Persic versions." MacDonald says, "Luke carefully guards the doctrine of the Virgin Birth with his precisely worded **Joseph and His mother,** as read by the King James tradition, following the majority of manuscripts" (MacDonald, bold type his).

Luke 4:4 "'But Jesus answered him, saying, 'It is written, 'MAN SHALL NOT LIVE BY BREAD ALONE, BUT BY EVERY WORD OF GOD.'" αλλ επι παντι ρηματι θεου (but by every Word of God) is in 90.7%, A, (D), TR, HF, RP, NKJV // ℵ, B, W. NU, NASB, NIV, ESV omit this phrase. Aland says, "The answer Jesus gave to the devil in Luke 4:4 and the traditional version was: 'Man shall not live by bread alone, but every word of God.' Modern versions omit the last phrase. This conforms to both external evidence and internal requirements. The expanded text is derived from Matt. 4:4, where Deut. 8:3 is cited in full…. If the phrase had been in the original text, what reason could there have been for its removal?" (Aland, pp. 308-309). Is it not easier to believe that a scribe accidentally omitted it rather than inserted it?

Luke 4:44 "And He was preaching in the synagogues of Galilee." γαλιλαιας (Galilee) is in (94.7%), A, D, TR, HF, RP // Ιουδαιας (Judea) is in ℵ, B, C, Q, $\mathfrak{P}^{75}$, NU, NASB. The parallel passages in Matthew 4:23 and Mark 1:39 say that Jesus was preaching in Galilee. Therefore, the reading in the Luke variant that states he was preaching in Judea is a geographical error. Metzger says that the NU editors chose "Judea" because it "is obviously the more difficult and the copyists have corrected it … in accordance with the parallels in Mt 4:23 and Mk 1:39" (Metzger, cited by Pickering, p. 319, who calls this "an error of fact").

Luke 5:4-6 "Launch out into the deep and let down your nets for a catch. (δικτυα, nets, plural) is in TR, HF, RP, WH, NU // "I will let down the net." δικτυον (net, singular) is [98%] A, C, TR, HF, RP // δικτυα (net, plural) ℵ, B, W, $\mathfrak{P}^{75}$, NU. "Their net was breaking." δικτυον (net, singular) is in [98.5%] A, C, TR, HF, RP // δικτυα (net, plural) ℵ, B, (D) W, $\mathfrak{P}^{75}$ NU. If the Byzantine text type is correct (singular), Peter was partially obedient. If the Alexandrian text type is correct, Peter was completely obedient (ℵ and B have plurals in verses 5 and 6)

Luke 8:43 "Now a woman, having a flow of blood for twelve years, who had spent all her livelihood on physicians and could not be healed by any." ιατροις (εις εατρους TR) προσαναλωσασα ολον τον βιον (had spent all her livelihood on physicians) is in 99.7% (א), A, (C), W, (TR), HF, RP, [NU], NKJV, ESV // omitted in B, (D), $\mathfrak{P}^{75}$, NASB, NIV.

Aland said, "In Luke 8:43, the detail that the woman with a hemorrhage 'had spent all of her living (in vain) on physicians' is single-bracketed in the Greek text (and correspondingly in modern versions). The witnesses for the omission—B (and D, with a single variation) s⁸ and sa—and by $\mathfrak{P}^{75}$, make their combined weight definitely stronger. And yet the motif of wasting money on doctors is already a part of the Marcan account, where it is stated even more emphatically in 5:26. Luke 8:43 can hardly be explained (as so frequently) by the influence of parallel texts, especially when the phrase is so freely and freshly expressed, even including a hapax legomenon [only used once]. It was a genuine Lucan warning about it, so it is an open question whether in the second century, to borrow a modern analogy, the medical profession had the phrase deleted or, to echo another modern complaint, the phrase was inserted as a protest against the rising cost of ineffective medical services (is this the reason for the hapax legomenon προσαναλωσασα?). The single brackets reflect the indecision of the editors of the new text at this point" (Aland, p. 309).

Luke 9:10 "And the apostles, when they had returned, told Him all that they had done. Then He took them and went aside privately into a deserted place belonging to the city called Bethsaida." κατ ιδιαν (private) εις τοπον (place) ερημμον (desert) πολεως (city) καλουμμενης (called) βηθσαιδα is in [94%], C, N, W, TR, HF, RP // ερημον (desert place) is in א. B, $\mathfrak{P}^{75}$, NU omit ερημον (desert place).

Westcott and Hort said this is a conflated reading that combines τοπον ερημον (desert place) in A and πολεως καλουμενης (city called) in B, $\mathfrak{P}^{75}$,

NU. (NASB: "He withdrew by Himself to a city called Bethsaida; NIV: "They withdrew by themselves for a town called Bethsaida; ESV: "He took them and withdrew apart to a town called Bethsaida").

Miller says that given the support for the Byzantine text type, Hort's position can only be held by assuming it beforehand" (Miller in Green, p. H-7). Pickering says, "NU has Jesus and company going to Bethsaida, but in verse 12, the disciples say that they are in a deserted area; thus, a contradiction is introduced. NU here is also at variance with NU in parallel passages" (Pickering, p. 325).

Luke 11:54 "lying in wait for Him, and seeking to catch Him in something He might say, that they might accuse Him." αυτον ζητουντες (seeking) is in [90%] A, C, W, TR, HF, RP // (και [6%] TR.) // αυτον ζητουντες (seeking) is in B, $\mathfrak{P}^{45}$, $\mathfrak{P}^{75}$ and omitted in ℵ // ινα κατηγορησωσιν αυτου (that they might accuse Him) is in [96.5%], C, TR, HF, RP. W // omitted in ℵ, B, $\mathfrak{P}^{45}$, $\mathfrak{P}^{75}$, NU.

Westcott and Hort contend that this is a conflated reading, combining the seeking of Him and the accusation against him. Hence, NASB: "plotting against Him to catch *Him* in something he might say; NIV: "waiting to catch him in something he might say; ESV: "lying in wait for him, to catch him in something he might say." Burgeon says, "Are we to understand ℵ B and the Coptic version, outweigh every other authority which can be named?" (Burgeon, cited in Green, p. H-8).

Luke 12:18 "So he said, 'I will do this, I will pull down my barns and build greater, and there I will store all my crops and my goods." τα γενημματα (crops) μμου και τα αγαθα (goods) μου. γενημματα (crops) is in [91%] ℵ, A, D, N, Q, W, TR, HF, RP // τον σιτον is in (B), $\mathfrak{P}^{75}$, NU.

"Westcott and Hort list this as a conflated reading. Lachmann, Tischendorf, and Alford retained the Byzantine Text. So does Tregelles. And so do Westcott and Hort, except they substitute τον οιτον for τα γενηματα. So, there has been no 'Syrian conflation' here. Cod. B has a substitution, and Cod. ℵ has an omission. That is all" (Miller in Green, p. H-8).

Luke 17:36 "Two *men* will be in the field: the one will be taken and the other left." This verse is in the TR, KJV, NKJV, but not in the MT, RP, BT, or f³⁵. In his English translation of f³⁵, Pickering said that perhaps only about 20% of Greek manuscripts have verse 36. He says that he believes this paragraph deals with the Rapture and that Jesus is addressing those who are left behind but who had expected to go. In other words, this is immediately after the Rapture.

Luke 22:43-44 "Then an angel appeared to Him from heaven, strengthening Him. And being in agony, He prayed more earnestly. Then his sweat became like great drops of blood falling down to the ground." Verses 43-44 are in (98.7%), (ℵ), D, Q, TR, HF, RP, NU. They are omitted in ℵ, B, N, P, W, 𝔓⁶⁹, 𝔓⁷⁵, and they are placed after Matthew 26:39 in C.

The Cambridge Bible for Schools and Colleges says, "This and the next verse are not of absolutely certain authenticity, since they are omitted in ℵ, B, and by the first corrector of ℵ and Jerome and Hilary say that they were omitted in 'very many' Greek and Latin MSS. Their omission may have been due to mistaken reverence, or the Evangelist himself may have made their insertion in a later recension."

Luke 23:45 "Then the sun was darkened, and the veil of the temple was torn in two." εσκοτισθη (darkened) is in 98.6%, A, D, Q, W, TR, HF,

RP, f³⁵ // εκλιποντος (eclipse) is in ℵ, C, 𝔓⁷⁵, NU; NASB: "was obscure;" NIV: "stopped;" ESV: "light failed." εκλειποντος is in B. Jesus was crucified during the Passover and the Passover is always at a full moon. Therefore, "eclipse" is a "scientific error" (Pickering, p. 319).

Luke 24:53 "and were continually in the temple praising and blessing God. Amen." αινουντες και ευλογουντες τον θεον αμμην (praising and blessing God) is in 99.6%, A, (D), W, TR, HF, RP // αινουντες και (praising and) is missing in ℵ, B, C, 𝔓⁷⁵, NU., Which means that the Alexandrian text type reads "blessing God." αινουντες (praising) is in D. Westcott and Hort listed this verse as one of the eight verses they said were examples of conflated readings.

In other words, the Western text type reads "praising God," the Alexandrian text type reads "blessing God," and the Byzantine text type conflated them into "praising and blessing God." "It is evident that there has been an omission of two words from the complete account by the different witnesses. The Evangelist employed both words in order to emphasize the gratitude of the apostles" (Miller, in Green, p. H-8, capital his).

John 1:18 "No one has seen God at any time. The only begotten Son, who is in the bosom of the Father, He has declared *Him*." ο μμονογενης υιος (the only begotten Son) is in (99%), A, (W), TR, HF, RP, NKJV, NIV: "the one and only Son, who is himself God's" // μονογενης θεος (only begotten God) is in ℵ, B, C, NU, NASB: "the only begotten God;" ESV: "the only God."

Cambridge Bible for Schools and Colleges says, "The question of reading here is very interesting. Most MSS and versions have 'the only-begotten Son' or 'only-begotten Son.' But the three oldest and best MSS and two others of great value have 'only-begotten *God*.' The test of the value of a MS, or group of MSS, on any disputed point is the extent to which it admits false readings on other points not disputed. Judged by this test, the group of MSS which read 'only-begotten God' is very strong, while the far larger group of MSS, which have 'Son' for 'God' is comparatively weak, for the same group of MSS might be quoted in defense of a multitude of readings which no one would think of adopting. Again, the revised Syriac, which is among the minority of versions that support 'God,' is here of special weight because it agrees with MSS from which it usually differs. We conclude, therefore, that the very unusual expression 'only-begotten God' is the true reading, which has been changed to the usual 'only-begotten Son,' a change which in an old Greek MS would involve the alteration of only a single letter. Both readings can be traced up to the second century, which again is evidence that the Gospel was written in the first century. Such differences take time to spread themselves widely."

Pickering says, "'An only begotten God' is so deliciously Gnostic that the apparent Egyptian provenance [origin] of this reading makes it doubly suspicious" (Pickering, p. 328).

John 5:2 "Now there is in Jerusalem by the Sheep *Gate* a pool, which is called in Hebrew, Bethesda, having five porches." Βηθεσδα (Bethesda) is in (98%), A, C, (N), TR HF, RP, KJV, NKJV, NASB, NIV, ESV // Βηθεσθα (Bethestha) is in (1.2%) // Βηθεσαιδα (Bethsaida) is in $\mathfrak{P}^{75}$, B, T, W, (.4%) // Βηδσαιδαν (Bedsaidav) is in $\mathfrak{P}^6$ // Βηθζαθα (Bethzatha) is in ℵ (.3%), WH, NU. Βelζeθα (Belzada) is in D.

NIV has Bethesda but adds "[5:2 Some manuscripts Bethzatha; other manuscripts Bethsaida]." ESV has Bethesda but adds "[5:2 Some manuscripts Bethzatha; other manuscripts Bethsaida]."

Hodges wrote, "Another factor militating against an uncritical acceptance of the oldest manuscripts is that they show a capacity to unite behind readings which—even in the eyes of modern scholars—are likely to be wrong. John 5:2 is a case in point. Here, the three oldest manuscripts extant are $\mathfrak{P}^{66}$ and $\mathfrak{P}^{75}$ (both about AD 200) and B (4th cent.). All three unite to read 'Bethesida,' in this verse instead of the familiar Bethesda found in the AV. But both of the most widely used critical editions of the Greek text, Nestlé's text and the United Bible societies text, reject 'Bethesda' in favor of the reading Bethzatha, supported—among extant Greek text—only by Aleph [א] (4th century, somewhat later than B) and the ninth-century minuscule 33. But even this reading is most likely to be wrong, as the prominent German scholar Joachim Jeremias has pointed out in his definitive monogram entitled, *The Rediscovery of Bethesda*. Jeremias confidently declares that the reading 'Bethesda' is original and adduces as evidence for this the Copper Scroll from Cave III at Qumran [the Dead Sea Scrolls]. This scroll, which paleography indicates to have been inscribed 'between AD 35 and 65, that is, between the life and ministry of Jesus and John's writing of his Gospel,' contains a Hebrew form of the name 'Bethesda' found on the Copper Scroll. Thus, the reading of the Majority Text, which is not found in any extant Greek manuscript before the fifth century, has, after all, the superior claim to originality in John 5:2. This is a classic example of how the great mass of later manuscripts, without any strain on the imagination, may be thought of as going back to other manuscripts more ancient than any we currently possess. The RSV may reasonably be charged with an error following the reading 'Bethzatha,' while the AV can continue to be followed here with considerable confidence.

"Furthermore, the occurrence of $\mathfrak{P}^{66}$, $\mathfrak{P}^{75}$, and B in the spurious reading 'Bethsaida' is not the type of variant reading which copy is normally produced by accident but is most likely the result of some kind of correction of the text. It is quite possible, then, that all three manuscripts ultimately derive from a single parent manuscript in which the emendation was originally made. Thus, there are numerous arguments against the Majority Text that are suspect on the ground that they may simply reproduce the reading of a single ancient copy—the extent of whose errors and revisions we do not know" (Hodges, 1968, pp. 338-339).

John 5:3-4 "In these lay a great multitude of sick people, blind, lame, paralyzed, waiting for the moving of the water. For an angel went down at a certain time into the pool and stirred up the water; then whoever stepped in first, after the stirring of the water, was made well of whatever disease he had." εκδεχομενων την του υδατος κινησιν ("waiting for the moving of the water") in verse 3 is in (99.3%), (D), W, TR HF, RP // these words are not in (.7%), ℵ, A, B, C, T, $\mathfrak{P}^{66}$, $\mathfrak{P}^{75}$, NU. Verse 4 is in (99.2%), (A) TR, HF, and RP // It is not in (.8%) ℵ, B, C, D, T, W, $\mathfrak{P}^{66}$, $\mathfrak{P}^{75}$, NU.

In his commentary on the Gospel of John, Leon Morris says, "Vv. 3b-4 form a very ancient explanation that has somehow crept into the text. The manuscript evidence makes it certain that it is not part of the original Gospel. But there is no reason for doubting that it explains the presence of the people (cf. v. 7)."

Burgon points out that verse 4 is in the Peshitta, the Syriac, most of the Old Latin, the Vulgate, and the Jerusalem versions, with Tertullian, Ammonius, Hillary, Ephraem the Syrian, Ambrose, Didymus, Chrysostom (8 times), Nilus (4 times), Jerome, Cyril of Alexandria, (five times), Augustine (twice), and Theodorus Studita of the Fathers" (Burgon, *The Traditional Text*, p. 38).

In my commentary on the Gospel of John, I wrote, "The phrase 'waiting for the moving of the water' in verse 3 and all of verse 4 is not in some Greek manuscripts. However, they are present in the majority of manuscripts and should be included in the text. Besides, if these words are eliminated, the man's words in John 5:7 would make little sense (Wiersbe). If that is the case, the problem created by this verse is the movement of the water."

John 6:11 "He distributed *them* to the disciples, and the disciples to those sitting down." τοις μαθηταις οι δε μαθηται is in [97%], D, TR, HF, RP // these words are omitted in ℵ, A, B, W, $\mathfrak{P}^{66}$, $\mathfrak{P}^{75v}$, NU, NASB, NIV, ESV. The parallel passages, Matthew 14:19, Mark 6:41, and Luke 9:16, state that Jesus handed the bread to the disciples, who then distributed it to the people. However, the omission of this detail in John suggests that Jesus directly distributed the bread to the people.

John 6:47 "Most assuredly, I say to you, he who believes in Me has everlasting life." εις εμε (in Me) is in (99.5%) A, C, D, N, TR, HF, RP, but those words are omitted in ℵ, B, T, W, $\mathfrak{P}^{66}$, NU. Pickering declares, "By omitting 'in Me' the NU text opens the door to universalism…. Since it is impossible to live without believing in something, everyone believes—the object of the belief is of the essence. The verb 'believe' does occur elsewhere without a stated object (the context supplies it), but not in a formal declaration like this. The shorter reading is probably the result of a fairly easy instance of homoioarcton [a scribe's eye skips from one occurrence of a word or phrase to the same or similar word or phrase further down the page]—three short words in a row beginning with *E*. And yet Metzger says of the words 'in me,' 'no good reason can be suggested to account for the remission'" (Pickering, p. 327).

John 7:8 "I am not yet going up to this feast." εγω ουπω αναβαινω (I am not yet going) is in [96.5%][, B, N, T, W, $\mathfrak{P}^{66}$, $\mathfrak{P}^{75}$, TR, HF, RP // εγω ουκ αναβαινω (I am not going) is in ℵ, D, NU. NASB: "I do not go up to this feast," NIV: "I'm not going up to this festival;" ESV: "I am not going up to this feast."

Two verses later (7:10), Jesus goes to Jerusalem. So, He knew in verse 8 that He was going to go. Therefore, the reading, "I am not yet going," is correct, and the variant, "I am not going," is incorrect, as it puts a lie in the mouth of Jesus.

The Cambridge Bible for Schools and Colleges says, "'Yet,' though very ancient, is possibly no part of the original text." it may have been inserted to avoid the charge of the heathen critic Porphyry that Jesus here shows fickleness or deceit, and therefore cannot be Divine. But the sense is the same, whether 'yet' is inserted or not. He means, 'I am not going now; not going publicly in the general caravan of pilgrims; not going with you, who do not believe on Me.' He does not say, 'I shall not go.' The next two verses show exactly what is meant by the negative."

Pickering observes, "Since the NU editors usually attach the highest value to $\mathfrak{P}^{75}$ and B, isn't it strange that they reject them in this case? Here is Metzger's explanation: 'The reading ['not yet'] was introduced at an early date (it is attested by $\mathfrak{P}^{66, 75}$) in order to alleviate the inconsistency between ver. 8 and ver. 10.' So they reject $\mathfrak{P}^{66,75}$ and B (as well as 96.5% of the MSS) because they perceive the 'inconsistency.' NASB, RSV, NEB, and TEV stay with the eclectic text here" (Pickering, p. 326).

John 7:53-8:11 These verses are in [85%], TR, HF, RP // they are omitted in ℵ, B, N, T, W, $\mathfrak{P}^{66, 75}$. The passage is in the vast majority of manuscripts. It is in over a thousand manuscripts of the Gospel of John (Farstad, p. 113). "The earliest Greek manuscript known to contain the passage is codex Bezea of the fifth or sixth century, which is joined by several Old Latin manuscripts" (Metzger, p. 224).

Nevertheless, Metzger says, "The account is lacking in the best Greek manuscripts: it is absent from $\mathfrak{P}^{66}$, $\mathfrak{P}^{75}$, ℵ, B, L, M, T, W, X [etc.].... Even more significant is the fact that no Greek Church Father for a thousand years after Christ refers to the periscope, including those who, like Origen, Chrysostom, and Nonnus (in his metrical paraphrase), dealt with the entire gospel verse by verse. Euthymius Zigabenus, who lived in the first part of the twelfth century, is the first Greek writer to comment on the passage, and even he declares that the accurate copies of the Gospel do not contain it (Metzger, p. 223).

The two problems with concluding the passage are not original: 1) What is the explanation for it being included? and 2) the omission renders the grammar of the passage nonsensical. Augustine wrote that it was omitted for fear it would promote immorality (Farstad, p. 113). If John 7 stops at verse 52, the text of John reads, "They answered and said to him, 'Are you also from Galilee? Search and look, for no prophet has arisen out of Galilee'" (Jn. 7:52). "Then Jesus spoke to them again, saying, 'I am the light of the world. He who follows Me shall not walk in darkness, but have the light of life'" (Jn. 8:12). Such a construction of the text has Jesus addressing the meeting of Nicodemus and the Sanhedrin, but Jesus was not in that meeting! (Farstad, p. 114).

As Pickering explains, "What is the antecedent of 'them' and what is the meaning of 'again'? By the normal rules of grammar, if 7:53-8:11 is missing, then 'them' must refer to the 'Pharisees' and 'again' means that there has already been at least one prior exchange. But 7:45 makes clear that Jesus **was not there** with the Pharisees. Thus, NU introduces an aberration. And yet, Metzger claims that the passage 'interrupts the sequence of 7:52 and 8:12ff.'" (Pickering, pp. 329-330, bold print his).

For a defense of the inclusion of this passage, see E. F. Harrison, "Jesus and the Woman Taken in Adultery" (*Bibliotheca Sacra*, number 412, October-December, 1946) and Zane C. Hodges, "The Woman Taken in Adultery (John 7:53-8:11): The Text." (*Bibliotheca Sacra*, vol. 136, October-December, 1979, pp. 318-32) and Zane C. Hodges "The Woman Taken in Adultery (John 7:53-8:11): Exposition." (*Bibliotheca Sacra*, vol. 137, January-March, 1980, pp. 41-53). See also Hodge and Farstad, *The New Testament According to the Majority Text*, pp. xxiii-xxxii).

John 10:29 "The Father who has given them to me is greater than all." ο πατηρ μου ος δεδωκεν μμοι μμειζων παντων εστιν. ος (who) is in (97.6%), A, $\mathfrak{P}^{66}$, $\mathfrak{P}^{75}$, TR, HF, RP // o (which) is in א, B, D, W. // μμειζων παντων (greater all) (98%), P66, TR, HF, RP. μμειζων (greater) is in B, NU // א, D, and W omit both words.

Godet declares, "One must be singularly blinded by prejudice" to favor the reading of B over the reading of TR. He also says that the reading in א

indicates God is a thing! He adds that not only do B and ℵ contradict one another, but the sense that is offered by the reading of B does not have the "least internal probability." According to the reading in B, John would be saying that "with the Father that given to Jesus is greater than all or everything. It would thus be the flock of Jesus, which is here called greater in the sense of being more precious and more excellent than all. What a strange expression! Believers are of more value than the whole universe, perchance. But the Scriptures never express themselves in this way. They glorified God, not man, even the most faithful men" (Godet on John 10:29, vol. 2, p.161).

Acts 8:37 "Then Philip said, 'If you believe with all your heart, you may.' And he answered and said, 'I believe that Jesus Christ is the Son of God.'" This verse is not in 88%, ℵ, A, B, C, P, $\mathfrak{P}^{45}$, $\mathfrak{P}^{74}$, HF, RP. f^{35}. Only one 16th-century manuscript has Acts 8:37 as it appears in the TR. C. I. Scofield omitted this verse (Carlson, p. 76).

Irenaeus (115?-202) says, "[Philip declared] that this was Jesus, and that the Scripture was fulfilled in Him; as did also the believing eunuch himself" and, immediately requesting to be baptized, he said, 'I believe Jesus Christ to be the Son of God'" (*Irenaeus, Against Heresies,* 3.12.8; https://files.romanroadsstatic.com/materials/romans/early-christianity/IrenaeusV1-0.pdf).

Pickering says, "The addition appears in 18 slightly different forms [the name 'Philip' appears in eleven MSS or 2.3%]. Since Phillip's house in Caesarea seems to have been something of a way-station for traveling Christians, he probably repeated the story hundreds of times; the information given in verse 37 is likely historically correct, but the Holy Spirit didn't have Luke include it in the inspired account."

Acts 9:5-6 "And he said, 'Who are You, Lord?' Then the Lord said, 'I am Jesus, whom you are persecuting. It *is* hard for you to kick against the goads.' So he, trembling and astonished, said, 'Lord, what do You want me to do?' Then the Lord *said* to him, 'Arise and go into the city, and you will be told what you must do.'"

The first part of verse 6 ("And he, trembling and astonished, said, Lord, what do You want me to do?") is not in any Greek manuscript. JFB say, "(The most ancient manuscripts and versions of the New Testament lack all these words *here* [including the last clause of Acts 9:5]; but they occur in Acts 26:14 and Acts 22:10, from which they appear to have been inserted here)."

The M-Text and the NU read, "And he said, 'Who are You, Lord?' And He said, 'I am Jesus whom you are persecuting, but get up and enter the city, and it will be told you what you must do'" (Acts 9:5-6; NASB).

"Note that this reading begins and ends the same as the TR, but lacks the whole section in the middle, 'it is hard for thee to kick against the pricks. And he, trembling and astonished, said, Lord, what wilt thou have me to do? And the Lord said unto him.' So, where did this longer reading come from? It seems to be a harmonization with a passage later in the book. In Acts 26, Saul recounts the story of his conversion. In this second telling of the story, the words are found (even in the M-Text and the NU) 'And when we had all fallen to the ground, I heard a voice saying to me in the Hebrew dialect, 'Saul, Saul, why are you persecuting Me? It is hard for you to kick against the goads.' And I said, 'Who are You, Lord?' And the Lord said, 'I am Jesus whom you are persecuting (Acts 26:14-15). Thus, it is not that most manuscripts lack this information; they just don't have it twice. They all have it in Acts 26:14-15, but the majority do not have it in Acts 9:5-6" (Wayne).

Acts 15:34 "However, it seemed good to Silas to remain there." 70.8%, ℵ, A, B, HF, RP, f³⁵, NU omit this verse. Pickering says, "Verse 33 seems to require that Silas returned to Jerusalem; 'they were sent back ... to the apostles,' and 'they' refer to Judas and Silas. The 'problem' is that in verse 40, Paul chooses Silas to accompany him, so he had to be in Antioch, not Jerusalem. Accordingly, the longer reading was created to solve the 'problem.' The 'some days' of verse 36 could well have been a month or two. From Antioch to Jerusalem would be a trip of some 400 miles. Silas had time to go to Jerusalem and back to Antioch."

Acts 16:12 "And from there to Philippi, which is the foremost city of that part of Macedonia, a colony." πρωτη (foremost) is in [84%], ℵ, A, C, TR, HF, RP // πρωτης (first)" Pickering says. "[none!] [NU] (NU has a conjecture)."

In his article "The Critical Text of Acts 16:12: When You Have None," James F. Davis says, "Many Majority Text (MT) advocates and those who want to give the MT a stronger voice in determining the text of the New Testament (NT) are concerned when textual decisions are made in the Critical Text (CT) that have a slim number of manuscripts (Mss.) for external support. One is sometimes left scratching his head, wondering whether the internal evidence is really strong enough to accept a reading with only a handful of manuscripts as its basis. A selected reading with only three, two, or even one manuscript for support increases one's skepticism significantly. But what about a case where a reading is selected with no Greek Mss. for support? In textual critical circles, this type of proposal is referred to as a conjecture. With so much Greek evidence available for the NT (over 5,500 Gk. Mss.), such a conjectural approach anywhere in the NT is highly questionable.

"So, it is both disappointing and disturbing that in Acts 16:12, the CT opts for a reading that doesn't have even one Greek manuscript to support it. As far as I know, this is the only place in the NT where the CT adopts such a conjectural emendation. In this writer's view, the CT's conjecture in Acts 16:12 is both unnecessary and unwise. To make matters worse, Louw and Nida, a standard Greek lexicon used by Bible translators, seem to accept the CT and the argument for it. They write, 'In Acts 16:12 ... the Greek New Testament published by the United Bible Societies has adopted a conjectural emendation, since the more traditional text πρωτη την μεριδον literally 'first of the district,' is not only misleading in meaning but does not reflect the historical fact that Philippi was a city in one of the four districts of Macedonia but was not a capital city" (Louw and Nida, *Greek Lexicon of the New Testament*, 16).

"This passage is found as part of the itinerary of Paul's second missionary journey and expansion of the church into Europe. After sailing from Troas, the missionary team comes to Neopolis and from there, enters the Roman colony of Philippi. The description of Philippi is said to be 'the foremost city of that part of Macedonia, a colony (NKJV).' The Majority Text reads ειν φιλιππουν ητιν εστι πρωτη την μεριδον την μεριδος της μακεδονιαν κολωνια. The CT reads ειν φιλιππουν, ητιν εστιν πρωτην την μεριδον την μακεδονιαν πολιν κολωνια Today's English Version (TEV) adopts the CT and translates the phrase as 'Philippi, a city of the first district of Macedonia.' (Note: in my limited survey of English Bible translations, the TEV was the only one following the CT here.)

"The controversy involves the text and meaning of πρωτη (foremost) (MT) and πρωτης (CT), the addition of one letter. The addition of the Greek sigma (ς) makes the noun a genitive case with the resultant meaning, according to the UBS Textual Commentary, 'a city of the first district of Macedonia.' The external evidence for the Majority Text reading of πρωτη could hardly be stronger and more geographically widespread. It includes Papyri 74, Aleph [א], B, A, C, etc. In fact, every Greek witness except one has πρωτη, except D, which reads κεφαλή (lit. head) also in the nominative case. Kurt and Barbara Aland have determined that there are over 600 complete Greek Mss. of the book of Acts, so there isn't a lack of Greek evidence for this passage" (Aland, *Text of the New Testament*, 83). The critical text is based on conjecture and three late Vulgate Mss. (UBS, *Textual Commentary*, 446).

"As Louw and Nida explain, the basic reason this is even an issue is the historical factor that Thessalonica was the capital of Macedonia and not Philippi. However, it is well known, based on a statement by Livy, that the Roman province of Macedonia was divided into four districts. Additionally, most commentators and translations acknowledge that the Greek does not necessitate a meaning of 'capital city' but lexically and naturally allows for a meaning of 'leading' or 'prominent city.' However, according to the textual commentary, some would argue that Amphipolis was more prominent than Philippi even within its own district.

"Dating at least as far back as W. M. Ramsay (*Saint Paul the Traveler and Roman Citizen*), commentators have made a good historical case that Philippi was a leading city of its district, if not the leading city. The city was named after the father of Alexander the Great (Philip II of Macedonia) but really gained significant and unusual importance in the Roman Empire when Caesar Augustus (also known as Octavian) granted it special status and privileges. In the first century B.C., his forces won major battles at Philippi, and the city was made a Roman colony in honor of the victory. It was eventually renamed Colonia Augusta Iulia Philippensium. The city was entitled to self-government, the same rights/privileges as the populations of Italian cities, and immunity from taxation (see Fitzmeyer, Acts, *Anchor Bible Commentary*, 584). At that time, these were no small matters. Thus, one can argue that at the time of Paul's journey, Philippi was established as not only a prominent city in its district but also likely considered especially privileged in all of Macedonia.

"To be fair, one has to note that the United Bible Society's *Textual Commentary on the NT* records a dissenting opinion by Kurt Aland and Bruce Metzger of the CT decision. In fact, they state their objection well by writing in part, 'it appears ill-advised to abandon the testimony of $\mathfrak{P}^{74}$, Aleph, A, C, 81 al, especially since the phrase can be taken to mean merely that Philippi was 'a leading city of the district of Macedonia'" (*Textual Commentary*, 446).

"The MT view is sometimes ridiculed as a position that merely wants to count manuscripts for textual decisions, and if that is all that the MT position was, I would not support it either. But really, the question is, 'should the number of Mss. be any factor at all (and if so, how much) when weighing the textual evidence?' When some textual critics answer this question in the negative by their practice, it fuels the concern that considerable amounts of valuable external evidence are being disregarded. Don't we have the right and obligation to say something?"

Conclusion: The basic meaning of πρωτη is "first." Since Thessalonica was the capital of Macedonia, the Critical Text conjectures that another word, which is in no Greek manuscript, should be the reading here. The KJV translates this part of the verse as "the chief city of that part of Macedonia." The NKJV renders it "the foremost city of that part of Macedonia." The NASB, NIV, and ESV translate it "a leading city of the district of Macedonia."

In the first place, although the primary meaning of πρωτη is "first," it could legitimately be rendered "the foremost city." Kurt Aland and Bruce Metzger contend that πρωτη is the correct reading and conclude, "the phrase can be taken to mean merely that Philippi was 'a leading city of the district of Macedonia'" (*Textual Commentary*, p. 446). In the second place, another possible solution is the one taken by the KJV and the NKJV, which is that Philippi was "chief" (KJV) or "foremost" (NKJV) "of *that part* of Macedonia" (italics added).

Acts 19:16 "Then the man in whom the evil spirit was leaped on them, overpowered them, and prevailed against them so that they fled out of that house naked and wounded." αυτων (them) is in 90%, TR, HF, RP, NIV, ESV // αμφοτερων (both of them) is in ℵ, A, B, D, NU, NASB: "subdued all of them;" NIV: "overpowered them all;" ESV: "mastered all of them.

"The sons of Sceva were seven, not two.... Most modern versions render 'both' as 'all.' NASB (sic) actually renders 'both of them,' making the contradiction overt!" (Pickering, pp. 322-323). It was the ASV, not the NASB, that said "both of them."

Acts 28:13 "From there we circled round and reached Rhegium." οθεν περιελθοντες (we circled) is in [95%], A, TR, HF, RP, NASB: "We sailed around" // Περιελοντες (taking away) is in ℵ*, B, D, NU.

Pickering says the verb Περιελοντες is transitive and here, it is meaningless.... The Greek letters θ and 0 are very similar, and being side-by-side in a word, it would be easy to drop one of them out, in this case, *theta* [θ]" (Pickering p. 327).

Romans 5:1 "Therefore, having been justified by faith, we have peace with God through our Lord Jesus Christ." ειρηνην εχομεν (we have peace, present active indicative) is in (57%), TR, HF, RP, NU // ειρηνην εχωμεν (let us have peace, present active subjunctive) is in (43%), f^{35}, ℵ, A, B, C. The difference is ο versus ω.

Aland points out that ο and ω are pronounced alike, adding, "Many scholars believe that in the original dictation of the letter Tertius may well have written εχωμεν [let us] for Paul's dictated εχομεν [we have] (Aland, p. 286).

The Bible for Schools and Colleges says, "The Gr. has an important and strongly supported *various reading: 'Let us have peace.'* Without attempting to discuss the documentary evidence here, we merely state the case thus:—There is, on the whole, a greater weight of MSS and ancient Versions in favor of '*let us have.*' But on the other hand there is a greater weight of internal evidence for '*we have.*' In other words, '*we have*' exactly *fits the context;* '*let us have*' is *foreign to it.* The whole context is one not of exhortation but of dogmatic assertion— 'we have access;' 'we rejoice;' 'the love of God has been poured out into our hearts;' 'we shall be saved;' 'we are reconciled;' 'we have received the reconciliation.'—

How then can we account for the 'Let us have'? Probably, by early failures to grasp the complex but consistent argument of the whole long context and the inevitable tendency due to such misapprehension to substitute aspiration or exhortation for (what the text speaks of) a present possession.—It is an obvious right principle, though calling for most cautious application, that no amount of MS. evidence ought ever to force on us a reading which mars the context.—A *single stroke* in the Gr. MSS makes the only visible difference between the readings" (italics his).

Romans 8:1 "Who walk not after the flesh, but after the Spirit." The last phrase of Romans 8:1 is in (94%), א^c, D^c, K, P, TR, HF, RP // It is not in א, B, or NU.

Many commentators interpret Romans 8:1 as a reference to justification by faith (for example, Sandy and Headlam). Part of why they do so is that they omit the last part of the verse from the text, claiming that it is not in the "best" manuscripts. Thus, the verse reads, "There is therefore now no condemnation to those who are in Christ." Granted, the phrase "who do not walk according to the flesh but according to the Spirit" is not in *some* Greek manuscripts, but it is in the majority. Furthermore, it is in verse 4!

Romans 8:1 says there is no servitude to sin to those in Christ (see this expression in Rom. 6:11) and who walk (Rom. 6:4) according to the Spirit. Actually, according to Romans 8:1, believers can either walk according to the flesh or according to the Spirit. "According to" means the norm or the standard by which something is done. Believers can walk according to the standard of the flesh, which is the sin principle in them (Rom. 7:14, 23, 25), or they can live by the standard of the Holy Spirit (Rom. 7:5). Thus, Romans 8:1 is not a reference to justification from the guilt of sin. It is a reference to deliverance from the power of sin's disposition in the believer (Bruce, p. 149; Showers, p. 109; see my commentary on Rom. 5:16 for proof that the Greek word translated "condemnation" in Rom. 8:1 means "penal servitude").

Romans 10:17 "and hearing by the word of God." θεου (of God) is in A [98%], TR, HF, RP, KJV, NKJV // Χριστου (of Christ) is in ℵ, B, C, 𝔓⁴⁶, NU, NASB, NIV, ESV.

"Erasmus realized that the *Vulgate* had 'word of Christ,' as a number of early fathers (what he did not know, however, that 𝔓⁴⁶, ℵ, and B, *also* had 'Christ'). Basically, Erasmus 'guested' and chose 'God,' explaining, 'it does not greatly affect the meaning except in the sense that the phrase 'voice of God' lends more dignity to the words of the Apostle and has a wider application'" (White, p. 58, italics his).

Romans 14:15 "Yet if your brother is grieved because of *your* food, you are no longer walking in love." δε is in [96%], TR, HF, RP // γαρ is in ℵ, A, B, C, NU: "But." NASB and ESV: "For if because of food your brother is hurt." NIV: "If your brother is distressed" (It ignores the word altogether!).

If "for" is correct, Romans 14:15 is a reason or explanation of verse 14, which is not the case. In his commentary on Romans (1886), Charles Hodge says, "Instead of de, *but*, which is found in the common text, Griesbach, Lachmann, and Tischendorf, on the authority of the majority of the Uncial MSS, read gap, *for*. As this verse, however, does not assign a reason for the principle asserted in ver. 14, but does introduce a limitation to the practical application about principle, the majority of commentators and editors retain the common text."

Romans 14:23-15:1 "But he who doubts is condemned if he eats because *he does* not *eat* from faith; for whatever *is* not from faith is sin. We then who are strong ought to bear with the scruples of the weak and not to please ourselves." See the following paragraphs.

Romans 16:25-27 "Now to Him who is able to establish you according to my gospel and the preaching of Jesus Christ, according to the revelation of the mystery kept secret since the world began." ℵ, A, B, C, TR, [NU], NKJV, NASB, NIV, ESV put Romans 16:24-26 after Romans 16:23 (A puts it in both places), but some manuscripts place Romans 16:24-26 after Romans 14:23" (94.8%), A, f^{35}, HF, RP. 𝔓^{46} puts Romans 16:25-26 after Romans 15:33.

"The NU (and thus modern translations based on it) agree with the KJV here. In the majority of Greek manuscripts, however, these verses are in a different order. What the KJV and all major modern translations say Romans 16:25-27 is not found at the end of Chapter 16, but instead is written between 14:23 and 15:1. Thus, in the M-Text, we would read all together at the end of Chapter 14 on into 15 something like: 'But he who doubts is condemned if he eats because his eating is not from faith and whatever is not from faith is sin. Now to him, that is of power to stablish you according to my gospel, and the preaching of Jesus Christ, according to the revelation of the mystery, which was kept secret since the world began, But now is made manifest, and by the scriptures of the prophets, according to the commandment of the everlasting God, made known to all nations for the obedience of faith. To God only wise, be glory through Jesus Christ forever. Amen. Now we who are strong ought to bear the weaknesses of those without strength and not just please ourselves.' Thus, this is a place where the TR agrees with modern textual critics that the minority of witnesses are here more reliable that the majority and that the reading found in the Byzantine tradition (and thus in the M-Text) is incorrect" (Wayne).

1 Corinthians 5:1 "such sexual immorality as is not even named among the Gentiles—that a man has his father's wife!" ονομαζεται (is named) is in 96.8%, TR, HF, RP // this word is omitted in ℵ, A, B, C, 𝔓⁴⁸ NU, NASB: "of such a kind as does not exist;" NIV: "of a kind that even pagans do not tolerate;" ESV: "a kind that is not tolerated even among pagans."

Pickering explains that 96.8% of manuscripts indicate this is a type of fornication is not what the Gentiles talk about, but ℵ, B, NU, etc., affirm that this type of incest does not even exist among the Gentile, "a plain falsehood" (Pickering, p. 320).

1 Corinthians 15:51 "Behold, I tell you a mystery: we shall not all sleep, but we shall all be changed." ου (not) κοιμηθησομεθα παντες δε (but) αλλαγησομεθα (changed) is in 96.4%, B, D, K, P, Ψ, TR, HF, RP, NU. Tertullian, etc // ου (not) κοιμηθησομεθα ου (not) παντες δε αλλαγησομεθα (we shall *not* all be changed) is in ℵ, A, C, F, G. 𝔓⁴⁶, and still others read "We shall not all rise, but we shall not all be changed (D).

Ephesians 1:1 "In Ephesus." εν εφεσω (in Ephesus) is in (99.2%) ℵ ᶜ, A, B³, D, G, K, P, Ψ, TR, HF, RP, [NU], Chrysostom, Cyril, etc. // these words are omitted in ℵ, B, 𝔓⁴⁶, 424ᶜ, 1739 (Marcion), (Tertullian), Origen.

1 Thessalonians 2:7 "But we were gentle among you, just as a nursing mother cherishes her own children." εγενηθημεν ηπιοι εν μεσω (we were gentle among you) is in 87.5%, A, f³⁵, TR, HF, RP, Origen, Christendom // **ν**ηπιοι (we were babes) is in 𝔓⁶⁵, ℵ, B, C, R, (10.8%), NU.

In the Greek text, the only difference between the two words is that one has an "n" in the front of it, and the other does not. Although the reading "We were *babes* among you" does not make sense because "babes" is in Vaticanus and Sinaiticus, which are older, some scholars argue that "babes" is the correct reading while admitting that "gentle" makes excellent sense (Lightfoot). Hiebert cites Mace, who says, "No manuscript is as old as common sense."

Since Aland's handling of this variant is a good example of the method of textual criticism, here is a summary of his explanation. He argues that the earliest manuscripts contain νηπιοι [babes] $\mathfrak{P}^{65}$ (from the third century), ℵ, C, D^D, as well as Ψ and 104 "all have νηπιοι [babes] in the original hand corrected to ηπιοι [gentle] by a later hand. Only Codex Alexandrinus (A) (with the Majority Text) read ηπιοι [gentle] in the original hand from the beginning, while codices Vaticanus (B), F, G, and I and the minuscule 2495 read νηπιοι [babes] unaltered from the beginning in company with Clement of Alexandria (and a great number of the Church Fathers).... Thus, the external evidence seems unequivocal."

Aland then argues, "This word [ηπιοι, gentle] is not part of the Pauline vocabulary. νηπιος [babes] is far more typically a Pauline word.... νηπιος [babes] occurs 15 times in the New Testament, 11 of which are in the Pauline letters (twice in Matthew and once each in Luke and Hebrews). In addition, νηπιαzw is used only by Paul (once in 1 Corinthians). In contrast, ηπιοι [gentle] is found only once in the New Testament and 2 Timothy.

Aland also argues, "νηπιοι [babes] is actually the harder reading ... and the exegete should accept it" (Aland, p. 284). He adds that this is an example "of the tendency we find so often New Testament manuscripts to make the text more polished and acceptable. In all such instances, the judgment of textual criticism can only be that the more polished and acceptable form of the text is secondary."

1 Timothy 3:16 "Great is the mystery of godliness: God was manifest in the flesh." θεος (God) is in (98.5%), A, C, F, G, K, L, P, Ψ, 7TR, HF, RP, Chrysostom // ος (which) is in ℵ (1%), NU, Origen, Jerome, but it is grammatically incorrect because this pronoun has no antecedent. "Who is nonsensical" (Pickering, p. 330). // o (who) is in D, Augustine, but it is also grammatically incorrect because "who" is masculine and "mystery" is neuter. Besides, a human being manifesting itself in the flesh is not a mystery. All human beings have bodies. "He" (NASB; NIV; ESV) was manifest in the flesh" is not in any Greek or Latin manuscript!

That leaves θεος (God), which is correct. Then how did the other readings get into some manuscripts? Christian scribes developed contractions for "sacred" words, such as God, Lord, Jesus, Christ, and Son. The contraction was made by writing only the first and last letters, the first two and last letters, or the first and last two letters with a horizontal line above the contraction (Metzger, pp. 13-14). Thus, "God was written θC (with a cross stroke above the two letters to indicate an abbreviation), 'who' was written OC, and 'that' was written O. The difference between 'God' and 'who' is just two cross strokes, and with a scratchy quill, those could easily be light (or the copyist could be momentarily distracted and forget to add the cross stroke)" (Pickering, p. 331).

For a detailed, scholarly explanation of 1 Timothy 3:16, see http://livingwater-spain.com/1Tim3_16.pdf. See also Pickering pages 116-117.

2 Peter 3:10 "Both the earth and the works that are in it will be burned up." και γη και τα εν αυτη εργα κατακαησεται (be burned up) is in (93.6%), A, 048, TR, HF, RP, NASB, ESV.

Pickering says ευσεβειαις (be found) is in א, B, 𝔓⁷², NU, NIV: "be laid bare." Pickering adds, "The NU reading is nonsensical; the context is clearly one of judgment. Metzger actually states that their text 'seems to be devoid of meaning in the context.' So why did they choose it? Metzger explains that there is 'a wide variety of readings, and one of which seems to be original'—presumably if 'shall be burned up' were the only reading, with unanimous attestation, he would still reject it, he can scarcely argue that it is meaningless. NU editors deliberately chose a variant they believed to be 'devoid of meaning in the context.' NASB abandons UBS here, giving the majority reading; NEB and NIV render 'will be laid bare'" (Pickering, p. 331).

1 John 1:4 "And these things we write to you that your joy may be full." υμων (your) is in (41%), A, C, some TR // ημων (our) is in (59%), א, B, some TR, HF, RP, OC. The difference between the two readings is a single letter (υ versus η).

1 John 5:7-8 "For there are three that bear record in heaven, the Father, the Word, and the Holy Spirit, and these three are one. And there are three that bear witness in earth, the Spirit, and the water, and the blood," and these three agree in one." This passage is not in 99%, א, A, B, HF, RP, f³⁵, NU.

This passage is only found in five late Greek manuscripts and in part of the Latin tradition from which it came. Cyprian seemed to quote the comma. "The Lord says, 'I and the Father are one;' and again it is written of the Father, and of the Son, and of the Holy Spirit, 'And these three are one.'" For the story of how it got into the TR, see the chapter on the Textus Receptus. For a detailed explanation of how this passage got into the Greek text, see White, pp. 60-62.

Jude 14-15 "Now Enoch, the seventh from Adam, prophesied about these men also, saying, "Behold, the Lord comes with ten thousands of His saints, to execute judgment on all, to convict all who are ungodly among them of all their ungodly deeds which they have committed in an ungodly way, and of all the harsh things which ungodly sinners have spoken against Him." παντας τους ασεβεις (all who are ungodly) in verse 15 is in (95.8%), A, B, C, TR, HF, RP, in NASB, NIV, ESV. // Παντας ψυχην (all souls) is in ℵ, $\mathfrak{P}^{72}$, 1852 (a total of three MSS). Note ℵ and B differ.

Jude is talking about the judgment of infiltrators (verses 4, 5, 6, 7, 11, 13). In verse 14, he introduces a prophecy about "these men." Therefore, verse 15 talks about those who are ungodly, not all souls. In his apparatus of the New Testament, Pickering points out, "Nestlé[25] and UBS[2] stated with the Majority reading 'all the ungodly.' UBS[3] changed to 'every soul' without comment! Is this not a curious proceeding? The UBS editors reversed an earlier position, following just three manuscripts and the Sahidic version, and they do not even mention it in the apparatus."

Revelation 13:18 "His number *is* 666." εξακοσιοι εξηκοντα εξ εστιν χξς (666) is in all manuscripts except two, TR, HF, and RP // εξακοσιοι δεκα εξ (616) in Codex C, $\mathfrak{P}^{115}$. In Against Heresies 5. 29-30, Irenaeus commented on Revelation 13:18 (AD 180). He says 666 is "found in all the most approved and ancient copies," and "those men who saw John face to face" have testified to its genuineness. He then declared 616 a corruption (https://www.thetextofthegospels.com/2015/09/revelation-1318-and-number-of-beast.html).

Revelation 22:19 "And if any man shall take away from the words of the book of this prophecy, God shall take away his part out of the book of life, and out of the holy city, and from the things which are written in this book." βιβλου της ζωης (book of life) is in the TR // ξυλου της ζωης (tree of life) HF, RP, etc. The Latin Vulgate reads "book" rather than "tree," which is where Erasmus got the reading, "but before Erasmus, the reading was unknown in the original Greek" (Wayne).

As Wayne explains, "When Erasmus compiled the first edition of what later came to be known as the TR, he had only one manuscript of Revelation. This manuscript was missing the last six verses, so Erasmus was forced to translate from the Latin Vulgate into Greek to fill in this section of the text. In so doing, Erasmus created a number of Greek readings that had never been seen in any manuscript before." Wayne explains that many such readings were corrected in later additions, but some were not, including the most famous, Revelation 22:19."

Summary: The differences between the Byzantine Text (TR; MT; BT, f^{35}) and the Vaticanus/Sinaiticus (CT) make a difference in interpreting many passages.

Every word in the Word of God is inspired and words can make a world of difference. In a divorce dispute, the Los Angeles Dodgers' ownership became contentious. After they were married, both Frank and Jamie McCourt signed an agreement. The 12th word of the second paragraph of the first exhibit read either "**in**clusive" or "**ex**clusive." The document had six copies: three read inclusive and three read exclusive. If the word was inclusive, Frank was the sole owner. If the word was exclusive, Jamie was co-owner. The difference was two letters in one word.

Verses Omitted from the CT

Matthew 17:21 "However, this kind does not go out except by prayer and fasting." 99.4% of translations, including C, D, W, TR, HF, RP, NKJV, and ESV, have this verse, while the NASB places it in brackets. In contrast, ℵ, B, NU, and NIV omit it. Aland says this is a "duplicate ending taken from the parallel text in Mark 9:29. Even there, it is a secondary form…. Yet, ℵ, B, 0274, k, and Clement of Alexandria are quite adequate support for the shorter term of Mark 9:29." He adds that Mark is changed in the majority of witnesses to make it a smoother text (Aland, p. 301).

Matthew 18:11 "For the Son of Man has come to save that which was lost." 98.5%, D, N, W, TR, HF, RP, and NKJV include this verse, and the NASB places it in brackets. ℵ, B, NU, NIV, ESV omit it.

Matthew 23:14 "Woe to you, scribes and Pharisees, hypocrites! For you devour widows' houses, and for a pretense, make long prayers. Therefore, you will receive greater condemnation." 98%, W, TR, HF, RP, and NKJV have this verse and the. NASB puts it in brackets // ℵ, B, D, NU, NIV, ESV omit this verse. Aland says, "This text is doubtless derived from parallel traditions in Mark 12:40 and Luke 20:45-47, and it was introduced here to satisfy the same tendency toward completeness that is also observed in the scribal tendencies to conflated readings (Aland, p. 302).

Mark 7:16 "If anyone has ears to hear, let him hear!" 98.8% of the translations (A, D, W, TR, HF, RP, and NKJV) include this verse, while the NASB places it in brackets. In contrast, א, B, NU, NIV, and ESV omit this verse. Aland says, "This saying is found repeatedly in the original text of the gospel (Matt. 11:15; 13:9; 13:43; Mark 4:9; 4:23; Luke 8:8; 14:35) and it is only too easy to understand how a part of the manuscript tradition would add it in contexts where it seems appropriate, as in the present passage (the evidence for the insertion is clearly inferior to that for the omission when internal criteria are considered)." (Aland, p. 302).

Mark 9:44 "where 'THEIR WORM DOES NOT DIE AND THE FIRE IS NOT QUENCHED." 96%, A, B, N, TR, HF, RP, and NKJV have this verse, and the NASB puts it in brackets // א, B, C, W, NU, NIV, ESV omit it.

Mark 9:46 "where 'THEIR WORM DOES NOT DIE AND THE FIRE IS NOT QUENCHED.'" 96%, A, D, N, TR, HF, RP, and NKJV have this verse, and the NASB puts it in brackets // א, B, C, W, NU, NIV, ESV omit it.

Mark 11:26 "But if you do not forgive, neither will your Father in heaven forgive your trespasses." 96%, A, (C), (D), (N), TR, HF, RP, and NKJV have this verse and the NASB puts it in brackets // א, B, W, and, NU, NIV, ESV omit it. Aland says, "Mark 11:26 represents an adaptation of Matt. 6:15, typical of the way parallel texts have influenced the Gospel of Mark. The evidence for omission is excellent and in view of eternal criteria, it is convincing" (Aland, p. 302).

Mark 15:28 "So the Scripture was fulfilled which says, "AND HE WAS NUMBERED WITH THE TRANSGRESSORS." 88.7%, TR, HF, RP, and NKJV have this verse and the NASB puts it in brackets // 11.1%, א, B, C, D, and NU, NIV, ESV omit it.

Aland says, "Here the verses derived from Luke 22:37, converting the prediction Jesus made here into a theological comment by recounting its fulfillment. The external attestation for the omission is clearly superior. The presence of the verse in the Byzantine text explains why it (like the others) is in the text printed by Erasmus and in subsequent editions of the Greek text, and consequently in the versions made in the centuries following" (Aland, p. 302).

Luke 17:36 "Two *men* will be in the field: the one will be taken and the other left." The USB apparatus says it is included in D and a number of minuscules. It is found in the TR, KJV, and NKJV. However, it is not in HF, RP, or f³⁵, and Pickering does not comment on it. ℵ, A, B, K, L, W, X, 𝔓⁷⁵, etc., NIV and ESV omit it.

Aland says, "Here the external evidence is so weak, as well as being divided, that there seems to be no necessity for the Nestle apparatus to cite the evidence for the text (i.e., all the witnesses not cited for the insertion). Luke 17:36 is derived from the parallel tradition at Matt. 24:40" (Aland, p. 303).

Luke 23:17 (for it was necessary for him to release one to them at the feast). 97.9% (ℵ), (D), (N), W, TR, HF, RP (with a variety of minor variations), and NKJV and the NASB put it in brackets // A, B, T, 𝔓⁷⁵, NU. NIV, ESV omit it.

Aland says, "In contrast to the parallel account, Luke has neither referred to Pilate's releasing of a prisoner at the festival nor yet mentioned Barabbas, so that the insertion is understandable. For one part of the tradition, this was felt to be inadequate, and introductory phrases from the narrative in Matt. 27:15 and Mark 15:6 were added in different places and in a slightly adapted form. Even though A reads the insertion, the evidence for the originality of the omission is the stronger by far" (Aland, p. 303).

John 5:3b-4, "waiting for the moving of the water. For an angel went down at a certain time into the pool and stirred up the water; then whoever stepped in first, after the stirring of the water, was made well of whatever disease he had." 99.2%, A, C³, K, L, X, etc., TR, HF, RP, NKJV have this verse, and the NASB puts it in brackets // ℵ, B, C*, D, T, P, W, 𝔓⁶⁶, 𝔓⁷⁵, NIV, ESV omit this verse.

Aland, who composed this list of verses eliminated by the Critical Text, says, "The insertions considered thus far have all been derived from parallel text, whether in other gospels or in the same gospel. But in John 5:3b-4, we need another category: expansion of the original text by various later legendary supplements developed from the account itself. From the attestation for the 'shorter text,' it should be clear that the expansion of the ending of verse 3 and the whole of verse 4 represents a later insertion. Note that D adds only the ending of verse 3 without adding verse 4, and that 𝔓⁶⁶, which frequently has a freer tendency ... agrees with 𝔓⁷⁵, which follows an exemplar strictly. The ending of verse 3 represents more or less an explanatory editorial comment, but verse 4 is a skillfully related supplement based on a suggestion in verse 7, where the sick man complains that he is no one to assist them into the pool when the water is stirred, and that when he finally gets there, he finds someone else has entered before him. From this, it is inferred that (1) the water in the pool and stirred, for which verse 4 indicates the cause, and (2) the first person to enter will, as verse 4 states explicitly. The secondary character of this verse is obvious. But rule 3 should be remembered: ... these are all later considerations because, in this instance, the decision has already been determined by the external evidence. When internal criteria confirm the decision (cf. rule 2), it becomes certain. If the internal criteria oppose the external evidence, both should be reviewed. If the external evidence retains its validity, then the probability should be considered that the internal criteria have been examined in all their aspects" (Aland, p. 303).

Wiersbe says, "While it is true that some manuscripts omit the end of Joh. 5:3 and all of Joh. 5:4, it is also true that the event (and the man's words in Joh. 5:7) would make little sense if these words are eliminated. Why would anybody, especially a man sick for so many years, remain in one place if nothing special were occurring? You would think that after thirty-eight years of nothing happening to *anybody,* the man would go elsewhere and stop hoping! It seems wisest for us to accept the fact that something extraordinary kept all these handicapped people at this pool, hoping for a cure."

Acts 8:37 "Then Philip said, 'If you believe with all your heart, you may.' And he answered and said, 'I believe that Jesus Christ is the Son of God.'" The only manuscript identical to the TR is the 1883 edition, a 16th-century manuscript. Others have variations, such as KJV, NKJV, and the NASB, which have it in brackets // 88%, ℵ, A, B, C, $\mathfrak{P}^{45}$, HF, RP, NU, NIV, ESV, omit this verse.

Aland says, "The external evidence is so weak that the Nestlé apparatus cites only the support for the insertion and not for the original omission. The uncial E, together with a limited number of minuscules that are not without a certain weight in their own right, does not give the insertion significant support to qualify it for a claim to originality.... Acts 8:37 is omitted by $\mathfrak{P}^{45}$, $\mathfrak{P}^{74}$, ℵ, A, B, C, D, ψ, 049, 056, 0142, a long sequence of minuscules including even the majority text and so forth, while the addition is variously divided in the tradition. The voice which speaks in Acts 8:37 is from a later age, with an interest in the detailed justification of the treasurer's desire for baptism" (Aland, pp. 303-304).

Acts 15:34 "However, it seemed good to Silas to remain there." Some minuscules, TR, and NKJV, have this verse, and the NASB puts it in brackets // 70.8%, ℵ, A, B, P, ψ, HF, RP, f^{35}, NU, NIV, ESV omit this verse.

Aland says, "The insertion of Acts 15:34 appears in a variety of forms in C and others represent what may be called the first stage. It states only that Silas remained in Antioch (this seems necessary because, in 15:40, it says that Paul chose Silas to accompany him, and according to 15:33, he had already departed); D and others attempt to deal with the inconsistency more directly by explaining that Silas remained (in Antioch), and Judas had departed. The origin of this text (and, accordingly, its secondary character) is therefore clear. Only the omission of Acts 15:34 (attested by even Majority Text!) can qualify as the original form of the text, quite apart from the unambiguous voice of the external attestation. Rule 8: only the omission can explain the alternative readings)" (Aland, p. 304).

Pickering says, "Verse 33 seems to require that Silas returned to Jerusalem; 'they were sent back … to the apostles,' and 'they' refer to Judas and Silas. The 'problem' is that in verse 40, Paul chooses Silas to accompany him, so he had to be in Antioch, not Jerusalem. Accordingly, the longer reading was created to solve the 'problem.' The 'some days' of verse 36 could well have been a month or two. From Antioch to Jerusalem would be a trip of some 400 miles. Silas had time to go to Jerusalem and back to Antioch."

Acts 24:6-8 "He even tried to profane the temple, and we seized him, and [wanted to judge him according to our law. (Acts 24:7) But the commander Lysias came by and, with great violence, took *him* out of our hands, (Acts 24:8) commanding his accusers to come to you.] By examining him yourself, you may ascertain all these things of which we accuse him." The words in […] are not in 58.9%, ℵ, A, B, HF, RP, NU, NIV, ESV.

Aland says, "The omission of Acts 24:6b-8 and the indictment by Tertullus is supported by evidence that is absolutely conclusive. It leaves no ground for questioning the secondary character of the text. The insertion was prompted by the conclusion of the speech in verse 8, which states that when Felix examined Paul, he would learn directly from him all the Jewish charges against him. This appears to be a hiatus between verse 6, which recounts Paul's arrest by the Jews, and verse 8. Verses 6a-8a fill in the details (cf. Acts 21:31ff.) By telling how Lysias had taken Paul from them and ordered the case to be tried before the government (Acts 23:23ff.). This is no more than stylistic polishing, contributing no new information despite the claim of many exegetes in the past" (Aland, p. 304).

Pickering says, "What about the context? The addition makes good sense, and it fits nicely. But it is not really necessary; that information Felix already knew. The text reads quite well without the addition. I conclude that the sho form was judged to be abrupt or incomplete, giving rise to the addition; presumably, the autograph did not contain it. Since Tertullus was an orator, he may well have actually said what is in addition, and a good deal more besides, but did Luke write it? (The incidences recorded in Acts were well known by many contemporaries, and there were many written accounts in circulation [Luke 1:1], so it was entirely predictable the variety of historically correct material would be added, here and there, to Luke's account.) The external evidence, though divided, is adequate to resolve this case: 58.9% against a severely fragmented 41.1%. The ancient versions, and being divided, do not help us much this time.... [The TR reading really has little to command it.]"

Acts 28:29 "And when he had said these words, the Jews departed and had a great dispute among themselves." 95.3%, TR, HF, RP, and NKJV have these verses // they are omitted by ℵ, A, B, NU, NIV, and ESV.

Aland says, "Here again, the external evidence is unequivocal: Acts 28:29 cannot have been a part of the original text of Acts. The transition from verse 28 to verse 30 was felt by the Majority text to be too abrupt. A concluding sentence was lacking, and it was supplied by repeating the content of verses 24-25" (Aland, p. 304).

Romans 16:24 "The grace of our Lord Jesus Christ *be* with you all. Amen." 96.8%, TR, HF, RP, and NKJV have this verse, and NASB puts it in brackets // ℵ, A, B, C, $\mathfrak{P}^{46}$, NU, NIV, ESV omit this entire verse.

1 John. 5:7-8 "For there are three that bear witness in heaven: the Father, the Word, and the Holy Spirit; and these three are one." This passage is in a few minuscules and the TR // 99%, ℵ, A, B, HF, RP, NU, NIV, ESV omit it.

The ESV omits all of these passages, and in addition, it omits Matthew 12:47, Luke 17:36, 22:44, Acts 15:34, 24:7 (see the section on the ESV in the next chapter).

Chapter 12

ENGLISH TRANSLATIONS

The two main issues in translating the Bible are 1) which Greek text is translated and 2) which translation theory is used. Since the Greek text issue has been discussed in detail in the previous chapters, this chapter will focus on the second of those two issues.

Translation Theory

The task of translators is to convey the content of one language into another. Their goal is to provide an accurate translation of what the original author said or wrote. It sounds simple, but this, too, is a complex problem. On one extreme is the literal method of translation. Since no two languages are identical in the meaning of corresponding words or structure, there can be no absolute, literal translation that is readable. An exact literal translation of the Bible would read like an interlinear! On the other extreme is a loose paraphrase, which contains as much interpretation as translation, such as the *Cotton Patch Version*. One extreme focuses on the original language, while the other extreme stresses the receiving language. Between these two extremes are numerous theories.

The terms usually used for these two methods of translation are "formal equivalence" (also called "complete equivalence") and "dynamic equivalence" (also called "impact translation"). Formal equivalence points out that written material consists of words and structure. This view contends that in an accurate translation, the elements of the translation should correspond as closely as possible to the elements of the original word for word, phrase for phrase, clause for clause, and sentence for sentence. Dynamic equivalence claims the accuracy issue is determined by the reader's response to the translation. Their concern is for the correspondence of thought and ideas—equivalence of effect. Thus, there are basically two philosophies of translation.

Formal Equivalence	Dynamic
Complete Equivalence	Impact

There are basically two translation theories, but it is not quite as simple as that.

1. Both have some mixture. No formal equivalence translation of the Bible can preserve the precise grammatical structure of the original Hebrew and Greek texts. Accommodations must be made in English structure for clear communication. All dynamic equivalence translations must have at least some formal equivalence to the original; otherwise, it would not qualify as a translation at all. Hence, every translation of the Scripture is a mixture of formal equivalence and dynamic equivalence.

Yet there is a difference. While it is true that no translation is completely literal or completely dynamic, at the same time, each translation was produced with one or the other theories in mind. The difference is kind, not degree.

2. The dynamic equivalence theory of translation has a legitimate point. Translators certainly do not want to be so slavishly tied to the

structure of the original that they produce something in English that is awkward and does not communicate what the original author intended.

There is, however, a danger. The tendency and temptation of dynamic equivalence is in the name of "equivalent effect" to explain too much. Once translators unnecessarily depart from the original structure, they begin to interpret instead of translating. Nevertheless, word order must be changed to produce an intelligent English sentence. When such changes are necessary, they should be made.

The problem is that once translators adopt the dynamic equivalence method, they almost always make unnecessary changes. Should sentences in the original not be translated as sentences? If the original author wrote complex sentences, shouldn't complex sentences appear in the translation? If the original author was ambiguous, shouldn't the translation reflect that? Does the translator have the right to omit important words like conjunctions, which are clues to meaning? Must the translator eliminate technical terms? If translators add words, should they not alert the reader to that fact by putting the added words in italics? The issue is, "Should the translators practice dynamic equivalence to the point that they make unnecessary changes?"

3. Conclusion. Translators should adopt a formal equivalence approach to translating the New Testament. They should convey to the reader what the original author said and, as much as possible, the way it was expressed. The New King James does that. A scholar who worked on the New King James Version said, "We want a Bible that gives us what the text *says*, not what some scholar thinks it means!" (Farstad, p. 7, italics his).

A dynamic equivalence translation has a place. Reading such a translation quickly to get the gist of the content can be beneficial. On the other hand, a dynamic equivalence translation is not accurate enough for a careful explanation of a passage, doctrinal studies, or standard church use in public reading or memorization (Farstad, p. 121).

In describing the NIV, Zondervan Publishers diagrammed the position of English translations between the two extremes of translation theory.

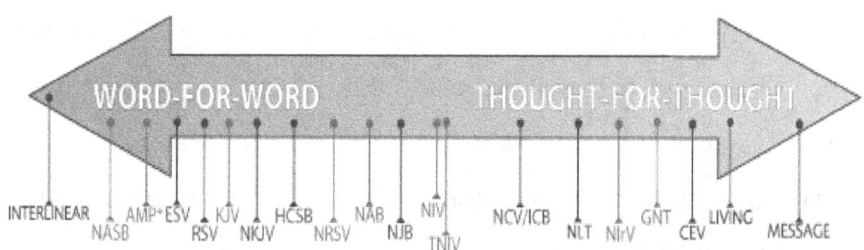

Here is an explanation of the abbreviations: NIV: New International Version; NIrV: New International Readers Version; KJV: King James Version; NKJV: New King James Version; NLT: New Living Translation; Updated NASB: New American Standard Bible; NRSV: New Revised Standard Version; AMP: Amplified; NAB: New American Bible; HCSB: Holman Christian Standard Bible; The Message; CEV: Contemporary English Version; GNT: Good News Translation; ESV: English Standard Version; NJB: New Jerusalem Bible; TNIV: Today's New International Version (Taken from material at http://www.zondervanbibles.com/translations.htm).

King James Version

The Greek Text In 1976, the Trinitarian Bible Society in London published a Greek text of the New Testament, which they said was the Greek text underlying the Authorized Version of 1611. In the preface, they explained which Greek text was used for the King James Version of the Bible. Here is a summary of their explanation.

Desiderius Erasmus produced the first printed edition in Basel in 1516. Erasmus also published four other editions (1519, 1522, 1527, 1535). His last two editions included some changes from the Complutensian Polyglot. Simon Colinaeus, a printer in Paris, published an edition of the Greek New Testament based on those of Erasmus and the Complutensian Polyglot (1534). His work was never reprinted.

Robert Stephens, Colinaeus' stepson, published four editions of the Greek New Testament in 1546, 1549, 1550, and 1551. His 1550 edition followed the text of the 1527 and 1535 editions of Erasmus, with marginal readings from the Complutensian Polyglot. The verse divisions first appeared in the 1551 edition, a reprint of the 1550 text.

Theodore Beza, Calvin's successor, published nine editions of the Stephens Greek text, with some changes, and a Latin translation of his own. These editions appeared in two formats: four in one format (1565, 1582, 1588, and 1598) and five in another format (1565, 1567, 1580, 1590, and 1604). "The editions of Beza, particularly that of 1598, and the two last editions of Stephens were the chief sources used for the English Authorized Version of 1611."

Elzevir brothers, Bonaventure and Abraham, published editions of the Greek text at Leyden (1624, 1633, and 1641). Except for a few changes from Beza's later revisions, they followed Beza's 1565 edition. In the preface to the 1633 edition, they stated that their text was based on the Textus Receptus, also known as the Received Text. Over time, the Stephens's text of 1550 became known by this name.

"The editions of Stephens, Beza, and the Elzevirs all present substantially the same text, and the variations are not of great significance and rarely affect the sense. The present edition of the Textus Receptus underlying the English Authorized Version of 1611 follows the text of Beza's 1598 edition as the primary authority and corresponds with 'The New Testament in the Original Greek according to the text followed in the Authorized Version,' edited by F. H. A. Scrivener ... and published by Cambridge University Press in 1894 and 1902.'"

In other words, the Greek text used to translate the King James Version in 1611 was based on a Greek text that went through multiple editions (five by Erasmus, one by Colinaeus, four by Stephens, and nine by Beza, for a total of 19) that made changes.

"Even accepting that the KJV derives from the TR and has most of its faults, it is reasonable to ask *which* TR it is based on. The usual simplistic answer is Stephens's or Beza's. F.H.A. Scrivener, however, who studied the matter in detail, concluded that it was none of these. Rather, it is a mixed text, closest to Beza, with Stephens in second place but not clearly affiliated with any edition. (No doubt the influence of the Vulgate and of early English translations is also felt here.) Scrivener reconstructed the text of the KJV in 1894, finding some 250 differences from Stephens. Jay P. Green, however, states that even *this* edition does not agree entirely with the KJV, listing differences at Matt. 12:24, 27; John 8:21, 10:16 (? —this may be translational); 1 Cor. 14:10, 16:1; also compare Mark 8:14; 9:42;

John 8:5; Acts 1:4; 1 John 3:16, where Scrivener includes words found in the KJV in *italics* as missing from their primary text" (taken from an article posted at https://www.skypoint.com/members/waltzmn/TR.html).

Another interesting fact: when it was first published, the King James Version contained 8,422 marginal readings (White, p. 209).

Revisions The KJV was revised in 1629, 1638, 1762, and 1769, which is the version used today (Farstad, pp. 25-26). The first English version to omit the apocryphal books was the 1629 edition of King James's Version (Robinson, *ISBE*, vol. 1, p. 600). There was an attempted American revision in 1833 by Noah Webster, the renowned producer of Webster's Dictionary and a devout Christian, but it was unsuccessful (Farstad, pp. 26-27). For the KJV story and an explanation of the revisions, see Farstad, pp. 21-29.

Problems

The translation of the King James Version was accurate at the time; however, since then, some English words, such as "thee" and "thou," as well as "shouldest," have become obsolete, and some English words have changed in meaning. In Romans 1:13, the Greek word rendered "let" (KJV) means "hindered" (NKJV). In 1 Thessalonians. 4:15, the Greek word translated "prevent" (KJV) means "precede" (NKJV).

Positions In his book *The King James Only Controversy,* James White defines five positions concerning the KJV: 1) "I like the KJV Best." For them, it is a personal preference or tradition. They would not deny the possibility of a better translation. 2) The Textual Argument. They say the underlying Hebrew and Greek texts used for the KJV translation are superior to all other original language texts. 3) Received Text Only. The Textus Receptus was supernaturally preserved. 4) The Inspired KJV

Group. KJV is inspired and, therefore, inerrant. 5) The KJV as New Revelation. The Greek and Hebrew texts should be revised to conform to the KJV (White, pp. 1-5).

The last two positions are extreme, but they have their defenders. For example, highly educated Waite says, "It is my own personal conviction and belief, after studying this subject since 1971, that the words of the Received Greek and Masoretic Hebrew texts that underlie the King James Bible are the very words which God has preserved down through the centuries, being the exact words of the originals themselves. As such, I believe they are inspired words" (Waite, *Defending the King James Bible,* pp. 48–49; see the article at http://textus-receptus.com/wiki/D._A._Waite). The most extreme view is that the King James Version itself, not just the Greek text under it, is the inspired Word of God. Peter Ruckman wrote, "*Mistakes in the A. V. 1611 are advanced revelations*! (Ruckman, p. 126, italics his). It is one thing to admire or prefer the KJV; it is something else to say that the TR under it is inspired or that it corrects the TR. That is going too far!

The New King James Version

The New King James Version uses a formal equivalence translation based on the Textus Receptus. For a detailed description of the NKJV, see *The New King James Version in the Great Tradition* by Arthur L. Farstad, Executive Editor of the New King James Version. In the Foreword I wrote for that book, I said, "In a most delightful manner, it will answer all your questions concerning the New King James version." Among many other interesting things, Farstad points out that one of the guidelines given to the scholars and editors of the NKJV was that they were to "Correct all departures from the Textus Receptus" (Farstad, p. 34) and that NKJV is the fifth major revision of the original Authorized Version (Farstad, p. 1).

Revision The NKJV has been revised. In 1979, when the New Testament was first published, it did not contain italics, which are used today to emphasize words or indicate foreign words. As a result of a public outcry, the NKJV was revised to include italics for words not in the Greek text (Farstad, p. 53).

Notes: The NKJV provides something no other translation does—namely, textual notes at the bottom of the page. In the first place, the NKJV translation is based on the Textus Receptus. "M" in the notes at the bottom of the page stands for the Majority Text, which is close to the TR except in Revelation. "NU" stands for the Nestlé-Aland and United Bible Society's Greek texts, which other modern translations use for their edition. For an example of all three options, see Acts 5:41. As Farstad points out, rather than labeling variant readings as "best" or "most reliable," the NKJV "clarifies them as to the school of thought which prefers these readings" (Farstad, p. 119).

The New American Standard Bible

The New American Standard Bible (NASB), published by the Lockman Foundation, is a revision of the American Standard Version (ASV). The New Testament was published in 1963, and the complete Bible in 1971. It is based on the Nestlé-Aland Greek text and uses a formal equivalence translation.

Revisions Minor text modifications were made in 1972, 1973, and 1975, and major text revisions were made in 1977, 1995, and 2020. Among other changes, the 2020 revision includes "gender accuracy" (adding "or sisters" in italics to passages that refer to "brothers").

Criticisms Carson commented, "But just as it is possible to be too loose, it is possible to be too literal. My chief complaint with the NASB, for example, is that it tries too hard to reflect the underlying Greek, Hebrew, and Aramaic; it often resorts to awkward English or unnecessarily stylized English. It attempts to render Greek imperfect consistently by English imperfect, a procedure not only insensitive to the flexibility of the Greek tenses but even more insensitive to English idiom. This fault was especially noticeable in the gospel" (Carson, p. 89). "In my judgment, the NASB is even more literal than the KJV" (Carson, p. 91).

I once wrote an article on Bible translations in which I said the NASB is the best literal translation of the wrong Greek manuscripts.

New International Version

According to Zondervan, the publishers of the NIV, there were 115 translators and their translation purpose was to "produce an accurate translation, suitable for public and private reading, teaching, preaching, memorizing, and liturgical use." They claim that the translation philosophy was a "balance between word-for-word and thought-for-thought (see their diagram earlier in this chapter).

Woudstra In an article entitled "A Teacher Looks at the NIV," Sierd Woudstra, a former Old Testament theology professor at Calvin Theological Seminary, says that as a teacher and exegete preacher, he has grave reservations about the NIV "because it often lacks the precision needed to make it a suitable tool for careful study and teaching. He accuses it of imprecision, "so imprecise as to make it difficult to teach from." He gives examples which he calls "disturbing weaknesses in the NIV" and says these weaknesses are caused because of the use of dynamic equivalence.

He concludes with some interesting observations, such as 1) Its translation of the Song of Solomon is outstanding. However, its translation of Ecclesiastes is something of a disaster. 2) I'm not rejecting the NIV. I still like it—but not for careful study and teaching purposes. 3) When I use it for Scripture reading from the pulpit, I have become reluctant to add, 'Thus says the Lord."

Martin In his small book, *Accuracy of Translation and the New International Version,* Robert Martin, a professor of biblical theology and a pastor, contends, "It is with the criteria of accuracy that we must begin to make a choice of a Bible version" (Martin, p. 2). Since that is the case, the issue is which method is most effective: formal equivalence or dynamic equivalence (Martin, pp. 6-7). The NIV claims to be a blend of both types of translation, but Martin says the translators were "heavily influenced by the dynamic equivalence philosophy of translation" (Martin, pp. 11-12).

To support his point, Martin identifies seven characteristics of dynamic equivalence translation and illustrates how the NIV exemplifies them. The seven are: 1) the elimination of complex grammatical structures, 2) the addition of words, 3) the omission of words, 4) the erosion of technical terms, such as propitiation, 5) the leveling of cultural distinctive, 6) the interpretation presented as Scripture, 7) paraphrasing (Martin, pp. 18-67).

Martin concludes that if accuracy is judged based on formal equivalence, the NIV must be judged inaccurate. He says, "While dynamic translations may have value, they should not be used as our primary study Bible or as the standard from which we derive our personal or corporate theology and practice" (Martin, p. 70).

Radmacher and Hodges In their book *The NIV Reconsidered*, Earl Radmacher and Zane Hodges give a more detailed evaluation. They, too, discuss the issue of dynamic equivalence. They agreed that the issue is accuracy (Radmacher and Hodges, p. 28). In example after example, the authors weigh NIV translations on the scale of general accuracy and reliability and find them wanting (Radmacher and Hodges, pp. 31-47). They are critical of the NIV's translation of prophetic passages, such as Psalm 16:10, Isaiah 7:14, Isaiah 53:11, Micah 5:2, and 2 Thessalonians 2:1-12 (Radmacher and Hodges, pp. 49-64). For example, the NIV translates Micah 5:2 as "from ancient times" instead of "from everlasting." There are also critical of the NIV's translation of New Testament passages, such as Matthew 19:9, John 3:5, Romans 3:25, 1 Corinthians 5:5, Ephesians 4:28, 1 Thessalonians 1:3, 1 Timothy 3:16, Hebrews 3:14, 11:1, Hebrews 10:10, 14, 29, 1 John 3:10, and 1 John 5:18 (Radmacher and Hodges, pp. 65-83). They have a whole chapter on the NIV translation of 1 Samuel 25:1-44 and another chapter on the NIV translation of Romans 8:1-17 (Radmacher and Hodges, pp. 101-132).

In the epilogue, they say, "Our conclusion is that the goal of accuracy frequently has been badly missed" (Radmacher and Hodges, p. 131).

English Standard Version

This is from https://en.wikipedia.org/wiki/English_Standard_Version. All the material is from that article, with slight editing, mainly involving the rearrangement of some of the material. All of the material under "controversy" remains unchanged.

Background In 1938, Clyde and Muriel Dennis founded Good News Publishers, working out of their home in Minneapolis, Minnesota. Years later, the name was changed to Crossway, now headquartered in Wheaton, Illinois. In the 1990s, Lane Dennis, Crossway's president, began exploring the possibilities of a new literal translation of the Bible. Dennis and Wayne Gruden negotiated with the National Council of churches to use the 1971 edition of the Revised Standard Version as the starting point for the new translation. Crossway officially published the English Standard Version (ESV) in 2001.

The Translators The original ESV translation committee consisted of 14 members, including Dr. Wayne A. Grudem (Research Professor, Theology and Biblical Studies, Phoenix Seminary), Dr. R. Kent Hughes (Senior Pastor Emeritus, College Church in Wheaton), Dr. J. I. Packer (Board of Governors Professor of Theology, Regent College, Vancouver, Canada), Dr. Vern Sheridan Poythress (Professor of New Testament Interpretation, Westminster Theological Seminary; Editor, Westminster Theological Journal), and Dr. Gordon Wenham (Old Testament Tutor at Trinity College, Bristol; Emeritus Professor of Old Testament, University of Gloucestershire).

Translation Theory: The ESV is a translation of the critical Greek text, employing a formal equivalence translation theory. They describe it as emphasizing "word for word" accuracy, using an "essentially literal translation philosophy."

Wayne Grudem claims that approximately eight percent (or about 60,000 words) of the 1971 RSV text being used for the ESV was revised in the first publication in 2001. Grudem states that the committee removed "every trace of liberal influence that had caused such criticism from evangelicals when the RSV was first published in 1952." Although, Grudem also states that much of the 1971 RSV text left unchanged by the committee "is simply 'the best of the best' of the KJV tradition."

The ESV translation committee states that "the goal of the ESV is to render literally what is in the original." The committee expands on this position, claiming that, although the ESV avoids using gender-neutral language (to preserve contextual meaning found in the original text), the translation utilizes gender-neutral language in specific cases. The committee further stated that their objective was "transparency to the original text, allowing the reader to understand the original on its own terms rather than in terms of our present-day Western culture." In 2008, Crossway published the ESV Study Bible.

The Controversy At the 2008 annual meeting of the Evangelical Theological Society, Mark L. Strauss presented a paper titled "Why the English Standard Version Should not Become the Standard English Version: How to Make a Good Translation Much Better." In the paper, Strauss criticizes the ESV for using dated language, among other perceived issues, such as inconsistent translation of gender-neutral language.

Regarding scholarly debate surrounding translation philosophy, ESV translator William D. Mounce responded to Strauss's criticism:

> While the content of the paper was helpful, I am afraid that it only increased the gap between the two "sides" of the [translation philosophy] debate.... He kept saying that the ESV has "missed" or "not considered" certain translational issues. While I am sure they were not intentional, these are emotionally charged words that do not help in the debate. They are, in essence, *ad hominem* arguments focusing on our competence (or perceived lack thereof) and not on the facts. He was not in the translation meetings and does not know if we in fact did miss or did not consider these issues.... The solution to this debate is to recognize that there are different translation philosophies, different goals and means by which to reach those goals, and the goal of the translator is to be consistent in achieving those goals. In all but one of his examples, our translation was the one required by our translation philosophy.

Strauss invited Mounce to publicly engage in the translation philosophy debate through participation at the following annual meeting. In 2009, Mounce presented his response paper, "Can the ESV and TNIV Co-Exist in the Same Universe?". In the paper, Mounce describes various points regarding his view of the need for both formal and functional translations.

Revisions In 2007, a revision that made minor changes was published. In 2011, another revision was issued "to correct grammar, improve consistency, or increase precision in meaning." Another revision was released in 2016.

Other Editions In 2013, Gideons International switched from the New King James Version to the ESV. At the time, Crossway gave Gideons International permission to modify the text of the ESV based on readings from the Textus Receptus. The Gideon edition uses over 50 alternative readings. In 2018, the Conference of Catholic Bishops of India published a Catholic edition of ESV (ESV-CE), which includes deuterocanonical books and modifications that adhere to Catholic teaching. In 2019, the Augustine Institute published the ESV-CE in North America as the *Augustine Bible*. In 2019, Anglican Liturgy Press published the ESV: Anglican Edition, which includes the Apocrypha.

For criticisms of the ESV based on its translations, see "Why the ESV is both excellent and terrible" at https://honza.pokorny.ca/2017/10/why-the-esv-is-both-excellent-and-terrible/.

For a critique of the ESV from someone who believes in the Textus Receptus, see the official website of the American Presbyterian Church (APC) at http://www.americanpresbyterianchurch.org/the-esv-is-a-perversion-of-the-word-of-god/. Apart from judging the ESV by the TR, this article has some helpful information, such as a list of the 17 New Testament verses the ESV omits. Here is that list and more: Matthew 12:47, Matthew 17:21, Matthew 18:11, Matthew 23:14, Mark 7:16, Mark 9:44, Mark 9:46, Mark 11:26, Mark 15:28, Luke 17:36, Luke 22:44, Luke 23:17, John 5:4, Acts 8:37, Acts 15:34, Acts 24:7, Acts 28:29, Romans 16:24.

After Mark 16:8, the ESV states, "Some of the earliest manuscripts do not include 16:9-20." Puff, there goes another 12 verses. And by the way, that is absolutely untrue! The book, *The Last Twelve Verses of the Gospel of Mark* by Dean Burgon, contains over 400 pages of documented evidence for Mark 16:9-20 that has never been refuted, nor will it ever be. After John 7:52, the NIV reads, "The earliest manuscripts do not include John 7:53-8:11." Puff, there goes another 12 verses! (from the APC article).

Summary: The KJV and NKJV are based on the Textus Receptus and employ a formal equivalence translation method; all other popular translations utilize the critical Greek text and, except for the NASB, employ a dynamic equivalence translation.

CONCLUSION

By now, the conclusion ought to be clear. The Greek text issue boils down to whether the Byzantine or the Alexandrian text type best reflects the autographs. As for English translations, the New King James Version is based on the Byzantine text and all other popular, modern translations are based on the Alexandrian text.

Although I accepted the Alexandrian text type in college and seminary years ago, Dean Burgon convinced me of the superiority of the Byzantine text type. (See the chapter on "The Traditional Text.") Also, the chapter "An Evaluation of Text Types" contains seven arguments to prove the case for the Byzantine text type.

1. The Area of Origin. The Byzantine text type originates from the area where almost all the autographs were originally written or where they were sent, and therefore, were first copied.

2. Early Existence. The Byzantine text type existed early in Greek manuscripts, translations, and the writings of Christians.

3. The Attitude of the Copyist. From the beginning, those who received the Scriptures were warned not to mishandle them.

4. The Majority of the Manuscripts. The Byzantine Text is the text type of 80 to 95 percent of all Greek manuscripts (Farstad, p. 109).

5. Unity. The Byzantine text type contains remarkable unity.

6. Use. The Byzantine text type has been used throughout the centuries. Did God hide the best manuscripts of the New Testament until 1859?

7. Divine Preservation. The Byzantine text type is the only text type that has been *continually* preserved. "The word of the Lord endures forever" (1 Pet. 1:25; see also Mt. 5:18; 24:35; Mk. 13:31; Lk. 16:17; 21:33).

Another way to present the case of the Byzantine text is to consider what the Scripture says more completely and to develop the data from history in more detail. What else did God say that relates to the transmission of the text? What else can we learn from history? Aland says that textual critics have "largely if not completely" ignored church history." He adds, "It is utterly amazing how many New Testament scholars failed to observe the historical implications of their theories, changing them as easily as they shift positions at their desks!" (Aland, p. 52).

The remainder of this chapter will discuss what the Scripture and history say about the transmission of the text of the New Testament. What follows expands on, repeats, and adds additional information to the material in Chapter 7.

The Scripture

Here are seven observations from the Scripture that need to be taken into consideration.

1. Inspiration. God inspired the Scripture. "All Scripture is given by inspiration of God" (2 Tim. 3:16). That verse does not say the *authors* of Scripture were inspired; it says the *Scriptures* are inspired. The Greek word translated "inspiration" means "God-breathed," and the one rendered "Scripture" means "that which is written—words, phrases, sentences (not

just ideas). That does not mean that God dictated the Scripture, as is evident from the distinct personalities of the authors of Scripture that are reflected in what is written. Yet, as they wrote, the Holy Spirit was at work. "Holy men of God spoke as they were moved by the Holy Spirit" (2 Pet. 1:21). The Holy Spirit worked through the human authors of Scripture so that what they wrote was what God intended to be recorded. The Bible is no ordinary book; it is God's Word.

2. The Original Language. The Old Testament was written in Hebrew, but the New Testament was written in Greek. Why did God not have the authors of His Word write the New Testament in Hebrew? Perhaps there is a clue in Galatians. "When the fullness of time had come, God sent forth His Son (Gal. 4:4). Christ arrived on the scene of human history at the time previously fixed by the Father. God waited for the right moment so that the gospel could rapidly spread. "The New Testament was written in Koine Greek, the Greek of daily conversation" (Aland, p. 52). The Greek language, Roman roads, and world peace made it a propitious time to spread the gospel.

3. The Original Recipients. As pointed out in Chapter 7, the Byzantine text type originates from the area where almost all the autographs were originally written or where they were sent, and therefore, was first copied. Sixteen books of the New Testament were either written from or to Asia Minor: Matthew, John, Galatians, Ephesians, Colossians, 1 and 2 Timothy, Philemon, 1 and 2 Peter, 1, 2, 3 John, Revelation, and probably James and Jude. The book of Revelation was written to seven churches in Asia Minor, including Ephesus, Smyrna, Pergamum, Thyatira, Sardis, Philadelphia, and Laodicea. Six books of the New Testament were written to Greece: 1 and 2 Corinthians, Philippians, 1 and 2 Thessalonians,

and Titus in Crete. Five books of the New Testament were connected with Rome, including Mark, Romans, probably Luke, Acts, and possibly Hebrews. In other words, 22 of the 27 books of the New Testament were either written from or to Asia Minor or Greece. The other five pertain to Rome.

4. Immediate Recognition. The New Testament writings were recognized as Scripture before the New Testament was completed. When Paul wrote 1 Corinthians in the early spring of AD 57, he considered it inspired (1 Cor. 2:13; 14:37).

Paul called Luke Scripture. He wrote, "For the Scripture says, "You shall not muzzle an ox while it treads out the grain," and, "The laborer is worthy of his wages" (1 Tim. 5:18). The first quotation is from Deuteronomy 25:4 and the second is from Luke 10:7. Meade considers this evidence of an early "Canon consciousness" (Meade, cited by Kruger, p. 68). John Meier notes, "The only interpretation that avoids contorted intellectual acrobatics or special pleading is the plain, obvious one. [1 Timothy] is citing Luke's Gospel alongside Deuteronomy as normative Scripture for the ordering of the church's ministry" (Meier, cited by Kruger, p. 69). Luke wrote his Gospel toward the end of Paul's imprisonment in Caesarea, around AD 59. Paul possibly wrote 1 Timothy in AD 62, meaning Paul referred to what Luke wrote as Scripture three years after Luke wrote it.

Peter called what Paul wrote Scripture. "As also our beloved brother Paul, according to the wisdom given to him, has written to you, as also in all his epistles, speaking in them of these things in which are some things hard to understand, which those who are untaught and unstable *people* twist to their own destruction, as *they do* also the rest of the Scripture" (2

Pet. 3:15-16). Peter penned 2 Peter about AD 64, which means Paul's epistles were recognized as Scripture soon after he wrote them, not only by Peter but also by others.

5. Collection. At least some of the books of the New Testament were collected together, even before the New Testament was completed. Peter spoke of "all his [Paul's] epistles" (2 Pet. 3:16; see the full quote in the previous paragraph). "This passage does not refer to just one letter of Paul, but to a *collection* of Paul's letters (how many is unclear) that had already begun to circulate throughout the churches—so much so that the author could refer to 'all his [Paul's] letters' and expected his audience will understand that to which he was referring.... He mentions it quite casually, offering no introduction, defense, or explanation of this idea" (Kruger, p. 66). "Meade even argues that the author of 2 Peter includes Petrine text within the category of Christian scripture by referring to Paul as 'our beloved brother' (3:15), a likely reference to the 'college' of apostles in which Peter certainly participated (*cf.* Pet. 1:16)" (Kruger, p. 67). Aland says, "The letters of Paul were apparently preserved from the very first *as a collection*" (Aland, p. 49, italics added).

6. Copied. The autographs were copied immediately, even before the New Testament was completed. Paul expected his writings to be read beyond the churches to which they were sent (1 Thess. 5:27; Col. 4:16; see "the churches of Galatia" in Gal. 1:2; "all the saints in Achaia" in 2 Cor. 1:1; "all who in every place" in 1 Cor. 1:2). John intended the same thing (Rev. 1:1-3; see "churches," plural in 2:7, 2:11, 2:17, 2:29; 3:6, 3:13, 3:22). So did Peter (1 Pet. 1:1).

For example, Paul instructed the church at Colossae to ensure that the letter he wrote to them was read in Laodicea (Col. 4:16). Did the church at

Colossae send the original letter to the church at Laodicea, or did they send a copy? Peter calls Paul's letters Scripture and speaks about them to a group of churches in such a way that indicates they had seen copies of them (2 Peter 3:15-16). "Copies of the original would be made for use in neighboring churches. The circulation of a book would be like the rippling of the stone cast into a pond, spreading out in all directions at once" (Aland, p. 55).

Pickering makes an intriguing suggestion. He says, "The idea of publishing a book in the form of multiple copies may be inferred from the epistles. 2 Corinthians was written to the church of God, which is at Corinth, with the saints who are in all Achaia (verse 1). How many congregations would there have been 'in all Achaia?' Was Paul thinking of [producing] multiple copies? 1 Corinthians was addressed to 'all those everywhere who call on the name of our Lord Jesus Christ' (verse 2). Now, how many copies would that take? Galatians was written to the 'churches of Galatia' (verse 2). Would a single copy get to all of them?" (Pickering, p. 92). After examining other passages that could be used to support this idea, Pickering concludes, "I believe all the New Testament books were released in the form of multiple copies, with the exception of the letters addressed to individuals" (Pickering, p. 94).

Pickering proposes another possibility. "Quite apart from the idea of 'publishing' via multiple copies, consider what would happen when a congregation received a copy of 1 Peter, James, or any of Paul's Epistles, accompanied by the instruction they would have to pass it on. If you were one of the elders of that congregation, what would you do? I would most certainly make a copy for us to keep. Wouldn't you? The point is that as soon as an inspired book began to circulate, the proliferation of copies began at once. That means a 'majority text' also began at once" (Pickering, p. 94 fn. 2).

7. Carefully Copied. From the beginning, those who received the Scriptures were warned not to mishandle them. Moses cautioned, "You shall not add to the word which I command you, nor take from it, that you may keep the commandments of the LORD your God which I command you" (Deut. 4:2). Later, he repeated the caution, "Whatever I command you, be careful to observe it; you shall not add to it nor take away from it" (Deut. 12:32). Proverbs echoes the admonition, "Every word of God *is* pure; He *is* a shield to those who put their trust in Him. Do not add to His words, Lest He rebuke you, and you be found a liar" (Prov. 30:5-6). The Old Testament saints were taught not to change the Scriptures.

"Josephus confirms that the Old Testament principle ... continued to be recognized in the first century" (Kruger, *The Early Text of the New Testament*, p. 72). Josephus wrote, "We have given practical proof of our reverence for our own Scripture. Therefore, although such long ages have now passed, no one has ventured either to add or to remove, or to alter a syllable" (*Ag. Ap.* 1.42).

The Masoretic manuscripts "agree with one another very closely." Between 1776 and 1780, Bishop Kennicott published the readings of 634 Hebrew manuscripts that demonstrated this. "He was followed in 1784-88 by De Rossi, who published correlations of 825 more manuscripts. No substantial variation among the manuscripts was detected by either of these two scholars" (Hills, p. 100, who cites F. G. Kenyon, *Our Bible and the Ancient Manuscripts*, p. 41).

Until the mid-20th century, the oldest known copy of the Hebrew Old Testament was a Masoretic Text dated to approximately AD 900. Then, the Dead Sea Scrolls were discovered. Among the Dead Sea Scrolls was a copy of Isaiah, dated between 100 and 200 BC. In other words, with the discovery of the Isaiah scroll, we have jumped 1000 years closer to the time when the original Hebrew manuscripts were written.

The Old Testament text found among the Dead Sea Scrolls is virtually identical to the medieval Masoretic texts, demonstrating textual consistency over centuries. For example, 4QGen, a manuscript of Genesis 1:1-28 (dated to the 1st century AD), is identical to the Masoretic text (dated to AD 1008) except for one spelling variant. The differences between the Masoretic text of Isaiah and the one found in the Dead Sea Scrolls are exceedingly minor, such as spelling differences (like "colour" in England versus "color" in America) and the addition of a single letter (the Hebrew letter ש, which is translated "and").

That's incredible! If that is true for the Isaiah manuscript, it is no doubt true of the remainder of the Masoretic Text of the Old Testament. There is little doubt that we have an accurate copy of the Hebrew Old Testament.

As mentioned earlier, regarding the New Testament, Paul claimed to have written Scripture. He said, "If anyone thinks himself to be a prophet or spiritual, let him acknowledge that the things which I write to you are the commandments of the Lord" (1 Cor. 14:37). "For this we say to you by the word of the Lord, that we which are alive and remain until the coming of the Lord will by no means precede those who are asleep" (1 Thess. 4:15).

"Not only do Pauline letters regularly make claims that they had been written with divinely given authority (Gal. 1:1; 1 Thess. 2:13; 1 Cor. 7:12, 14:37), but they also include commands that they be read publicly at the gathering of the church (Col. 4:16; 1 Thess. 5:27; 2 Cor. 10:9). This practice of reading *Scripture* in worship can be traced back to the Jewish synagogue, where portions from the Old Testament were routinely read aloud to the congregations (Lk. 4:17-20; Acts 13:15, 15:21). Indeed, 1 Timothy makes this connection clear when Timothy is exhorted to 'devote yourself to the public reading of Scripture' (1 Tim. 4:13:6)" (Kruger, p. 67). Paul called Luke Scripture (1 Tim. 5:18).

The point is that many of the books of the New Testament are referred to as *Scripture in the New Testament*. "Furthermore, the apostles and other early Jewish members of the Antioch church had the tradition of Israel's careful copying of the Scriptures as an example for their care" (Sturz, pp. 104-105).

Kruger argues Paul's statement that when it comes to covenants, "no one holds it adds to it once it has been ratified" (Gal. 3:15) echoes Deuteronomy 4:2 and "therefore, for Paul—and no doubt early Christians influenced by Paul or who shared Paul's Jewish background—covenant documents were not to be altered." He concludes, "The overall attitude for the reproduction of the Old Testament Scriptures—particularly the language of 'not adding or taking away'—is not abandoned when we reach the New Testament era but is reaffirmed and applied (implicitly or explicitly) by early Christians to the New Testament writings" (Kruger, p. 73).

Kruger is right. The Apostle John warned, "For I testify to everyone who hears the words of the prophecy of this book: If anyone adds to these things, God will add to him the plagues that are written in this book, and if anyone takes away from the words of the book of this prophecy, God shall take away his part from the Book of Life, from the holy city, and *from* the things which are written in this book" (Rev. 22:18-19). Would that not motivate believers to be careful when they were copying Scripture?

The New Testament books were carefully copied, even before the New Testament was completed. In the first place, if early Christians recognized that the New Testament was Scripture, would they not have carefully copied it? Of course. Beyond that assumption, there are indications in the New Testament that the authors were concerned about this issue.

Peter spoke of "untaught and unstable people" who "twist" what Paul had written "as they do also the rest of Scripture" (2 Pet. 3:16). Peter was probably focusing on the interpretation of what Paul had written, but that would, no doubt, involve the meaning of words, phrases, and sentences. If Peter was concerned about people verbally twisting Scripture, would he not have been even more concerned about people tampering with the written words of Scripture?

Paul was concerned that someone might twist his vocal words or write a letter in his name. He told the Thessalonian believers "not to be soon shaken in mind or troubled, either by spirit or by word or by letter, as if from us, as though the day of Christ had come" (2 Thess. 2:2). "By spirit" means "through" some spiritual gift, such as a prophetic or ecstatic utterance. "By word" means "through" something spoken. "By letter" means just that, "through" a letter supposedly written by Paul. He was concerned that anyone might not accurately convey his written words.

There are other reasons for believing that the New Testament was copied carefully. Roberts and Skeat "suggest that the adoption of the papyrus codex by Christians probably took place at Antioch not later than AD 100." (Metzger, p. 261 fn.). Skeat draws attention to the special features of New Testament manuscripts, such as the abbreviation of divine names "as being, together with the use of the codex, an indication of 'a degree of organization, conscious planning, and uniformity of practice among Christian communities which we have hitherto had little reason to suspect'" (Metzger, p. 261). Also, it is not "uncommon to find a colophon" [a statement at the end of a book, giving information about its authorship and printing] at the end of cursive manuscripts, "where the copyist calls on God for His mercy and even for His recognition and blessing" (Pickering, p. 196 fn. 1).

The other reason for believing the Scriptures were carefully copied is the providential preservation of God. God not only inspired His Word, but He also promised to preserve it. Jesus spoke of the preservation of the Old Testament. He said, "For assuredly, I say to you, till heaven and earth pass away, one jot or one tittle will by no means pass from the law till all is fulfilled" (Mt. 5:18) and "It is easier for heaven and earth to pass away than for one tittle of the law to fail" (Lk. 16:17). There is evidence that God providentially preserved the Old Testament. The Masoretes, a group of Jewish scribes, preserved the Hebrew text of the Old Testament, known as the Masoretic text of the Hebrew Bible.

Jesus also promised to preserve the New Testament. He said, "Heaven and earth will pass away, but My words will by no means pass away" (Lk. 21:33) and "Go therefore and make disciples of all the nations, baptizing them in the name of the Father and of the Son and of the Holy Spirit, teaching them to observe all things that I have commanded you; and lo, I am with you always, *even* to the end of the age" (Mt. 28:19-20). For Jesus to be with those teaching people to observe all He commanded until the end of the age requires that His commandments be preserved to the *end of the age*. The question is, "Did the Lord preserve the New Testament text like He preserved the Old Testament text? To answer that, consider what we know from history.

To sum up what the Scripture says, God inspired His Word in Greek, primarily in Greek-speaking Asia Minor and Greece, where it was immediately recognized as Scripture, collected, and carefully copied and God promised to preserve His Word forever.

The First Century

This concern for correctly copying Scripture extended beyond the New Testament. "One area that has been largely overlooked is the *attitude* toward that text that is actually expressed by Christians in the earliest literary sources, that is, statements about how they would have viewed their sacred writings, they would have understood the transmission and preservation of the text, and how they would have responded to the changes and alterations of the text. In other words, how much attention has been given to the literary products of early Christians (the text itself), less has been given to the literary culture of early Christians (their expressed attitude to the text)" (Kruger, pp. 63-64, italics added).

In the first century, even before the New Testament was completed, Christian *authors recognized New Testament books as Scripture*, which affected their attitude toward it.

Epistle to Diognetus (70-80) The *Epistle to Diognetus* has been dated from before 100 to 130; however, it mentions the Jews making blood sacrifices (3:5). These sacrifices ceased when the Temple was destroyed in AD 70, which could indicate that the *Epistle* was written before AD 70. If so, it is the earliest non-canonical Christian writing in existence.

The Epistle to Diognetus quotes 1 Corinthians 8:1, stating, "the apostle says" (12:5). Many words and phrases in the book are reminiscent of the New Testament. The author refers to "the observance of months and of days" (4:5; Gal. 4:10). He calls believers "sojourners" (5:5; 1 Pet. 1:1). He says, "their citizenship is in heaven" (5:9; Phil. 3:20). When they are reviled, they bless (5:5; 1 Pet. 2:23, 39; Mt. 5:11). They are in the world, but not of the world (6:3; Jn. 17:13-14). The One who was sent was "gentle and meek" (7:4; 2 Cor. 10:1). He was sent as loving, not as judging (7:5; Jn. 3:16-17). The Son died "the just for the unjust" (9:2; 1 Pet. 3:18). God sent "His only begotten Son" (10:2; Jn. 3:16). God promised the kingdom and will give it to those who love Him (10:2; Jas. 2:5). He says, "You love Him that so loved you before" (10:2; 1 Jn. 4:19). Believers are "imitators of God" (10:6; Eph. 5:1). "He sent forth the Word, that He might appear unto the world, who being dishonored by the people, and preached by the Apostles, was believed in by the Gentiles" (11:3; 1 Tim. 3:16). The Word was from the beginning (11:4; Jn. 1:1). "The apostles say, 'Knowledge puffs up, but charity edifies' (12:5; 1 Cor. 8:1). In other words, the author definitely knew 1 Corinthians and, no doubt, nine other New Testament books (Jn.; 2 Cor.; Gal.; Eph.; Phil.; 1 Tim.; Titus; Jas.; and 1 Pet.). The author was also aware he was quoting the apostle Paul. He quotes 1 Corinthians 8:1, "the apostle says" (12:5). He knew it was Scripture.

Didache (80-90) Although some date this work to the middle of the second century, many have argued for a date before AD 100, between AD 80-90, and even earlier. It speaks of apostles and prophets coming to minister (11:5-9). Ehrman says it appears to have been written "at the same time as or possibly even earlier than some of the books of the New Testament" (Ehrman, vol. 1, p. 165).

The Didache has quotations and numerous allusions to the Gospel of Matthew. For example, the author says, "Neither pray like the hypocrites, but as the Lord has commanded in His Gospel, in this way pray" (8:2). The author quotes the entire Lord's Prayer, including the ending omitted by the modern Critical Text (8:2-7). He also states, "The meek will inherit the land" (3:7). Several times, he mentions being double-minded (2:4; 4:4), reminiscent of James 1:8. There are allusions to other books of the New Testament, including slaves being told to be subject to their masters (4:11; Eph. 6:5; Col. 3:22), believers being told not to eat meat sacrificed to idols (6:3; Acts 15:29), believers being instructed that if people do not work, do not let them live with you idle (12:4; 2 Thess. 3:11-12), and prophets are worthy of their food as workmen are worthy of theirs (13:1-2; 1 Tim. 5:17). The author admonishes his readers: "And reprove one another not in wrath but in peace as you find in the Gospel, and let none speak with any who has done wrong to his neighbor, nor let him hear a word from you until he repents. But your prayers and alms and all your acts perform as ye find in the Gospel of our Lord" *(*Did. 15:3-4). Thiessen says, "It knows most of our New Testament books" (Thiessen, p. 13).

Clement of Rome (95) Clement of Rome quotes or alludes to Matthew, Mark, Luke, Acts, Romans, 1 Corinthians, 2 Corinthians, Galatians, Ephesians, 2 Timothy, Titus, Hebrews, James, 1 Peter, and Revelation. He wrote, "Take up the epistle of the blessed Apostle Paul. What did he write to you at the time when the Gospel first began to be preached? Truly, under the inspiration of the Spirit, he wrote to you concerning himself, and Cephas, and Apollos, because even then parties had been formed among you" (1 Clement 47:1-3). Clement of Rome said Paul wrote to the Corinthians "under the inspiration of the Spirit!" One author says, "Even by the end of the first century, a number of apostolic writings were already regarded as authoritative 'scripture'" and gives a detailed analysis of Clement of Rome to prove his point (see the article by Harter at https://etimasthe.com/2018/02/14/clement-of-romes-new-testament/).

Papias (95-100) According to Irenaeus (115?-202), Papias was "the hearer of John and a companion of Polycarp" [Irenaeus, *Ag. Her.* 5.33.4; see also Eusebius (264-340), *Eccl. Hist.*, 33.39.1]. Scholars disagree concerning the date for Papias. In an article entitled "The Date of Papias: A Reassessment," Robert W. Yarborough lists the reasons for a late date and gives the evidence for an early date (Yarborough, *JETS*, volume 26, pp. 181-182). Yarborough lists a number of arguments, including that Papias knew Philip's daughters, who were adults and would have been in their 50s, which means that he was alive and well before the end of the first century (Eusebius, *Eccl. Hist.*, 3.39.9). The Eusebius section says Papias mentions Matthew and Mark, quotes 1 John, 1 Peter, and knows John's Gospel (Thiessen, p. 13). Most agree Papias refers to the story of the women taken in adultery (Morris, *John,* p. 883; he cites Eusebius, *Eccl. Hist.*, 3:39, 17).

To summarize the data from the first century, Christian authors recognized New Testament books as Scripture, which undoubtedly affected their attitude toward it. The Didache and Papias cited the Byzantine text type, proving it existed in the first century.

The Second Century

Early into and throughout the second century, the Byzantine text type existed in Greek manuscripts, translations, and writings of Christians.

The Manuscript Evidence The second-century Chester Beatty Papyri contains "many Byzantine readings which previously had been regarded as late readings. Twenty-six Byzantine readings occur in the Gospels, eight in Acts, and 31 in the Pauline epistles (Hills, Introduction, p. 50). The Bodmer II Papyri contains 22 papyrus manuscripts discovered in Egypt in 1952. These manuscripts have been dated as early as about AD 200, although some have been dated later. While the text type has been identified as Alexandrian, there are Byzantine text type readings. Hills says, "To be precise, Papyrus Bodmer II contains thirteen percent of all the alleged readings of the Byzantine text in the area it covers (18 out of 138). Thirteen percent of the Byzantine readings, which most critics have regarded as late, have been proven by Papyrus Bodmer II to be early readings" (Hills, Introduction, p. 54).

Sturz lists 150 distinctively Byzantine readings that have early Egyptian papyri support (Sturz, pp. 61, 145-159) and lists corrections in papyri from a Byzantine text type to an Alexandrian text type (Sturz, p. 63; see Appendix IV for examples of corrections).

Mark 6-9 of $\mathfrak{P}^{45}$ (where extant), there is 38% agreement with Codex D, 40% with the TR, 42% with B, 59% with f^{13}, and 68% with W^3. In Mark 5-16 of codex W, there is 34% agreement with B, 36% agreement with D, 38% with the TR and 40% with ℵ (Pickering, p. 43). Pickering lists more on page 44.

> $\mathfrak{P}^{45}$ agrees with ℵ 19 times, with B 24 times, and with TR 32 times
> $\mathfrak{P}^{66}$ agrees with ℵ 14 times, with B 29 times, and with TR 33 times
> $\mathfrak{P}^{75}$ agrees with ℵ 9 times, with B 33 times, and with TR 29 times
> $\mathfrak{P}^{45,66,75}$ agree with ℵ 4 times, with B 18 times, and with TR 20 times

$\mathfrak{P}^{45,66}$ agree with ℵ 7 times, with B 3 times, and with TR 8 times

$\mathfrak{P}^{45,75}$ agree with ℵ 1 time, with B 2 times, and with TR 2 times

$\mathfrak{P}^{66,75}$ agree with ℵ 0 times, with B 8 times, and with TR 455 times

The Early Translation Evidence The Peshitta is the Syriac version of the New Testament. Syria was part of what became known as the Byzantine Empire. The date of the Peshitta is debated. Most critics today date it from the fifth century, but there is proof that it's probably dated from the second century.

In 1864, Westcott assigned Peshitta to the early second century "in accordance with the general opinion of the scholarly world of the time" (Pickering, p. 306, who cites Westcott's *The Bible in the Church*, p. 132). According to Britannica, the accepted Bible of the Syrian church, the Peshitta, dates from the end of the third century (see the article at https://www.britannicacom/topic/Peshitta).

However, "Because the Peshitta witnesses the 'Byzantine' text, Hort had to get it out of the second and third centuries. Accordingly, he posited a late recension to account for it. F. C. Burkitt went further than Hort and specified Rabbula, Bishop of Edessa from AD 411-435, as the author of the revision" (Pickering, p. 23). The following is an edited version of Hills' explanation and reputation of that hypothesis (Hill's Introduction, pp. 55-57).

Burkitt (1904) contended that the Peshitta did not exist before the fifth century because it was a revision made by Rabbula from 411 to 435. Modern scholarship has generally adopted this hypothesis. There is, however, a difficulty with it, namely that the Peshitta was regarded as authoritative Scripture by both the Nestorians and the Monophysites.

In the fifth century, a controversy arose in the Syrian Church concerning the nature of Christ's person. The Nestorius (d. 451), Bishop of Constantinople, was accused of teaching that Christ not only had two natures but was also two persons. The Monophysites asserted that Christ was only one person; His divine and human natures were fused together to be one. Although the Nestorians and Monophysites were divided over Christology, they were united in using the Peshitta as their authoritative Scripture.

Hills explains, "It is hard to see how this could have come to pass on the hypothesis that Rabbula was the author and chief promoter of the Peshitta. For Rabbula was a decided Monophysite and a determined opponent of the Nestorians. It is almost contrary to reason, therefore, to suppose that Nestorian Christians would adopt so quickly and so unanimously the handiwork of their greatest adversary.

"Due to this historical difficulty, Burkitt's hypothesis was rejected by such competent scholars as A. Mingana (1915) and A. C. Clark (1933). Its complete overthrow, however, seems to have been accomplished in recent years by the research of A. Voobus, who published his results in several important monograms of the origin and early use of the Peshitta. In his first work (1947), Voobus denies that Rabbula was the author of the Peshitta and even contends that he did not use it at all. In the second study (1948), Voobus converts Burkitt's statement that after the time of Rabbula, only the Peshitta was used by the Syrian writers. Burkitt, he says, made this assertion on insufficient grounds. And in a third treatment of the same subject (1951), he disputes Burkitt's dictum, 'before Rabbula no trace of the Peshitta.' Voobus finds traces of the Peshitta in an Armenian translation of the writings by Aitallaha, Bishop of Edessa, who died about

346. This work was not known until 1911 and was not available to Burkitt when he formulated his theory.

"If Voobus is correct in his findings [and they have been accepted at least in part by M. Black (1951) and other authorities in the field], and especially if he is right in his contention that the Syrian Christians did not unanimously adopt the Peshitta until after the fifth century, there is only one theory which can explain how both the Nestorians and the Monophysites came to receive it as their official text. This is the traditional view that the Peshitta was made in the second century and is the oldest Syrian version. The other Syrian versions (the Diatessaron and the so-called Old Syriac) were foreign importations that may, for a time, have eclipsed the Peshitta and its popularity but never drove it out of circulation altogether. In the sixth century, after the Nestorian and Monophysites had broken off their relationship with the Greek church, both groups returned to the ancient version, which they knew to have been the text of their fathers. Indeed, they vied with each other in doing so; each party sought to demonstrate that they were truly Orthodox. Thus, recent studies of the Peshitta tend to re-establish it is the oldest of the ancient versions and thus a very important witness to the antiquity of the Byzantine text from which it is made" (Hills, Introduction, pp. 56-57).

Aland agrees, "Since the Peshitta was used by both parts of the divided Syriac church, ... its origin and acceptance as authoritative must have occurred before their division, i.e., by the mid-fifth century at the latest.... It is certain ... as it stands today, [it] cannot have been entirely his [Rabbula] .... [It] follows "an exemplar of a (mainly) Koine [Byzantine] type-text" (Aland, p. 197).

Since the Peshitta follows the Byzantine text type, if it is a second-century document, the Byzantine text type existed in the second century. For a free copy of the Peshitta, see https://www.dukhrana.com/peshitta/.

Metzger says that on May 6, 1897, there was a debate at Oxford. Edward Miller and several others were on one side, holding up Burgon's position and William Sandy and A. C. Headlam were on the other. As Metzger explains, "One of the chief points of contention was the date of the Peshitta Syriac version of the New Testament. Miller maintained this version, which is a witness to the Syrian type of text, goes back to the second century. Therefore, the Syrian type of text did not originate with Lucian and his contemporaries at the beginning of the fourth century. Sandy acknowledged the date of the Peshitta was the 'sheet anchor' of Miller's position but was unable to produce convincing evidence for its late origin" (Metzger, pp. 136-137 fn., who cites *The Oxford Debate on The Textual Criticism of the New Testament*, 1897, p. 28).

The Writings of Second-Century Christians These authors *recognized New Testament books as Scripture*, which affected their attitude. They also had Byzantine text type readings. First, consider how much of the New Testament the second-century authors knew.

1. Polycarp (110). Polycarp (ca 69-155) was a disciple of the Apostle John. Irenaeus, who was Polycarp's pupil, wrote, "Polycarp was instructed by the apostles, and was brought into contact with many who had seen Christ" (Irenaeus, *Ag. Her.* 3.3; see also Eusebius, *Eccl. Hist.* 4.14). Polycarp was the "Bishop" of Smyrna for many years. In 110, Polycarp wrote an epistle to the Philippians. He refers to Paul being at Philippi and writing them a letter (Chapter 3) and to the Apostle John. There are about sixty quotations from the New Testament, of which thirty-four are from

Paul's writings (Cairns, p. 75). To be more specific, he quotes 14 books of the New Testament, including Matthew, Luke, Acts, Romans, 1 Corinthians, Galatians, Ephesians, Philippians, 1 Timothy, 2 Timothy, 1 Thessalonians, 2 Thessalonians, 1 Peter, and 1 John (Thiel claims that Polycarp alludes to all 27 books of the NT; for his proof see www.COGwriter.com, accessed 7/24/2010). He says, "Only, as it is said in these Scriptures, Be angry and sin not, and Let not the sun set on your wrath" (Chapter 12). The word "Scriptures" is in the plural. In other words, he is citing two passages of Scripture. The first, "Be angry and sin not," is from Psalm 4:4, and the second, "Let not the sun go down on your wrath," is from Ephesians 4:26. Polycarp called Ephesians 4:26 Scripture!

2. Ignatius (110-115). Ignatius (67-ca 116) wrote epistles between 110-115. He quotes Matthew 13:33 (Eph. 14), 1 Cor. 6:9-10 (Eph. 16), 2 Cor. 4:18 (Rom. 3), and 1 Thess. 5:17 (Polycarp 1). In Ephesians 5, he quotes, "God resists the proud" (Prov. 3:34; Jas. 4:6; 1 Pet. 5:5). He alludes to Matthew 18:19 (Eph. 5), 1 Pet. 2:5 (Eph. 9), and John 12:7 (Eph. 17). Writing to the Ephesians, Ignatius uses phrases from the New Testament book of Ephesians (*cf.* his Eph. 1 with Eph. 5:2).

3. The Epistle of Barnabas (*ca.* 130). In Chapter 4, the author says, "As it is written, 'Many are called, but few were chosen'" (Mt. 20:16 or 22:14). This is introduced by a formula that is common for the quotation of Old Testament Scripture—'as it stands written' (*The Epistle of Barnabas*, 4:14)." In Chapter 5, he says, "He came not to call the righteous, but sinners to repentance" (Mt. 9:13; Mk. 2:17; Lk. 5:32). In Chapter 7, he writes, "The Lord says, 'Behold, I will make the last like the first'" (Mt. 20:16). There is a possible allusion to Colossians 1:16 (Barnabas 11). Thiessen says, "It quotes Matthew, and there are echoes of Romans, 1 and

2 Corinthians, and Ephesians. The writer perhaps knew 1 Peter and certain passages reminded us of John" (Thiessen, p. 17).

4. Second Clement (*ca.* 140). There's no relationship between 1 Clement and 2 Clement. This Clement quotes Matthew 7:21 (2 Clem. 4:2), Matthew 7:23 (2 Clem. 4:5; see Lk. 13: 26-27), Matthew 9:13, calling it Scripture (2 Clem. 2:4), Matthew 10:16 (2 Clem. 5:2), Matthew 10:32-33 (2 Clem. 3:2), Matthew 12:50 (2 Clem. 9:11), Matthew 16:26 (2 Clem. 6:2), Matthew 21:13, calling it Scripture (2 Clem. 14:1), Mark 9:44 (2 Clem. 17:5), Luke 12:4 (2 Clem. 5:4), Luke 16:13 (2 Clem. 6:1), Luke 1610 (8:5), 1 Corinthians 2:9 (2 Clem. 11:7) and alludes to 1 Corinthians 9:24-27 (2 Clem. 7:5) and 2 Peter 3:10 (2 Clem. 16:3). In 2:4, he says, "Another Scripture says."

5. Justin Martyr (*ca.* 100-165). Justin refers to the "Memoirs of the Apostles," that is, the Gospels and quotes Matthew 2:1 (Justin, *Dialog.* 106:4), Mark 3:16-17 (Justin, *Dialog.* 106:4), Luke 22:44, 42 (Justin, *Dialog.* 103:8), John 3:3 (Justin, *First Apology* 61:4). He does not quote, but he refers to the book of Revelation (Justin, *Dialog.* 81.4). Justin Martyr writes that just as Abraham believed the voice of God, "In like manner, we having believed God's voice spoken by the apostles of Christ" (*Apology*, 1.66). He believed in the inspiration of the Scriptures. In *Dialogue with Trypho*, he writes, "To persuade you that you have not understood anything of the Scripture, I will remind you of another psalm, dictated to David by the Holy Spirit" (*Trypho*, 34). He also wrote, "There was a certain man with us, his name was John, one of the apostles of Christ, who prophesied by a revelation that was made to him, that those who believe in Christ would dwell a thousand years in Jerusalem" (*Trypho*, 120). "It also seems

clear from *Trypho*, 120 that Justin considered the New Testament writings to be Scripture" (Pickering, p. 96).

6. Athenagorus of Athens (177). He writes, "We are not even allowed to indulge in a lustful glance for says the Scripture, 'He who looks at a woman lustfully, has already committed adultery in his heart" ("*Plea for Justice*" 32).

7. Theophilus of Antioch (168-182). He quotes 1 Timothy 2:1 and Romans 13:7 as "the divine word (*Apology to Autolycus*, iii.14) and he quotes from the Gospel of John, saying that John was "inspired by the Spirit" (ii, 22). He also says, "The statements of the Prophets and of the Gospels are found to be consistent because they are inspired by the one Spirit of God" (ii.9; ii.35; iii.17).

8. Irenaeus (177). Irenaeus (115?-202) was brought up in Smyrna, was a pupil of Polycarp and Papias, and became bishop of Lyons in Gaul (now France) in 177. Irenaeus says, "The Scriptures are indeed perfect since they were spoken by the Word of God and His Spirit" (Irenaeus, *Ag. Her.* 2.28.2). Nowhere in the extant writing of Irenaeus is there a list of New Testament books, but "he had a clear notion of their identity" (Bruce, CS, p. 173). He does not list the letters of Paul, "but he evidently accepted the whole corpus of thirteen letters; the only letter he does not mention is the short letter to Philemon, which he had no occasion to cite" (Bruce, CS, p. 176). He quotes Paul 206 times (Kelly, p. 58). Irenaeus declares that there are four gospels and no more than four. "It is not possible that the Gospels can be either more or fewer in number than they are" (Irenaeus, *Ag. Her. 3.11.1*). He goes on to name Matthew, Mark, Luke, and John and quotes from them. Latourette says Irenaeus even recognized some questioned portions of the Gospel of John (Latourette, p. 133).

Miller says Irenaeus made 1800 quotations from the New Testament and recognized the four Gospels, Acts, 13 Pauline epistles, 1 Peter, 1 John, and Revelation as canonical Scripture" (Miller cited by Baker, p. 84). Harrison argues that the lack of mention of a few books is not proof of their non-canonical standing in the eyes of Irenaeus since he does not furnish a formal list of New Testament writings (Everett Harrison, pp. 99-100).

To sum up, thus far, Christian authors writing throughout the second century quoted or alluded to every book of the New Testament. Most of these second-century authors were from Greek-speaking Asia Minor (Polycarp was Bishop of Smyrna, Ignatius was from Antioch, Athenagorus was from Athens, Theophilus was from Antioch, and Irenaeus was originally from Smyrna).

Second-century Christians were also concerned about the accuracy of Scripture. Polycarp said, "Whoever perverts the sayings of the Lord ... that one is the firstborn of Satan (Polycarp, 7:1). "Dionysius, Bishop of Corinth (168-176), complained that his own letters had been tampered with, and worse yet the Holy Scriptures also.... Irenaeus said that the doctrine of the apostles had been handed down by the succession of bishops, being guarded and preserved, without any forging of the Scriptures, allowing neither the addition nor curtailment, involving public reading without falsification (*Against Heresies* IV. 32:8). Tertullian also says, "I hold sure title-deed from the original owners themselves ... I am the heir of the apostles. Just as they carefully prepared their will and testament, and committed it to a trust ... even so I hold it" (Pickering, p. 100).

After citing quotations pertaining to tampering with the text from six ancient authors, Sturz comments, "Note how these quotes, bridging the close of the second and beginning of the third centuries, reflect in opposition to the emendation of the Scripture for any reason…. These early Fathers … are voicing strong disapproval of any tampering with the text of Scripture…. This high regard for the Scripture, on the part of the early Fathers, may have worked toward a more careful handling of the K-text [Byzantine] than has generally been acknowledged. In fact, it is the conviction of some textual critics that the editing of the Byzantine text actually appears to have been less dramatic than that which is found in other main text types" (Sturz, pp. 120-121).

Metzger says, "In order to ensure accuracy in transcription, authors would sometimes add at the close of their literary works an adjuration [a solemn oath] directed to future copyists. So, for example, Irenaeus attached to the close of his treatise *On the Ogdad* the following note: 'I adjure you who shall copy out this book, but our Lord Jesus Christ and by his glorious advent when it comes to judge the living and the dead, that you compare what you transcribe, and corrected carefully against the manuscript from which you copy; and also that you transcribe the adjuration and insert it in the copy'" (Metzger, p. 21).

After quoting Metzger, Pickering notes, "If Irenaeus took such extreme precaution for the accurate transmission of his own work, how much more would he be concerned with the accurate copy of the Word of God? In fact, he demonstrated his concern for the accuracy of the text by defending the traditional reading of a single letter" (Pickering, p. 100). Pickering goes on to explain that in Revelation 13:18, the difference between 666 and 616 is a single Greek letter, adding, "Irenaeus asserts that 666 is found 'in all the most approved and ancient copies' and that 'those men who saw John face-to-face' bear witness to it. And he warns those who made the change (of a single letter) that 'there shall be no light punishment upon him who either adds or subtracts anything from the Scripture' (xxx. 1). Presumably, Irenaeus is applying Revelation 22:18-19" (Pickering, pp. 100-101).

Irenaeus was a pupil of Polycarp and Polycarp (*ca.* 69-155) was a disciple of the apostle John. With that in mind, Pickering suggests that, given Polycarp's intimacy with John, his personal copy of Revelation would probably have been taken from the autographs and given Irenaeus's relationship with Polycarp, his personal copy of Revelation was taken from Polycarp's. "He was clearly in a position to identify a faithful copy and to declare with certainty the original reading—this in AD 186." (Pickering, p. 101).

After a chapter explaining unintentional and intentional errors in Greek manuscripts, Metzger says, "It ought to be noted that other evidence points to a careful and painstaking work on the part of many faithful copyists." After giving several examples, Metzger concludes, "These examples of dogged fidelity of the part of scribes could be multiplied (Metzger, p. 206). Aland says, "One of the characteristics of the New Testament textual tradition is tenacity, i.e., the stubborn resistance of readings and text types to change" (Aland, p. 69).

Pickering proposes four factors crucial for ensuring the faithful transmission of the text: access to the autographs, proficiency in the source language, the strength of the church, and an appropriate attitude toward the text.

1. Access to the autographs. "Who held the autographs? Speaking in terms of regions, Asia Minor may be safely said to have had twelve (John, Galatians, Ephesians, Colossians, 1 and 2 Thessalonians, and Titus in Crete), Rome may be safely said to have two (Mark and Romans)—as to the rest, Luke, Acts, and 2 Peter were probably held by Asia Minor or

Rome; Matthew and James by either Asia Minor or Palestine; Hebrews Rome or Palestine; while it is hard to state even a probability for Jude, it was quite possible held by Asia Minor. Taking Asia Minor and Greece together, the Aegean area helps the autographs to at least eighteen (two-thirds of the total) and possibly as many as twenty-four of the twenty-seven New Testament books. Rome held at least two and possibly up to seven. Palestine may have helped up to three (but in AD 70, they would have been sent away for safekeeping, quite possibly to Antioch). Alexandria (Egypt) held **none.** We may reasonably assume that in the earliest period of the transmission of the 'NT text, the most reliable copies would have been circulating in the region that held the autographs" (Pickering, pp. 102-103, bold type his; he also says, based on Tertullian's comment, this was true to AD 200 and beyond).

Pickering adds, "So, in the year 200, someone looking for the best text of the 'NT would presumably go to the Aegean area; certainly not Egypt.... Aland states, 'Egypt was distinguished from other provinces of the church, so as far as we can judge, by the early dominance of gnosticism.' He further informs us that 'at the close of the 2nd century' the Egyptian church was 'dominantly gnostic' and then goes on to say: 'the copies existing in the gnostic communities could not be used because they were under suspicion of being corrupt.'…. What Aland is telling us, in other words, is that up to AD 200, the textual tradition in Egypt could **not be trusted**" (Pickering, p. 103, see also fn. 1, bold type his).

2. Proficiency in the source language. "Any divine solicitude for the precise form of the NT Text would have to be mediated through the language of the autographs—Greek. Evidently, ancient versions (Syriac, Latin, Coptic) may cast a clear vote with reference to major variants, but

precision is possible only in Greek (in the case of the 'NT).... To copy a text by hand in a language you do not understand is a tedious exercise—it is almost impossible to produce a perfect copy.... You virtually have to copy letter by letter and constantly check your place.

"Consider the case of $\mathfrak{P}^{66}$. This papyrus manuscript is perhaps the oldest (c. 200) extant N. T. manuscripts of any size (it contains most of John). It is one of the worst copies we have. It has an average of roughly two mistakes per verse—many being obvious mistakes, stupid mistakes, and nonsensical mistakes. From the pattern of mistakes, it is clear that the scribes copied syllable by syllable. I have no qualms in affirming that the person who produced $\mathfrak{P}^{66}$ did not know Greek. Had he understood the text, he would not have made the number and sort of mistakes that he did" (Pickering, p. 103).

Pickering says, "Now consider the problem from God's point of view. To whom should He entrust the primary responsibility for the faithful transmission of the N. T. Text (recall 1 Chronicles 16:15)? If the Holy Spirit was going to take an active part in the process, where should He concentrate His efforts? Presumably, fluent speakers of Greek would have the inside track, and areas, where Greek would continue in active use would be preferred. For a faithful transmission to occur, the copyist had to be proficient in Greek and over the long haul. So, where was the Greek predominant? Evidently, in Greece and Asia Minor.... The dominance of Greek in the Aegean area was guaranteed by the Byzantine Empire for many centuries, in fact, until the invention of printing. Constantinople fell to the Ottoman Turks in 1453.... (For those who believe in Providence, I would suggest that we have a powerful case in point here.)

"How about Egypt? The use of Greek in Egypt was already declining by the beginning of the Christian era. Bruce Metzger observes that the Hellenized section of the population in Egypt 'was only a fraction in comparison with the number of native inhabitants who used only the Egyptian language.' By the third century, the decline was evidently advanced." After giving another illustration, this time concerning $\mathfrak{P}^{75}$, Pickering says, "Aland agrees that before 200, the tide had begun to turn against the use of Greek in the areas that spoke Latin, Syriac, or Coptic, and 50 years later, the changeover to local languages was well advanced" (Pickering, p. 104).

3. The strength of the church. Pickering says, "If the selection of churches to receive the glorified Christ's 'letters' (Revelation 2 and 3) is any guide, the center of gravity of the church seems to have shifted from Palestine to Asia Minor by the end of the first century." Pickering sites Aland who says that about 180 the greatest concentration of churches was in Asia Minor and even around AD 325 the scene was still largely unchanged. Asia Minor continued to be "the heartland of the church." … "C. H. Roberts, in a scholarly treatment of the Christian literary papyrus of the first three centuries, seems to favor the conclusion that the Alexandrian church was weak and insignificant to the Greek Christian world in the second century" and Aland says that "at the close of the 2nd century" the Egyptian church was "dominantly gnostic." So Pickering says again "up to AD 200 the textual tradition in Egypt **could not be trusted**" (Pickering, p. 105, bold type his).

In this regard, Pickering also cites Metzger, who says, "To judge by the comments made by Clement of Alexandria, almost every deviant Christian sect was represented in Egypt during the second century;

Clement mentions Valentinians, the Basilidians, the Marcionites, the Peratae, the Encratites, the Docetists, the Haimetites, the Cainites, the Ophites, the Simonians, and the Eutychites. What proportion of Christians in Egypt during the second century were orthodox is not known." Pickering adds, "It is almost enough to make one wonder whether Isaiah 30:1-3 might not be a prophecy about 'NT textual criticism!'" (Pickering, p. 106).

4. Attitude toward the text. "Being followers of Christ, and believing that they were dealing with Scripture, to a basic honesty would be added reverence in their handling of the text come from the start. And to these would be added vigilance, since the Apostles had repeatedly and emphatically warned them against false teachers [Acts 20:27-32, Gal. 1:6-12, 2 Tim. 3:1-4:4, 2 Pet. 2:1-2, 1 Jn. 2:18-19, 2 Jn. 7-11, Jude 3-4, 16-19].... The rise of the so-called 'school of Antioch' is a relevant consideration. Beginning with Theophilus, a bishop of Antioch who died around 185, the Antiochians began insisting upon the literal interpretation of Scripture. The point is that a literalist is obligated to be concerned about the precise wording of the text since his interpretation or exegesis hinges upon it. It is reasonable to assume that this 'literalist' mentality would have influenced the churches of Asia Minor and Greece and encouraged them in the careful and faithful transmission of the pure text that they had received. For example, the 1000 MSS of the Syriac Peshitta are unparallel in their consistency (by way of contrast, the 8000+ MSS of the Latin Vulgate are remarkable for their extensive discrepancies and in this, they follow the example of the old Latin MSS)" (Pickering, p. 107).

On the other hand, "Since Philo of Alexandria was at the height of his influence when the first Christians arrived there [Egypt], it may be that his allegorical interpretation of the O.T. began to rub off on the young church already in the first century. Since an allegorist is going to impose his own ideas on the text anyway, he would presumably have fewer inhibitions about altering it—precise wording would not be a high priority. The school of literary criticism that existed at Alexandria would also be a negative factor, if it influenced the church at all, and W. R. Farmer argues that it did. 'But there is ample evidence that by the time of Eusebius the Alexandrian text-critical practices were being followed in at least some of the scriptoria with the New Testament manuscripts were being produced. Exactly when the Alexandrian text-critical principles were first used ... is not known.' ... The point is, the principles used in attempting to 'restore 'the works of Homer would not be appropriate for the NT writings when appealed to the autographs, or exact copies made from them, was still possible" (Pickering, p. 108).

The Greek New Testament was translated into other languages during the second century. Aland says the early versions, the Latin, Syriac, and Coptic, were about AD 180. Later, other translations were produced, including the Gothic, Slavonic, Armenian, and Georgian (Aland, p. 185). "By AD 250, the church in the West was a Latin church" (Aland, p. 68). Metzger says, "Though at one time Greek was the *lingua franca* of the Roman Empire, by the sixth century, it was scarcely understood beyond the borders of the Byzantine Empire" (Metzger, p. 292).

Someone copying a text in a language not his native language would predictably make meaningless mistakes. $\mathfrak{P}^{66}$ is an example. It has an average of two mistakes per verse and is virtually impossible to use (Pickering and Freitas, p. 49). Colwell said $\mathfrak{P}^{66}$ was copied syllable by syllable and $\mathfrak{P}^{75}$ was copied letter by letter, which means that neither of the copyists knew Greek. Mistakes in $\mathfrak{P}^{66}$ are "stupid mistakes, nonsense, without meaning" (Pickering and Freitas, p. 51).

Augustine complained, "For in the early days of the faith, every man who happened to get his hands upon a Greek manuscript, and who thought he had any knowledge, were it ever so little, of the two languages, ventured upon the work of translation" (Augustine, *On Christian Doctrine*, II. XI. 16, AD 397; https://www.ccel.org/ccel/augustine/doctrine.xii_1.html). When Aland cites this quote and, he makes clear that Augustine was referring to translations into Latin (Aland, p. 187). Augustine was in Africa

To summarize the data from the second century, Greek manuscripts, translations (Peshitta), and writings of Christians indicate that Byzantine text type existed in the second century and the writings of Christian authors indicate they weer concerned about the accuracy of Scripture.

The Third Century

At the beginning of the third century, there is evidence that at least some of the autographs of the New Testament still existed! There is even an indication that some of the autographs still existed at the end of the third century.

Beginning of the Third Century In Chapter 36 of *Prescription against Heretics,* Tertullian (*ca* 155-220) wrote, "The very thrones of the apostles are still pre-eminent in their places, in which **their own authentic writings are read**, uttering the voice and representing the face of each of them severally. Achaia is very near you (in which) you find Corinth. Since you are not far from Macedonia, you have Philippi (and there, too), you have the Thessalonians. Since you are able to cross to Asia, you get Ephesus.

Since, moreover, you are close to Italy, you have Rome **from which there comes even into our own hands the very authority** (of apostles themselves). How happy is its church, on which apostles poured forth all their doctrine along with their blood? Where Peter endures a passion like his Lord's! Where Paul wins his crown in a death like John's where the Apostle John was first plunged, unhurt, into boiling oil and thence remitted to his island-exile! See what she has learned, what she taught, what fellowship has had with even (our) churches in Africa! One Lord God does she acknowledge, the Creator of the universe, and Christ Jesus (born) of the Virgin Mary, the Son of God the Creator; and the Resurrection of the flesh; the law and the prophets she **unites in one volume with the writings of evangelists and apostles**, from which she drinks in her faith" (Tertullian**,** bold type added). Pickering says that Tertullian wrote this "around the year 208" (Pickering, p. 101, bold type added), that is, at the beginning of the third century.

Daniel Wallace, an authority on textual criticism, points out that Tertullian, who wrote about AD 180, said, "Come now, you who would indulge a better curiosity if you would apply it to the business of your salvation, run over [to] the apostolic churches, in which the very thrones of the apostles are still pre-eminent in their places, in which their own authentic writings are read, uttering the voice and representing the face of each of them severally." Wallace adds that "Tertullian goes on to discuss each of these 'authentic writings' as being found in the very churches to which they were written. He mentions Corinth, Philippi, Thessalonica, Ephesus, and Rome. He urges his readers to visit these sites to check out these authentic writings. This seems to suggest that he believed that these documents were the autographs. In the least, it suggests that by his day, carefully done copies of the originals were considered important for verifying what the apostles meant, and such copies had a strong connection to the churches to which they were originally written. One still has to wonder why Tertullian focuses on the very churches that received the originals if he didn't mean by the comment that these churches still preserved the autographs." Wallace concludes, "From the context and from lexical usage, Tertullian meant the autographs" (see Wallace, "Did the Original New Testament Manuscripts still exist in the Second Century?" See the article at https://bible.org/article/did-original-new-testament-manuscripts-still-exist-second-century-0.).

Eusebius of Caesarea (265-339) cites an anonymous work written about 230 that says, "They have tampered with the divine Scripture without they have set aside the rule of primitive faith; they have not known Christ…. [They] corrupt the simple faith of the divine Scripture with the craftiness of godless men…. They lay hands fearlessly on the divine Scriptures, saying they had corrected them…. For anyone who will collect several copies together and compare them one with another will discover marked discrepancies…. For either they do not believe that the divine Scriptures were spoken by the Holy Spirit, and, therefore, are unbelievers; or they consider themselves wiser than the Holy Spirit, and what is that but devil possession?" (Sturz, pp. 118-119). Commenting on this quotation, Sturz notes, "that boldness in correcting is condemned in such strong terms suggests that at the time and locale of this writer the orthodox did not exercise freedom in this direction" (Sturz, p. 120).

End of the Third Century Wallace also says that Peter, Bishop of Alexandria, who died the last year of the Diocletian persecution in AD 311, "speaks of the autograph of the Gospel of John as still existing in his day.

The copy itself that was written by the hand of the evangelist, which, by the divine grace, has been preserved in the most holy church of Ephesus, and is there adored by the faithful" (https://bible.org/article/did-original-new-testament-manuscripts-still-exist-second-century-0). Galen (AD 129-216) spoke of papyri manuscripts lasting 300 years (see the article at "Galen on a 300-year-old papyrus roll," at https://www.roger-pearse.com/weblog/2011/02/02/galen-on-a-300-year-old-papyrus-roll/).

The significance of this information from Tertullian and Peter, Bishop of Alexandria, lies in the fact that the original autographs were still in the churches to which they were written—the very area that produced the Byzantine type-text. Other text types, Egyptian and Western, came from areas where the text is said to have been corrupted.

The Fourth Century

All agree that the Byzantine text type existed in the fourth century. "Scholars from Hort to Aland have recognized that any Byzantine 'recension' could not have been created later than the 4th century" (Pickering, p. 176), which means it existed in the fourth century. Pickering says, "The Aegean area was the best qualified to protect, transmit, and attest the true text of the NT writings. This was true in the 2nd century. It was true in the 3rd century; it continued to be true in the 4th century" (Pickering, p, 108).

Pickering concludes, "'Byzantine' readings are recognized (most notably) by the Didache, Diognetus, and Justin Martyr in the first half of the second century, the Gospel of Peter, Athenagotus, Hegesippus, and Irenaeus (heavily) in the second half; by Clement of Alexandria,

Tertullian, Clementines, Hippolyus, and Origen (all heavily) in the first half of the third century; by Gregory of Thaumaturgus, Novatian, Cyprian (heavily), Dionysius of Alexandria and Archelaus in the second half; by Eusebius, Athanasius, Macarius Magnus, Hillary, Didymus, Basil, Titus of Bostra, Cyril of Jerusalem, Gregory of Nyssa, Apostolic Canons and Constitutions, Epiphanius and Ambrose (all heavily) in the fourth century" (Pickering, pp. 67-68).

Miller listed "2630 citations from 76 Fathers or sources, ranging over a span of 300 years (AD 100-400), supporting readings of the 'Byzantine' text as opposed to those of the critical text of the English Revisers (which received 1753 citations)" (Pickering, p. 66).

From the Fifth to the Tenth Century

From Chrysostom Forword "An overwhelming proportion of the variants common to the great mass of cursive and late uncial Greek MSS are identical with the readings followed by Chrysostom" (ob. 407)" (Hort, p. 91). In other words, Chrysostom and those who came after him used the Byzantine text.

All Critics Agree The Byzantine text type is called Byzantine "because all modern critics acknowledge that this was the Greek New Testament text in general use throughout the greater part of the Byzantine Period (312-1453)" (Hills, Introduction, p. 20).

The Quinisext Council The church resisted changes in the text after AD 200 (Sturz, p. 122). This concern for careful properties continued through the centuries. Manuscripts written on parchment were sometimes reused by scraping and washing off the original writings so that another document could be written on it. Such manuscripts are called palimpsest. The Quinisext Council, held at Constantinople in AD 692, condemned using a Scripture manuscript for some other purpose. Granted, that was many years later, but it illustrates Christians' attitude toward the manuscripts of Scripture.

Burgon's Concept Burgon contends, "a majority of extant documents is more likely to represent the majority of ancestral documents, then *vice versa* (Burgon, p. 254, italics his). Assuming the Westcott and Hort view that the Traditional Text was fabricated at Antioch about AD 350, then for 1532 years (350 to 1882), the *Antiochian* standard has been faithfully retained and transmitted and "it will be impossible to assign any valid reason why the inspired Original itself the apostolic standard should not have been faithfully transmitted and obtained from the *Apostolic* age to the Antiochian" (Burgon, p. 296).

From the Tenth to the Sixteenth Century

The Byzantine Text is the text type of 80 to 95 percent of all existing Greek manuscripts (Farstad, p. 109). These are dated late, between 900 and 1500, but their characteristics reveal something significant about them.

The Majority of the Manuscripts. How does one explain that the vast majority of manuscripts support the majority text type? Westcott and Hort explained away the majority by claiming it was a late, edited edition. Later theories claim that the Byzantine text type evolved slowly over a long period of time. Is there not a better explanation that this text type was closer to the original and, therefore, there was more time to produce more copies?

The Declaration of Independence was written in 1776. Suppose there was no printing press at that time and people began to copy the Declaration of Independence by hand. Then, imagine that somewhere around 1820, someone made a copy that contained changes, and it began to be copied. All things being equal, which document would produce the most manuscripts today, the original 1776 document or the copy that was changed in 1820?

Adam Boyd says imagine that 20 people made a copy of a document and each of them asked 20 people to copy their copy. If 95% read one way and 5% read another way, common sense says that 95% is almost certainly the correct copy (https://www.youtube.com/watch?v=rz2DfD_ej14).

Unity The Byzantine text type contains remarkable unity. Hort said, "An overwhelming proportion of the text in all known cursive MSS except a few is as a matter of fact identical, most especially in the Gospels and Pauline epistles, however, we may account for the identity. Further, the identity of readings implies identity of origin" (Hort, p. 143). The Byzantine text "has maintained a high degree of homogeneity. It has not undergone an extensive cross-fertilization from other text types" (Sturz, p. 125).

Furthermore, the majority of Greek manuscripts consist of a smooth Greek text with no grammatical, historical, or geographical errors. Hort says it has "completeness" and removes "all stumbling blocks out of the way of the ordinary reader.... New omissions, accordingly, are rare, and where they occur, are usually found to contribute to the apparent simplicity. Both in manner and in diction the Syrian text is conspicuously a full text. It delights in pronouns, conjunctions, and expletives and supplies the links of all kinds, as well as in more steerable additions. It presents the New Testament in the form smooth and attractive." It is "Entirely blameless on either literary or religious grounds as regards vulgarised or unworthy diction" (Hort, p. 135). "In themselves, Syrian readings hardly ever offend at first. With rare exceptions, they run smoothly and easily in form, and yield at once to even a careless reader a passable sense, free of surprises and seemingly transparent" (Hort, pp. 115-116). Yet, "The very smoothness and completeness of the text led these scholars [Westcott and Hort] to believe it [Byzantine text type] was late, edited, and hence corrupt" (Farstad, p. 108).

Metzger says that scribes corrupted the Vulgate and that, in an attempt to purify it, a number of recensions were produced during the Middle Ages. "Unfortunately, however, each of these attempts to restore Jerome's original version resulted evidently in still further textual corruption through a mixture of several types of Vulgate text, which had come to be associated with various new European centers of scholarship. As a result, the more than 8000 Vulgate manuscripts which are extant exhibit the greatest amount of cross-contamination of textual types" (Metzger, p. 76). The majority of Greek manuscripts display more uniformity than the Vulgate, an official fourth-century edition of the Latin manuscripts by Jerome. That's incredible!

Used throughout the Centuries The Byzantine text type has been used throughout the centuries. That's why it's called the Traditional Text. Everyone agrees that it was used in the fourth century (Chrysostom) and throughout the Middle Ages. It was the text of the Protestant Reformation. Luther used it to translate the New Testament into German. Tyndale used it to translate the New Testament into English. It was the text used to translate the King James Version. It was the text used during the Wesleyan

Revivals, the Great Awakening, and the modern missions movement. Is it not interesting and impressive that throughout history, until the latter part of the nineteenth century, the church used the Byzantine Text? It is the only family of the New Testament manuscripts that has had continuous use throughout church history, at least from about 500 (some argue even earlier). Hills asks, "How did it (the Byzantine text) become the text of the whole Greek-speaking church, in all nations, in all the Christian communities, during the greater part of the Byzantine Period (312-1453)?" (Hills, Green, p. 35).

Divine Preservation The Byzantine text type is the only text type that has been *continually* preserved. Several verses say that God would preserve His Word (Mt. 5:18; 24:35; Mk. 13:31; Lk. 16:17; 21:33; 1 Pet. 1:24-25). Perhaps it could be argued that God preserved His Word in a manuscript such as Vaticanus or Sinaiticus, even though those text type manuscripts were not used throughout church history. That would be like God putting His Word in a safety deposit box to be opened centuries later.

Hills argues "that it was through the usage of the Church that Christ has fulfilled His promise always to preserve the true New Testament and that therefore the Byzantine text found in the vast majority of Greek Testament manuscripts is the true text" (Hills, Introduction, pp. 65-66). That only appeals to people who believe in the inspiration and preservation of the Word of God, but as has been said, "To what better kind of person would you want to appeal?"

Summary: Based on the historical evidence, the Greek autographs of the New Testament originated and/or were sent to Greek-speaking Asia Minor, where they were immediately recognized as Scripture, carefully copied, and preserved, and from a biblical point of view, God was providentially preserving His Word.

Aland concedes, "Asia Minor and Greece, the centers of early Christianity, undoubtedly exercise a substantive if not critical influence on the development of the New Testament text, but it is impossible to demonstrate because the climate in those regions has been unfavorable to the preservation of any papyri from the early period" (Aland, p. 67). But he is the one who said textual critics have "largely if not completely" ignored church history." He adds, "It is utterly amazing how many New Testament scholars failed to observe the historical implications of their theories, changing them as easily as they shift positions at their desks!" (Aland, p. 52). Perhaps he should consider early church history more carefully.

Pickering concludes, "The present printed Majority Text (whether H-F or R-P) is a close approximation to the original, free from the error of fact and contradiction discussed above. (All modesty aside, I consider my Greek text to be even closer.)" (Pickering, p. 337).

Nevertheless, textual critics reject the Byzantine text type. What are their objections?

The Oldest is the Best One objection to the Byzantine text type being preferred is that the Alexandrian text type (basically א and B) is older, and, therefore, it is to be preferred. But just because a couple of manuscripts are old does not mean they are the best. Pickering pointed out that the oldest can be the worst (Pickering and Freitas, p. 36). All the oldest manuscripts *come from Egypt*. They include Chester Beatty Papyri, Bodmer Papyri, Vaticanus, Sinaiticus, Alexandrinus, Ephraem Syrus, and Freer Washington.

Burgon collated the five oldest uncials in his day (ℵ, A, B, C, D). He found they repeatedly displayed confusion and disfigurement (Pickering, p. 133). Hort found that the confusion of Mark 14:30, 68, 72a, b (in ℵ, A, B, C, D, L, D) was so great that no two had the same text in all four places (Pickering, p. 134). Hort said that the "singular readings of B ... by no means [had] a high standard of accuracy" (Hort, p. 233).

$\mathfrak{P}^{66}$ has nearly 200 nonsense readings and 400 spelling errors. To that "could be added those singular readings whose origin baffles speculation, readings that can be given no more exact label than carelessness leading to absorbed variant reading. A hurried count shows $\mathfrak{P}^{45}$ with 20, $\mathfrak{P}^{75}$ with 57, and $\mathfrak{P}^{66}$ with 216 purely careless readings. As we have seen, $\mathfrak{P}^{66}$ has, in addition, more than twice as many 'leaps' from the same to the same as either of the others" (Colwell, cited by Pickering, pp. 130-131).

The scribe of $\mathfrak{P}^{45}$ "omits adverbs, adjectives, nouns, participles, verbs, and personal pronouns—without any compensating habit of additions. He frequently omits phrases and clauses. He prefers the singular to the compound word. In short, he favors brevity. He shortens the text in at least fifty places in **singular readings alone**" (Colwell, Pickering, p. 132, bold print his).

$\mathfrak{P}^{46}$ abounds with scribal blunders, omissions, and also additions (Zuntz, cited by Pickering, p. 132).

According to Aland, concerning $\mathfrak{P}^{47}$, "We need not mention the fact that the oldest manuscript does not necessarily have the best text. $\mathfrak{P}^{47}$ is, for example, by far the oldest of the manuscripts containing the full or almost full text of the Apocalypse, but it is certainly not the best" (Aland, cited by Pickering, p. 133).

No Early Byzantine Text Types The other objection to the Byzantine text type being preferred is that critics claim there are no extant "witnesses" of the Byzantine text type before the fourth century. "Witnesses" are Greek manuscripts, translations, and quotations from early Christian writers. What exactly is the testimony of these witnesses?

In the first place, according to Aland, there were no text types before the third/fourth century. He says, "The text of the early period prior to the third/fourth century was, then, in effect, a text not yet channeled into types because, until the beginning of the fourth century, the church still lacked the institutional organization required to produce one.... Until the third/fourth century, then, there were many different forms of the New Testament text, including some which anticipated or were more closely akin to the D text, but not until the fourth century, following the decades of peace prior to the Diocletianic persecutions, that the formation of text types begin" (Aland, p. 64).

Furthermore, these papyri are from Egypt, where the text is said to have been corrupted and only represents their local situation. Metzger says, "Inasmuch as almost all extant Greek papyri have been preserved in Egypt, their general lack of 'Western' readings proves no more than that the general absence of such reading in that geographical area of the early church" (Metzger, p. 294).

Nevertheless, all agree there are Byzantine-type *readings* before the fourth century. All the Greek manuscripts from before the fourth century are papyri. The Chester Beatty Papyri contain many Byzantine readings that had not previously been regarded as late readings. "Twenty-six of these Byzantine readings occur in the Gospel section of the Chester Beatty Papyri, 8 in Acts and 31 in Paul's epistles" (Hills, Introduction, p. 50).

The Bodmer II Papyri contain 22 papyrus manuscripts discovered in Egypt in 1952. These manuscripts have been dated as early as about AD 200, although some have been dated later. While the text type has been identified as Alexandrian, there are Byzantine text type readings. Hills says, "To be precise, Papyrus Bodmer II contains thirteen percent of all the alleged readings of the Byzantine text in the area which it covers (18 out of 138). Thirteen percent of the Byzantine readings most critics have regarded as late, have been proven by Papyrus Bodmer II to be early readings" (Hills, Introduction, p. 54).

Sturz has demonstrated, and Metzger acknowledges (Metzger, p. 292), that there are approximately 150 passages throughout the New Testament where Byzantine readings are supported by one or more of the papyri. Whenever B and $\mathfrak{P}^{75}$ disagree, one or the other always has the Byzantine reading. They each have approximately the same number of Byzantine readings, which suggests that the Byzantine text originated in AD 220 (Pickering and Freitas, p. 69).

To be specific, the first hand of $\mathfrak{P}^{66}$ was "extensively corrected and both hands are dated around AD 200. The first hand is almost half 'Byzantine' (a. 47%). But the 2nd hand regularly changed 'Byzantine' readings to 'Alexandrian' and vice versa, i.e., changed 'Alexandrian' to 'Byzantine,' repeatedly. This means that they must have had two exemplars, one 'Alexandrian' and one 'Byzantine'—between the two hands, the 'Byzantine' text received considerable attention (in the year 200!!)" (Pickering, p. 137).

What about translations? Aland says, "It must be emphasized that the value of the early versions for establishing the original Greek text and for the history of the text has frequently been misconceived, i.e., they have been considerably overrated. An inadequate appreciation of how their linguistic structures differ from those of Greek has all too often permitted early versions to be cited in the critical apparatuses of the Greek text when the evidence is irrelevant. Westcott and Hort's assumptions can no longer be maintained either for the Old Syriac or the Old Latin. And yet, the importance of the versions is substantial. They are authoritative in confirming the identity of the regional or provincial text where they are produced (e.g., the Coptic version of the Egyptian texts)" (Aland, p. 6, 186).

What about quotations from the early writers? This objection is dealt with in detail in the chapter "The Evaluation of Text types" and earlier in the Conclusion. A study done by Aland can be added to that. He tabulated the patristic citations in the New Testament, dealing with Marcion, Irenaeus, Clement of Alexandria, Origen, Basil, Chrysostom, and others. With the exception of Marcion, each used the Byzantine text type more than the Alexandrian text type. Even Clement and Origen, who were in Egypt, preferred the Byzantine text over the Egyptian (Pickering, p. 144, who adds, "This is startling because it goes against almost everything we have been taught for over a century."

By the way, Chrysostom (347-407) preached in Antioch in AD 380 and later in Constantinople in AD 397. There are no earlier Antiochian Fathers than Chrysostom, whose literary remains are extensive enough so that New Testament quotations may be analyzed as to the type of text they used (Sturz, p. 80).

The factor often overlooked in this discussion is that Greek manuscripts were destroyed because of persecution. As Robinson pointed out, various persecutions, especially the Diocletian persecutions, eliminated a large number of New Testament Greek manuscripts. So, naturally, the Greek manuscripts from the Byzantine area would have been destroyed. Nevertheless, the Byzantine text type did exist at the beginning of the fourth century. Even Aland concedes that "toward the end of the third or the beginning of the fourth century, the Byzantine text type "first took form in Antioch" (Aland, pp. 50-51). Granted, he does not concede that it existed before then, but he acknowledges that it existed at that time. Since there is not one shred of evidence that it resulted from a recension, based on what we know, it is safe to assume that these were surviving manuscripts from the Byzantine area.

Diocletian ordered the destruction of Christian manuscripts throughout his empire (303–310). Some leaders refused to give up their manuscripts, even when tormented. The Diocletian campaign probably succeeded in destroying less valuable manuscripts. The best manuscripts in the care of serious leaders no doubt protected them at all costs; thus, the campaign purified the text's transmission (Pickering and Freitas, p. 77).

Aland explains how the Byzantine text became so widespread in the fourth century, "The major text types trace their beginning to the Diocletianic persecution in the Age of Constantine, which followed. It seems paradoxical. The period of persecution, which lasted almost ten years in the West and much longer in the East, was characterized by the systematic destruction of church buildings (and church centers), and any manuscripts that were found in them were publicly burned. Church officials were further required to surrender to the public, burning all holy books in their possession or custody…. The result was a widespread scarcity of New Testament manuscripts, which became all the more acute when the persecution ceased." Aland explains that after the persecution, there was "a sudden demand for large numbers of New Testament manuscripts in all provinces of the empire." The exegetical school of Antioch provided bishops for many dioceses throughout the East, and each of these bishops took the Lucian text with him to his dioceses. "In this way, it rapidly became widely disseminated even in the fourth century (Aland, p. 65).

Like virtually all modern textual critics, Aland assumes there was a Lucian recension, but there is no evidence that such a recension happened. So, if there was no recension, then the Byzantine text type that was so widely distributed during the fourth century was none other than a copy of the autographs that survived up until the fourth century.

APPENDIX I: THE WESTCOTT-HORT THEORY

In 1881, Brooke Westcott and Fenton Anthony published *The New Testament in the Original Greek*. In 1882, they released Volume II, *The New Testament in the original Greek: Introduction and Appendix [to] the Text Revised by Brooke Foss Westcott and Fenton John Anthony Hort* (a.k.a. *Introduction and Appendix*; for a downloadable free copy, see https://archive.org/stream/newtestamentinor82west/newtestamentinor82west_djvu.txt).

This appendix contains notes and quotes from Volume II. While Westcott and Hort claim responsibility for the "principles, arguments, and conclusion" in Volume II, they say Hort wrote the second volume (Hort, p. 18). Since Hort was the author of Volume II, his name alone will be in references to it. Pages numbers after his name are from Volume II.

The opening statement of the Introduction states, "This edition is an attempt to present exactly the original words of the New Testament, so far as they can now be determined from surviving documents" (Hort, p. 1). He adds this is necessary because the witnesses are "full of complex variation, the original text cannot be elicited from it without the use of criticism, that is, of a process of distinguishing and setting aside those readings which have originated in some link in the chain of transmission" (Hort, p. 1).

Hort insists that the "great bulk" of the words of the New Testament do not need textual criticism. He estimates that 7/8 of the words are accepted "above doubt," that the great part of the remaining 1/8 is "formed in great part by changes of order and other comparative trivialities," and that "if the principles followed in this present edition are sound, this area may be very greatly reduced." He concludes the "substantial variations" are a "small fraction" of the whole that can "hardly form more than a thousandth part of the entire text" (Hort, p. 2).

Part I: The Need for Criticism

Hort discusses "Transmission by writing" (manuscripts) and "Transmission by printed editions" (text). Pointing out the autographs do not exist, he argues that the originals must have been lost early because no second or third-century author mentions them, although there were many motives for appealing to them and passages that are supposed to say that they do are misinterpreted (Hort, p. 4). He says the loss of "intrinsic purity of text from mixture with other text" (conflated readings) "has taken place on a large scale in the New Testament" (Hort, p. 8). Other manuscript problems include the destruction of manuscripts at the beginning of the fourth century, the obsoleteness of form, the use of uncial, and palimpsest. He also says, "In the ordinary course of things, the most recent manuscripts would at all times be the most numerous, and therefore the most generally accessible" (Hort, p. 10).

As far as the printed editions, "In his haste to be the first editor, Erasmus allowed himself to be guilty of strange carelessness" and the numerous editions that came after that were "chiefly of a common late text" (Hort, pp. 11-12). Hort briefly mentions textual criticism. He mentions that: 1. Simon (1689-1695) had a large share in discrediting acquiescence in the accepted text" (Hort, p. 12). He adds that in 1831, with

Lachmann, for the first time, "a text was constructed directly from the ancient documents without the intervention of any printed edition" and that for the first time a "systematic was made to substitute scientific method for arbitrary choice in the discrimination of various readings" (Hort, p. 13). Tischendorf and Tregelles "produce text substantially free from the later corruptions" (Hort, p. 7).

Because of the "untrustworthiness of the 'received' texts,' ... "no other guides than Lachmann's text, and the second of the four widely different texts of Tischendorf," Hort says that they began their work in 1853 (Hort, p. 16). They "privately" gave their work in installments to the members of the revision of the English New Testament and "to a few other scholars." They issued the Gospels in July 1871, Acts in February 1873, the Catholic Epistles in December 1873, the Pauline Epistles in February 1875, and the book of Revelation in December 1876. The complete work was published in 1881 (Hort, p. 18).

Part II: The Methods of Textual Criticism.

Hort lists 1) Internal Evidence of Reading, 2) Internal Evidence of Documents, 3) Genealogical Evidence. Other divisions of Part II are an expansion of one of those three methods [see 4) Internal Evidence of Groups, 5) Recapitulation of Methods in Relation to Each Other, 6) errors and Antecedent to Existing Text, pp. 60-72.]

1. Internal evidence of reading is corruption either caused by the author or the copyist. "Authors are not always grammatical, or clear, or consistent, or felicitous.... Thus, the best words to express

and offer meanings need not, in all cases, be those which he actually employed (Hort, p. 21). "The most obvious causes of corruption are clerical or mechanical, arising from a carelessness of the transcriber" (Hort, p. 24).

2. Internal evidence of documents is "the comparative trustworthiness of the documentary authority.... Knowledge of documents precede final judgment upon readings. The most prominent fact known about a manuscript is its date" (Hort, p. 31). "Specially important loss of homogeneousness occurs whenever the transmission of a writing his been much affected by what we have called the mixture, the irregular combination into a single text of two or more text belonging to different lines of transmission" (Hort, p. 38).

3. Genealogical evidence is "ceasing to treat Documents independently of each other, and examining them connectedly as part of a single whole in virtue of their historical relationships" (Hort, p. 39). Manuscripts are part of a "genealogical tree of transmission" (Hort, p. 40). Hort emphatically states, "ALL TRUSTWORTHY RESTORATION OF CORRUPTED TEXT IS FOUNDED ON THE STUDY OF THEIR HISTORY" (Hort, p. 40, all capitals are his). He explains that if a treatise existed in ten manuscripts and a reading appeared in nine of them versus another reading in only one of them, if the nine were copied from one manuscript, they only count as one "documentary evidence." Thus, the "ten documents resolve themselves virtually into two witnesses" (Hort, p. 41). This "enables us, on the one hand, to detect the late origin and therefore irrelevance of some parts of the *prima facie* documentary evidence" (Hort, p. 43). "It would be

difficult to insist too strongly on the transformation of the superficial aspect of numerical authority" (Hort, p. 43).

"Knowledge of the Genealogical of Documents ... can sometimes be obtained to a certain extent from external sources ... but it is chiefly gained by a study of the text in comparison to each other" (Hort, p. 46; see pp. 60-62). "The clearest evidence for tracing the antecedent factor of the mixture in the text is afforded by readings which are themselves mixed or, as they are sometimes called, 'conflate,' that is, ... [a] combination of the readings of both documents into a complete whole" (Hort, p. 49). "Whenever a text is found in a plurality of documents, there is a strong probability that some of them are descended from a single lost original" (Hort, p. 53). "The preservation of a comparatively small number of documents would probably suffice for the complete restoration of an autograph text" (Hort, p. 57).
Toward the end of Part II, Hort says, "Personal judgment inevitably takes a large part in the final decision," and "personal discernment would seem the surest ground for confidence" (Hort, p. 65).

In Part III, Hort applies the principles of criticism to the text of the New Testament. He describes Greek manuscripts (Hort, pp. 74-78), versions (Hort, pp. 78-86), and fathers (Hort, pp. 87-89). The "four great" Uncials of the fourth and fifth centuries are Vaticanus (B), Sinaiticus (ℵ), Alexandrinus (A), and Ephraemi (C) (Hort, pp. 74-75). The cursives range from the ninth to the sixteenth centuries (Hort, p. 76). The three principal classes of versions are the Latin, the Syriac, and the Egyptian (Hort, p. 78).

"Numerous verses of the New Testament are rarely or never quoted by the Fathers" (Hort, p. 88).

"An overwhelming proportion of the variants common to the great mass of cursive and late uncial Greek MSS are identical with the readings followed by Chrysostom" (ob. 407)" (Hort, p. 91). "The fundamental text of late extant Greek MSS generally is beyond all question identical with the dominant Antiochian or Grieco-Syrian text of the second half of the fourth century" (Hort, p. 92).

For Hort, conflated readings are proof of the lateness of the Syrian text type (versus the Western and neutral text types). He gives eight examples of conflated readings in the New Testament: Mark 6:33, 8:26, 9:38, 9:49; Luke 9:10, 11:54, 12:18, 24:53 (Hort, pp. 95-107). He identifies three text types: Western, Syrian, and Alexandrian (Hort, pp. 108-115). Origen does not exhibit any "clear and tangible traces of the Syrian text" (Hort, p. 114). "The Syrian conflated readings have shown the Syrian text to be posterior to at least two ancient forms of text still extant, one of them being 'Western'" and the Syrian text type is not found in the middle of the third century (Hort, p. 115).

"In themselves, Syrian readings hardly ever offend at first. With rare exceptions, they run smoothly and easily in form, and yield at once to even a careless reader a passable sense, free of surprises and seemingly transparent" (Hort, pp. 115-116).

"It follows that all distinctively Syrian readings may be set aside at once as certainly originating after the middle of the third century, and therefore, as far as transmission is concerned, corruptions of the apostolic text" (Hort, p. 117). "All distinctively Syrian readings must be at once rejected. The variations between the Pre-Syrian text raise much more different questions, which can be answered only by careful examination of the special characteristics of several text" (Hort, p. 119).

At this point, Hort discusses text types (Hort, pp. 120-135).

1. "The chief and most constant characteristic of the Western readings is a love of paraphrase. Words, causes, and even whole sentences were changed, omitted, and inserted with astonishing freedom" (Hort, p. 122). "Another equally important characteristic is the disposition to enrich the text at the cost of its purity by alterations or additions taken from traditional and perhaps from apocryphal or other nonbiblical sources" (Hort, p. 123; for example, see the long interpolation after Matthew 20:28). "Many curious Western interpolations [are] in the Acts, a certain number of which, having been taken up capriciously by the Syrian text, are still current as part of the Received text" (Hort, p. 123). "The Western text generally are due to a corruption the apostolic text" (Hort, p. 127).
2. The neutral text is a pre-Syrian text (Hort, p. 127). "That a purer text should be preserved at Alexandria than in other churches would not in itself be surprising. There, if anywhere, it was to be anticipated that, owing to the proximity of an exact grammatical school, a more than usual watchfulness over the transmission of the writings of apostles and apostolic men would be suggested and alive, but the rapid total extinction of comparatively pure text in all of the places would undeniably be a riddle hard of solution" (Hort, p. 127). Hort later says, that "in remote antiquity, the non-Western text was by no means confined to Alexandria" (Hort, p. 128).

3. On the grounds of Intrinsic and Transcriptural Probability alike, the readings that we call Alexandrian are certainly, as a rule, deprived from the other non-Western Pre-Syrian readings and not *vice versa*. The only documentary authority assisting them with any approach of constancy and capable of being assigned to a definite locality are quotations by Origen, Cyril of Alexandria, and occasionally other Alexandrian Fathers and two principal Egyptian versions, especially that of Lower Egypt" (Hort, pp. 130-131). "Had D of the Gospels and Acts and $D_2E_4F_2G_2$ of the Pauline Epistles all in like manner perish, it would have been in like manner far harder than now to form a clear conception of the Western text, and consequently of early textual history" (Hort, p. 131). "The more startling characteristics of the Western corruption are almost wholly absent from the Alexandrian readings" (Hort, p. 131).

4. "The qualities which the authors of the Syrian text seem to have most desired to impress on it are lucidity and completeness. They were evidently anxious to remove all stumbling blocks out of the way of the ordinary reader, so far as this could be done without recourse to violent measures. They are apparently equally desirous that he should have the benefit of instructive matter contained in all the existing text, provided it did not confuse the context or introduce seeming contradictions. New omissions are rare and, where they occur, are usually found to contribute to the apparent simplicity. New interpolations, on the other hand, are abundant, most of them being due to harmonic or other assimilation, fortunately, capricious and incomplete. Both in manner and in diction, the Syrian text is conspicuously a full text. It delights in

pronouns, conjunctions, and expletives and supplies links of all kinds, as well as in more steerable additions. As distinguished from the bold figure of the 'Western' scribes and refined scholarship of the Alexandrians, the spirit of its own corrections is at once sensible and feeble. Entirely blameless on either literary or religious grounds as regards vulgarised or unworthy diction, yet showing no marks of either critical or spiritual insight, it presents the New Testament in the form smooth and attractive but appreciably impoverished incense and force more fitted for curious for perusal or recitation than for repeated and diligent study" (Hort, p. 135).

5 "The Syrian version, like the Latin version, underwent revision long after its origin, and ... our ordinary Syriac MSS represents not the primitive but the altered Syriac text.... We find large and peculiar coincidences between the revised Syriac text and the text of the Antiochian Fathers of the latter part of the fourth century and strong indication that the revision was deliberate and in some way authorized.... The final process was apparently completed by 350 or thereabouts. At what date, between 250 and 350, the first process took place, it is impossible to say with confidence.... Whether, however, Lusianus [martyred in 312] took a leading part in the earlier stage of Syrian revision or not, it may be assigned with more probability either to his generation or that which immediately followed than to any other" (Hort, pp. 136-137).

Throughout the rest of Part III, Hort makes numerous observations to support his view of the text types. Here are samples of his comments.

"Four great early Bibles [are] ABAC" (Hort, p. 141).

"Before the close of the first century ... a Greek text not materially differing from the authority at Antioch, and exercise much influence elsewhere.... With one memorable exception, that of the Story of the Woman taken in Adultery, there is evidence of but few and unimportant modifications of the Antiochian text by the influence of other ancient text before it became the current text of the East generally." Hort says the two causes of this were 1) "The West became exclusively Latin, as well as estranged from the East" and 2) "the use and knowledge of the Greek language died in Western Europe" (Hort, p. 142).

"The Revised Syriac is the first version to betray clearly the existence of the Greek Syrian revision.... The only versions, besides the Italian and the Vulgate Latin, in which the complete Syrian text is clearly and widely represented are definitely known to be the fourth century or later centuries, that is, the Gothic, Ethiopic, Armenian, and Harklean Syriac." The date of the Jerusalem Syriac is unknown (Hort, p. 159).

"The first point to decide with respect to each reading is whether it is Pre-Syrian or not" and if it is, it is "to be rejected at once as proven to have a relatively late origin" (Hort, p. 163). "B very far exceeds all other documents in the neutrality of text... And a long interval after B, but hardly a less interval before all other MSS, stands A." As for other manuscripts, the ones having the "most Alexandrian readings have usually also [the] most neutral readings" (Hort, p. 171).

"The Syrian text as a whole must, we believe, be condemned by Internal Evidence of Groups almost assuredly is by the evidence connected with the history of text" (Hort, p. 191). "It is our belief (1) that readings of AB should be accepted as the true reading until strong internal evidence is found to the contrary, and (2) that no reading of AB can safely be rejected absolutely, though it is sometimes right to place them only on an alternative footing, especially where they received no support from Versions or Fathers" (Hort, p. 225).

"When therefore a text of late degenerate type, such as the Received Text of the New Testament, consists consciously and unconsciously taken as the standard document belonging to a purer stage of the text must by the nature of the case had the appearance of being guilty of omissions; and the near the document stands to the autographs, the more numerous must be the omissions laid to its charge" (Hort, p. 235).

"So many readings of B by themselves commend themselves on their own merits that it would be harsh to reject any hastily, though undoubtedly not a few have to be rejected" (Hort, p. 238). [Note" "not a few?"] B and A started from "a common source not much later than the autographs" (Hort, p. 247).

"There are many sub-singular readings of B that cannot claim more than a secondary rank of alternative readings which may possibly be genuine, and there are many others that may be safely rejected" (Hort, p. 244). [Note" "many others?"] In A, "the singular readings are very numerous, especially in the Apocalypse, and scarcely ever command themselves on internal grounds" (Hort, pp. 246-247). "There are a few passages where it is difficult to think that either B or A has preserved the reading of the common original. But these coincidences are likely to be only exceptional" (Hort, p. 248).

In the Pauline epistles, there are places where "the Western element of B has displaced its fundamental or neutral element" (Hort, p. 257).

"Taking all kinds of indications together, we are inclined to surmise that B and a were both written in the West, probably at Rome; that the ancestors of B were a wholly Western (in geographical, not textual sentence) up to a very early time in the; and that the ancestors of a were in great part Alexandrian, again in the geographical, not textual sense" (Hort, p.0 267).

There is good reason to believe that true readings have not perished, but there is a textual error in all extant documents (Hort, pp. 276-280, for example, 2 Peter 3:10, where "exposed" rather than "burned up" is the "most original of recorded readings, ... yet itself corrupt"). In a few passages in Matthew, not all the words have apostolic authority (Mt. 12:40 [13:35], 23:35, 27:9 and the second part of 27:49), but in these words, the autograph has been exactly preserved (Hort, p. 282). "There are no signs of deliberate falsification of the text for dogmatic purposes" (Hort, p. 282).

In Part IV, Hort discusses the nature and details of their edition of the Greek text. Hort states that their aim was to "obtain it once the closest possible approximation to the apostolic text itself" (Hort, p. 288). The three classes of readings are omission, insertion, and substitution (Hort, p. 291).

The end of Mark 16 is preserved in five languages. "In style, it is unlike the ordinary narrative of the Evangelist, the comparable to the four introductory verses of St. Luke's gospel.... Whatever may be the cause of the present abrupt termination of the gospel at v. 8, it was intended by the Evangelists to end at this point ... not only the book in the paragraph only but also the last sentence is incomplete" (Hort, pp. 298-299).

Concerning the woman taken in adultery, "no interpolation is more clearly Western, though it is not Western of the earliest type.... Not the slightest allusion to it has been discovered in the whole of Greek theology before the twelfth century. The earliest Greek MSS containing it, except the Western Codex Bezea, are from the eighth century…. In the West, it was well known in the fourth century and doubtless long before. It has no right to a place in the text of the Four Gospels: yet it is evidently from an ancient source…. There is no evidence of its existence in ancient times except in Western text…. The text [they printed] thus obtained is perhaps not sure, but it is at least purer than any which can be found on the basis supplied chiefly by the MSS of the Greek East" (Hort, pp. 299-300).

APPENDIX II: RULES OF TEXTUAL CRITICISM

Textual critics operate on a set of rules that function as their presuppositions. Aland lists 12 basic rules (Aland, pp. 280-281). Here is a summary of his rules with my observations in brackets.

1. Only one reading can be original.
2. Only the reading that best satisfies the external and internal criteria requirements can be the original. [Yes, but the next principal will say that the external evidence is more important.]
3. Criticism of the text must always begin from the evidence of the manuscript tradition [external evidence] and only afterward consider internal criteria. [His practice indicates that if the external evidence is ℵ and/or B, the external evidence determines the correct reading. See his comments at the end of this list of his rules.]
4. Internal criteria (the context of the passage, its style and vocabulary, the theological environment of the author, etc.) can never be the sole basis for critical decisions, especially in opposition to external. [His practice indicates that he has predetermined that the external evidence of ℵ and/or B determines the correct reading. See his comments at the end of this list of his principles.]
5. The primary authority for a critical text decision lies with the Greek manuscript tradition [external evidence of ℵ and/or B], with the

versions of the Fathers serving no more than a supplementary and collaborative function, particularly in passages where underlying Greek text cannot be reconstructed with absolute certainty.

6. Furthermore, manuscripts should be weighed and not counted, and the particular traits of each manuscript should be duly considered. However important early papyri, or a particular uncial or minuscule, maybe, no single manuscript or group of manuscripts can be followed mechanically, even though certain combinations of witnesses deserve greater consideration than others. Instead, decisions in textual criticism must be worked out fresh, passage by passage (the local principle). [This principle establishes that the Byzantine text type is secondary, and the "traits" of ℵ and/or B automatically make them primary.]

7. The principle that the original reading may be found in a singular manuscript version when it stands alone or nearly alone is only a theoretical possibility. Any form of eclecticism that accepts this principle hardly succeeds in establishing the original text of the New Testament; it will only confirm the view of the text that it presupposes. [But in practice, he allows ℵ and/or B to be the determining factor even when they are alone.]

8. The construction of a stemma of readings for each variant (the genealogical principle) is an extremely important device because the reading that can most easily explain the deviation of the other forms is itself most likely the original.

9. Variants must never be treated in isolation but always considered in the context of the tradition. Otherwise, there is too great a danger of reconstructing a "test tube text" which never existed in time or

place. [In other words, "tradition," i.e., the external evidence of ℵ and/or B is primary.]

10. There is truth in the maxim: "The more difficult reading is the more probable reading." However, this principle must not be taken mechanically, with the most difficult reading adapted as its original simply because of its difficulty.

11. The venerable maxim: "The shorter reading is the most probable reading," is certainly right in many instances. But here again, the principle cannot be applied mechanically. It is not valid for witnesses whose text is otherwise very significantly from the characteristic pattern of the textual tradition, with frequent omissions or expansions reflecting editorial tendencies (e.g., D).

12. A constantly maintaining familiarity with the New Testament manuscripts themselves is the best training to protect from criticism. In textual criticism, theoreticians often do more harm than good.

Then Aland makes statements like this: Some things are inserted into the text "under the influence of the Koine or Byzantine Imperial text." In other words, he and virtually all other textual critics presuppose that the Byzantine text type is secondary. Aland also says that Bible readers "should not insist on keeping as part of the New Testament the readings which scholars have long recognized as late additions to the text" (Aland, p. 306). As is evident from his illustrations, Aland presupposes that ℵ and/or B are "primary" (his word for "superior") and the Byzantine text type is "secondary" (his word for "inferior) and, therefore, only rarely to be accepted as the correct reading.

Matthew 5:44 reads, "But I say to you, love your enemies, bless those who curse you, do good to those who hate you, and pray for those who spitefully use you and persecute you" With slight variations (see the treatment of this verse in the chapter "What Difference Does It Make?"), "bless those who curse you, do good to those who hate you) is in 91.2%, W, HF, RP, and NKJV. // ℵ, B, NU, NASB, NIV, ESV omit it.

Aland says, "This is nothing more than an adaptation from the parallel text of Luke 6:27-28. Variety of forms in which this occurs in the manuscript tradition only underscores the secondary character of the expansion is undoubtedly made for a more edifying tax, but it is not in the original Gospel of Matthew. Admittedly, the section of Greek manuscripts preserving the original text is not very large (ℵ, B, f¹, and a few others), but representatives of all the early versions support them. As in the ending of Mark and frequently elsewhere as well, the expanded text is more impressive and 'better' than the original form, and few manuscripts have been able to withstand the momentum. Furthermore, the conclusive argument here (as in so many similar instances) is that if the expanded form were actually the original text, what would have been the motive for altering it? Accidental omission is hardly a possible cause (although a scribe could certainly have omitted a phrase by sheer chance, as described above, and his manuscript could have been copied by other scribes because the shorter text is found in all parts of the early church. Further, an important point for all similar examples is the variety of forms the expansion assumes, which is an irrefutable argument for its secondary character" (Aland, p. 306). Notice Aland makes his decision based on ℵ and B. Everything else he says is a presupposition.

APPENDIX III: SINAITICUS AND VATICANUS

This appendix lists some of the mistakes in Sinaiticus and Vaticanus. Underlying New Testament references indicate that either Vaticanus, Sinaiticus, or both are demonstrably defective in that verse. For a detailed explanation of the ones in this appendix, see Chapter 11. Many more could be added to this list.

Matthew 1:7 says, "Abijah begot Asa," but ℵ and B say, "Asaph. Asa was from the tribe of Judah. Asaph was from the tribe of Levi.

Matthew 1:8 says, "Asa begot Jehoshaphat." ℵ and B say, "Asaph."

Matthew 1:10 says, "Manasseh begot Amon." ℵ and B say, "Amos."

Textual critics say these are examples of nothing more than misspelled words. Pickering says, "Not counting Asa and Amon (see v. 10), Codex B misspells 13 names in this chapter; Aleph misspells 10" (Pickering p. 323).

Matthew 5:22 says, "Whoever is angry with his brother without a cause shall be in danger of the judgment." ℵ and B do not have "without a cause." If the omission is correct, Jesus says it is always wrong to get angry. If that is true, Jesus was a sinner (Mk. 3:5), and Paul contradicted Jesus (Eph. 4:26). On the other hand, if the inclusion is correct, there is a "righteous indignation."

Matthew 6:13b says, "For Yours is the kingdom and the power and the glory forever. Amen." The doxology at the end of the Lord's Prayer is not found in ℵ or B, but it is present in Luke, the Didache —a document many believe was written before AD 100 —and in translations of the New Testament, which were much earlier than the fourth century. Without the doxology, the prayer concludes with the words "evil" or "evil one," which seems odd, especially in light of the fact that it is traditional to end a Jewish prayer with praise to God (Farstad, p. 115). Farstad asks, "Since most manuscripts do contain the ending, isn't it easier for Christians to believe that some manuscripts dropped off the ending simply by careless copying?" (Farstad, pp. 115-117).

Matthew 13:35 says, "This was to fulfill what was spoken by the prophet." Instead of "prophet." ℵ^a has Isaiah. (ℵ^a means the reading of the original scribe.) This verse quotes Psalm 78:2, which Asaph, not Isaiah, wrote. "This is a manifest error" (Adam Clarke).

Matthew 19:17 says, "So He said to him, 'Why do you call Me good? No one *is* good but One, *that is,* God," but ℵ and B have "Why do you ask me about the good? One is good." Pickering explains, "The church in Egypt during the second century was dominated by Gnosticism. That such a 'nice' Gnostic variant came into being is no surprise, but why do modern editors embrace it? Because it is the 'more obscure' one (Metzger, p. 49)" (Pickering, p. 322).

Mark 1:1 says, "The beginning of the gospel of Jesus Christ, the Son of God. υιου του θεου (the Son of God) is in 98.4%, A, TR, HF, RP. KJV, NKJV, NASB, NIV, ESV // υιου θεου (Son of God) is in B, D, W (.4%). The phrase is not in ℵ (.8%). WH" [υιου θεου]. NIV: [some manuscripts do not have *the* Son of God]. ESV: [some manuscripts omit *the* Son of God]. Burgon points out, "Irenaeus (AD 170) unquestionably read υιου του θεου in this place. He devotes a chapter of his great work to the proof that Jesus is the Christ, very God, and very man" (Burgon, p. 279; cited by Fuller, p. 78).

Mark 1:2 says, "As it is written in the Prophets," but ℵ and B have "in Isaiah the prophet." In this verse, Mark quotes two prophets. The first quote is from Malachi (Mal. 3:1). The second quote is from Isaiah (Isa. 41:3). "Written in Isaiah the prophet is a factual error. Did the Holy Spirit inspire that?

Mark 6:22 says, "when Herodias' daughter herself came in," but ℵ and B read [his (daughter) Herodias]. Matthew 14:6 states that the girl was the daughter of Herodias, who had been the wife of Philip, Herod's brother, but was now living with Herod. In other words, she was not Herod's daughter. She was his stepdaughter, but ℵ and B make her Herod's daughter.

Mark 16:9-20 ℵ and B do not have these verses. Pickering gives the manuscript evidence for this passage. "It is contained in every extant Greek MS (about 1700) except three (really only two, B and 304—Aleph is not properly extant because it is a forgery at this point). [In a footnote, Pickering points out, "Tischendorf ... warned that the folded sheets containing the end of Mark and beginning of Luke appeared to be written by a different hand with different ink than the rest of the manuscript."] Every extant Greek lectionary (about 2000?) contains them (one of them, 185, doing so only in the Menologian). Every extant Syriac MS except one (Sinaitic) contains them. Every extant of the Latin MS (8000?) except one (k) contains them. Every extant Coptic MS except one contains them" (Pickering, pp. 327-328). In Vaticanus, there is a blank space for it, the only blank space in the whole manuscript!

If the Gospel of Mark ends with Mark 16:8, it ends with the Greek word *gar* (for), which would be abrupt and abnormal. "To end a book on this word seems most unlikely" (Farstad, p. 113). It is usually the second word in the sentence. Metzger says, "To terminate a Greek sentence with the word **gar** is most unusual and exceedingly rare—only a relative few examples have been found in all of the vast range of Greek literary works, and no instances have been found where **gar** stands at the end of the book. Moreover, it is possible that in verse 8, Mark uses the verb εφοβουντο to mean 'they were afraid of'(as he does in four of the other occurrences of this verb in his gospel). In that case, obviously, something is needed to finish the sentence" (Metzger, p. 228). Even Hort, who believes the book ends with verse 8, observes that it ends with "singular abruptness," adding that the sentence is not even complete.

Taylor says that Lightfoot cites examples of sentences ending with "for," but none of them stand at the end of a book. He points out that there is no parallel in the conclusion of any Markan periscope, John, Jewish, or Hellenistic literature. He adds, "It is incredible that Mark intended such a conclusion." Cole says ending Mark in verse 8 is abrupt linguistically and theologically. If Mark ends with Mark 16:8, it ends with the disciples being afraid (16:8). Can you imagine Mark doing that?

In his commentary on Mark, Hort says, "It cannot have been meant to conclude thus" either some accident may have prevented its completion, or a leaf of the original copy may have been lost." Alexander, the famous Princeton Theological Seminary professor of the 19th century, said that to suppose that Mark ends with verse 8 is "folly."

Luke 1:26 says Nazareth is a city of Galilee, which is true; א says Nazareth is "a city of Judea," which is factually wrong.

Luke 3:33 says, "The son of Amminadab, *the son* of Ram." ℵ and B read, "The son of Amminadab, the son of Admin, the son of Arni." Pickering explains, "The fictitious Admin and Arni are introduced into Christ genealogy" (p. 321), an egregious error" (p. 322).

Luke 2:33 says, "and Joseph and his mother marveled at these things which were spoken of him." (ℵ) and B read, "his father and the mother." A. T. Robinson wrote, "Luke had already used 'parents' in Luke 2:27. He by no means intends to deny the Virgin Birth of Jesus so plainly stated in Luke 1:34-38. He merely employs here the language of ordinary custom." MacDonald, however, says, "Luke carefully guards the doctrine of the Virgin Birth with his precisely worded **Joseph and His mother,** as read by the King James tradition, following the majority of manuscripts" (MacDonald, bold type his).

Luke 4:44 says, "And He was preaching in the synagogues of Galilee," but ℵ and B read "Judea" instead of Galilee. The parallel passages in Matthew 4:23 and Mark 1:39 say that Jesus was preaching in Galilee. Therefore, the reading in the Luke variant that says He was preaching in Judea is a geographical mistake. Pickering calls this "an error of fact" (p. 319).

Luke 9:10 says, "And the apostles, when they had returned, told Him all that they had done. Then He took them and went aside privately into a deserted place belonging to the city called Bethsaida." κατ ιδιαν (private) εις τοπον (place) ερημμον (desert) πολεως (city) καλουμμενης (called) βηθσαιδα is in [94%], C, N, W, TR, HF, RP // ερημον (desert place) is in ℵ. B, $\mathfrak{P}^{75}$, NU omit ερημον (desert place). Pickering says, "NU has Jesus and company going to Bethsaida, but in verse 12, the disciples say that they are in a deserted area; thus, a contradiction is introduced. NU here is also at variance with NU in parallel passages" (Pickering, p. 325).

Luke 23:45 "Then the sun was darkened, and the veil of the temple was torn in two." εσκοτισθη (darkened) is in 98.6%, A, D, Q, W, TR, HF, RP, f^{35} // εκλιποντος (eclipse) is in ℵ, C, 𝔓^{75}, NU; NASB: "was obscure;" NIV: "stopped;" ESV: "light failed." εκλειποντος is in B. Jesus was crucified during the Passover and the Passover is always at a full moon. Therefore, "eclipse" is a "scientific error" (Pickering, p. 319).

John 6:11 says, "He distributed *them* to the disciples, and the disciples to those sitting down." These words are omitted in ℵ and B. The parallel passages, Matthew 14:19, Mark 6:41, and Luke 9:16, say Jesus handed the bread to the disciples, who distributed it to the people, but omitting that in John makes Jesus distribute the bread to the people.

John 7:8 says, "I am not yet going up to this feast," but ℵ does not have "yet." Two verses later (Jn. 7:10), Jesus goes to Jerusalem. So, He knew in verse 8 that He was going to go. Therefore, the reading, "I am not yet going," is correct, and the variant, "I am not going," is incorrect and puts a lie in the mouth of Jesus.

John 7:53-8:11 These verses are in the vast majority of manuscripts, over a thousand manuscripts of the Gospel of John (Farstad, p. 113), but they are omitted in ℵ and B. Augustine wrote that these verses were omitted for fear it would promote immorality (Farstad, p. 113). If John 7 stops at verse 52, the text of John reads, "They answered and said to him, 'Are you also from Galilee? Search and look, for no prophet has arisen out of Galilee'" (Jn. 7:52). "Then Jesus spoke to them again, saying, 'I am the light of the world. He who follows Me shall not walk in darkness, but have the light of life'" (Jn. 8:12). Such a construction of the text has Jesus addressing the meeting of Nicodemus and the Sanhedrin, but Jesus was not in that meeting! (Farstad, p. 114).

John 10:29 says, "The Father who has given them to me is greater than all." Instead of "who," ℵ and B have "which." Godet declares that "which" indicates "God is a thing."

Acts 19:16 says, "Then the man in whom the evil spirit was leaped on them, overpowered them, and prevailed against them so that they fled out of that house naked and wounded." Instead of them, ℵ and B have "both of them," but "The sons of Sceva were seven, not two.

Romans 5:1 says, "Therefore, having been justified by faith, we have peace with God through our Lord Jesus Christ." Instead of "we have peace," ℵ and B have "let us have peace." *The Bible for Schools and Colleges* says, "'We have' exactly *fits the context; 'let us have' is foreign to it.* The whole context is one not of exhortation but of dogmatic assertion—'we have access;' 'we rejoice;' 'the love of God has been poured out into our hearts;' 'we shall be saved;' 'we are reconciled;' 'we have received the reconciliation'" (italics his).

Romans 8:1 says, "Who walk not after the flesh, but after the Spirit," but is not in ℵ and B. Without this last phrase, Romans 8:1 is taken to refer to justification, but the context of Romans 6-8 is sanctification. See the full explanation of this verse in Chapter 11.

1 Corinthians 5:1 says, "Such sexual immorality as is not even named among the Gentiles—that a man has his father's wife!" The word "named" is omitted in ℵ and B, which makes the verse mean this type of incest does not even exist among the Gentile, "a plain falsehood" (Pickering, p. 320).

1 Corinthians 15:51 says, "Behold, I tell you a mystery: we shall not all sleep, but we shall all be changed." Instead of "we shall all be changed," which is in B, ℵ says, we shall *not* all be changed, which is not true

1 Thessalonians 2:7 says, "But we were gentle among you, just as a nursing mother cherishes her own children." Instead of "we were gentle among you," ℵ and B have "we were babes," which is obviously incorrect.

1 Timothy 3:16 says, "Great is the mystery of godliness: God was manifest in the flesh." Instead of "God," ℵ has "which" and D has "who." "Which" is grammatically incorrect because this pronoun has no antecedent. "Who" is nonsensical" (Pickering, p. 330). It is also grammatically incorrect because "who" is masculine and "mystery" is neuter.

2 Peter 3:10 says, "Both the earth and the works that are in it will be burned up." Instead of "burn up," ℵ and B have "be found," which is "nonsensical" (Pickering, p. 331).

Jude 14-15 "Now Enoch, the seventh from Adam, prophesied about these men also, saying, 'Behold, the Lord comes with ten thousands of His saints, to execute judgment on all, to convict all who are ungodly among them of all their ungodly deeds which they have committed in an ungodly way, and of all the harsh things which ungodly sinners have spoken against Him." Instead of "all who are ungodly," which is in B, ℵ as "all souls." Jude is talking about the judgment of infiltrators (verses 4, 5, 6, 7, 11, 13). In verse 14, he introduces a prophecy about "these men." Therefore, verse 15 talks about those who are ungodly, not all souls.

Summary: ℵ and B contain many mistakes, some factual inaccuracies.

APPENDIX IV: PAPYRUS

A papyrus manuscript was written on papyrus (see "papyrus" in Job 8:11). Papyri manuscripts are named using the Gothic letter 𝔓 followed by a number, for example, $𝔓^{66}$. As of 2021, about 140 papyrus manuscripts have been found.

Collections

The Chester Beatty papyri are named after the man who purchased them from an Egyptian dealer in the 1930s.

$𝔓^{45}$ contains 30 fragmentary leaves, two small leaves of Matthew 20-21, 25-26, a portion of Mark 4-9, 11-12, portions Luke 6-7, 9-14, portions John 4-5, 10-11, and a portion of Acts 4-17. The Gospels are in the Western order: Matthew, John, Luke, Mark, and Acts. These fragments are from the first half of the 3rd century.

$𝔓^{46}$ contains Romans 5–6, 8-15, all of Hebrews, Ephesians, Galatians, Philippians, Colossians, virtually all of 1–2 Corinthians and 1 Thessalonians 1–2, 5. P_{47} contains Revelation 9-17 and is dated to the 3rd century. The order of Hebrews after Romans and Galatians after Ephesians is unique. These date to *ca.* AD 200.

$𝔓^{47}$ contains Revelation 9-17 and is dated to the 3rd century.

While there are other text type readings in these papyri, there are also 26 Byzantine readings in the Gospels, eight in Acts, and 31 in

301

Paul's epistles. Some scholars have argued that these are Caesarea in readings, but that is not true in Acts or Paul's epistles.

The Bodmer papyri is named after the man who purchased them in Egypt in 1952.

𝔓⁶⁶ contains John 1:1–6:11, 6:35b–14:26, 29–30; 15:2–26; 16:2–4, 6–7; 16:10–20:20, 22–23; 20:25–21:9, 12, 17. First, it was dated around A. D. 200, but Hunger claimed the handwriting should be dated earlier (early or middle second century). Nongbri argued that the format, construction techniques, and provenance (origin) of the codex, along with the handwriting, indicates it was produced "in the early or middle part of the fourth century" (https://en.wikipedia.org/wiki/Papyrus_66). It contains the Alexandrian text type. "In John's Gospel, it has over 900 indisputable errors" (Pickering adds that the scribe did not know Greek, p. 155).

𝔓⁵² is the oldest copy of the Gospel of John. It omits John 5:3b-4 and 7:53-8:11.

𝔓⁷² is the earliest known copy of Jude, 1 and 2 Peter.

𝔓⁷⁵ is a partial codex containing most of Luke and John.

Individual Manuscripts

𝔓⁴⁵ contains two small leaves of Matthew 20-21, 25-26, portions of Mark 4-9, 11-12, portions of Luke 6-7, 9-14, portions of John 4-5, 10-11, and a portion of Acts 4-17. These fragments are from the first half of the 3rd century. It is the oldest manuscript of Mark (*ca.*

AD 200). The doxology is at the end of Romans 15, not Romans 14.

𝔓⁴⁶ contains Romans 5–6, 8-15, all of Hebrews, Ephesians, Galatians, Philippians, Colossians, virtually all of 1–2 Corinthians and 1 Thessalonians 1–2, 5. It is the oldest manuscript of Paul's letters (*ca.* AD 200).

𝔓⁴⁷ contains Revelation 9-17, which is the oldest manuscript of Revelation (3rd century).

𝔓⁵² contains John 18:31-33, 18:37-38, dated AD 90-150 (Wallace, speech). It is the size of a credit card and is the earliest extant Greek manuscript.

𝔓⁶⁶ contains a large portion of the Gospel of John, dated about AD 200.

𝔓⁷² contains the earliest known copy of Jude, 1 and 2 Peter.

𝔓⁷⁵ contains most of Luke and John and a partial codex of Acts

Byzantine Readings

Sturz lists some Byzantine readings (Sturz, pp. 57-58).

𝔓⁴⁵ has a Byzantine reading at Mark 7:31.

𝔓⁴⁵ has a Byzantine reading at Luke 10:42. (A.D. 240, Burkitt, cited by Sturz, p. 57).

𝔓⁴⁵ has a Byzantine reading at John 11:19.

𝔓⁴⁶ has Byzantine readings.

Corrections

Sturz points out that among the papyri, there are corrections from a Byzantine text type to an Alexandrian text type (Sturz, pp. 63-64).

$\mathfrak{P}^{66}$ has a correction in John 7:39 from Byzantine to Alexandrian.

$\mathfrak{P}^{66}$ has a correction in John 7:40 and 8:54 from Byzantine to Alexandrian and Western.

$\mathfrak{P}^{66}$ has a correction in John 12:9 from Byzantine to a single reading or one very lightly attested.

$\mathfrak{P}^{46}$ has a correction in Ephesians 2:12 from Byzantine to a Western form.

$\mathfrak{P}^{46}$ has a correction in Hebrews 12:25 from Byzantine to an Alexandrian form.

$\mathfrak{P}^{13a}$ has a distinctively Byzantine reading in Hebrews 11:4.

$\mathfrak{P}^{46}$ has a distinctively Byzantine reading in Hebrews 11:4.

$\mathfrak{P}^{13c}$ has a reading from a distinctively Byzantine reading to one by Clement of Alexandria.

$\mathfrak{P}^{66}$ has a correction in John 8:21 and 19:4 from Western to Byzantine.

$\mathfrak{P}^{66}$ has a correction in John 19:11 away from the singular or lightly supported reading of the Byzantine.

For an article on the earliest New Testament manuscripts, see correctionshttps://biblearchaeologyreport.com/2019/02/15/the-earliest-new-testament-manuscripts/.

APPENDIX V: TR AND MT DIFFERENCES

If the Textus Receptus (TR) and the Majority Text (MT) are both within the same text type of Greek manuscripts of the New Testament, what is the differences between the two? Wallace counts 1838 differences between the TR and MT (see Wallace's "The Majority Text Theory" History, Methods, and Critique," in Ehrman & Holmes, *The Text of the New Testament in Contemporary Research*, Studies & Documents, Eerdmans, 1995. See note 28 on p. 302.) In a conversation with Hodges, when I asked him what was the most significant difference, he said "holy, holy, holy" in Revelation was nine "holys" instead of three.

Differences Between the MT and the TR

Luke Wayne writes, "While it would be impossible to give an exhaustive list of all the differences between the M-Text and TR, it is worth noting just a few of the more important variants and a sample list of some examples representing the different *kinds* of variants that occur, both significant and trivial." He then discusses in some detail 1 John 5:7, Revelation 22:19, Acts 9:5-6, and "some other sample readings" ("Bethsphage" versus "Bethphage").

Then Wayne says, "The following list is not given to say that the Majority Text is always right in these readings and the TR always wrong. It is given only to help demonstrate that the TR is not *the same thing* as the Majority Text and, thus, Majority Text arguments do not, in fact, favor the KJV. This list is *far* from exhaustive but is representative of many of the various types of differences that occur. It also helps to show how often, on the one hand, the M-Text and the NU agree against the TR and, on the other hand, how often the TR actually agrees with the NU (and thus with modern translations) in favoring a minority reading over against the Majority Text. It should also be noted that all three of these texts agree far more often than they disagree and that the vast majority of the New Testament will read exactly the same way no matter which text you end up siding with" (Wayne, italics his).

Wayne also says, "One should always note that most of the differences between the TR and the M-Text (as with most differences between *any* manuscripts) are inconsequential and often can't even be translated. Even among those that *can* be translated, most are simple matters of word order (like 'Christ Jesus' versus 'Jesus Christ') or mere spelling conventions, often of names ('Bethsphage' versus "Bethphage' or 'Barsabbas' versus 'Barsabas'). Many others, though they do effect the *wording* of the translation, have a little effect on the *meaning*" (Wayne, italics, see his entire article at https://carm.org/king-james-onlyism/differences-between-the-majority-text-and-the-textus-receptus/).

Matthew 3:11 M-Text omits "and fire."

Matthew 4:10 M-Text "Get behind me!" instead of "Away with you!"

Matthew 5:47 M-Text "Friends" instead of "Brethren."

Matthew 6:18 M-Text and NU both omit "openly."

Matthew 7:14 M-text and NU both read "How narrow" instead of "Because narrow."

Matthew 8:15 M-text and NU both read "him" rather than "them."

Matthew 9:36 M-text and NU both read "harassed/distressed" rather than "weary."

Matthew 10:8 M-text omits "raise the dead."

Matthew 10:25 M-text and NU both read "beelzabul" rather than "Beelzebub."

Matthew 12:5 M-text and NU both omit "even."

Matthew 12:24 M-text and NU both read "beelzabul" rather than "beelsebub."

Matthew 13:15 M-text and NU both read "would" rather than "should."

Matthew 18:19 M-text and NU read "assuredly I say" instead of just "I say."

Matthew 21:1 M-text reads "bethsphage" rather than "Bethphage."

Matthew 23:21 M-text reads "dwelt" rather than "dwells."

Matthew 23:25 M-text reads "unrighteousness" rather than "self-indulgence."

Matthew 25:44 M-text and NU both omit "him."

Matthew 26:26 M-text reads "gave thanks for" rather than "blessed."

Matthew 26:52 M-text reads "die" rather than "perish."

Matthew 27:35 M-text and NU both lack "that it might be fulfilled which was spoken by the prophet" 'They divided My garments among them, And for My clothing they cast lots.'"

Matthew 27:41 M-text says "the Pharisees" between "the scribes" and "the elders."

Matthew 27:42 M-text and NU both read "believe in Him" rather than "believe Him."

Matthew 28:19 M-text lacks "therefore" (# 23).

Mark 4:4 M-text and NU both lack "of the air."

Mark 4:9 M-text and NU both lack "to them."

Mark 6:15 M-text and NU both read "a prophet, like one of the prophets" rather than "the Prophet, or like one of the prophets."

Mark 6:33 M-text and NU both read "they" instead of "the multitudes."

Mark 6:44 M-text and NU both lack "about."

Mark 8:14 M-text and NU both read "they" instead of "the disciples."

Mark 9:40 M-text reads "you" and "your" rather than "us" and "our."

Mark 11:1 M-text reads "Bethsphage" rather than "Bethphage."

Mark 11:4 M-text and NU both read "a colt" rather than "the colt."

Mark 13:9 M-text and NU both read "stand" rather than "be brought."

Mark 15:32 M-text reads "believe Him" rather than just "believe."

Mark 16:8 M-text and NU both lack "quickly" (#35).

Luke 3:2 M-text and NU both read "in the high priesthood of Annas and Caiaphas." rather than "while Annas and Caiaphas were high priests."

Luke 4:8 M-text and NU both lack "for."

Luke 6:9 M-text reads "to kill" rather than "to destroy."

Luke 6:10 M-text and NU both read "him" rather than "the man."

Luke 6:26 M-text and NU both lack "to you," M-text also lacks "all."

Luke 7:31 M-text and NU both lack "and the Lord said."

Luke 8:3 M-text and NU both read "them" rather than "Him."

Luke 9:23 M-text lacks "daily."

Luke 10:12 M-text and NU both lack "but."

Luke 10:20 M-text and NU both lack "rather."

Luke 10:22 M-text reads, "and turning to His disciples He said" before "All things have been delivered..."

Luke 11:15 M-text and NU both read "Beelzebul" rather than "Beelzebub."

Luke 13:15 M-text and NU both read "hypocrites" rather than "hypocrite."

Luke 13:35 M-text and NU both lack "assuredly."

Luke 14:5 M-text and NU both read "son" rather than "donkey."

Luke 14:15 M-text reads "dinner" rather than "bread."

Luke 17:4 M-text lacks "to you."

Luke 17:9 M-text lacks "Him" while NU lacks "Him? I think not."

Luke 17:36 M-text and NU both lack this entire verse.

Luke 19:29 M-text reads "Bethsphage" rather than "Bethphage."

Luke 20:5 M-text and NU both lack "then."

Luke 20:19 M-text reads "were afraid" rather than "feared the people."

Luke 20:31 M-text and NU both read "also left no children" rather than "also; and they left no children."

Luke 22:50 M-text and NU both read "a rooster" rather than "the rooster."

Luke 23:25 M-text and NU both lack "to them" (#60).

John 1:28 M-text and NU both read "Bethany" rather than "Bethabara."

John 2:17 M-text and NU both read "will eat" rather than "has eaten."

John 2:22 M-text and NU both lack "to them."

John 6:45 M--text reads "hears and had learned" rather than "has heard and learned."

John 7:16 M-text and NU both read "So Jesus" rather than just "Jesus."

John 7:29 M-text and NU both lack "but."

John 7:33 M-text and NU both lack "to them."

John 8:2 M-text reads "very early" rather than just "early."

John 8:4 M-text reads "we found this woman" rather than "this woman was caught."

John 8:5 M-text and NU both read "to stone such" rather than "that such should be stoned." M-text also reads, "In our law, Moses commanded" rather than "Moses, in the law, commanded," and "What do you say about her?" rather than just "What do you say?"

John 8:5 M-text and NU both lack "as though he did not hear."

John 8:7 M-text reads "He looked up" rather than "He raised Himself up."

John 8:9 M-text and NU both lack "being convicted by their conscience."

John 8:10 M-text reads, "He saw her and said" rather than "and saw no one but the woman, He said" (the NU lacks this clause entirely), M-text and NU both lack "of yours" after "accusers."

John 8:11 M-text and NU both read "go, and from now on sin no more" rather than just "go and sin no more."

John 8:54 M-text and NU both read "our" instead of "your."

John 10:8 M-text lacks "before me."

John 13:25 M-text and NU both read "thus back" rather than just "back."

John 16:3 M-text and NU both lack "to you."

John 16:15 M-text and NU both read "takes of Mine and will declare" rather than "will take of mine and declare."

John 16:33 M-text and NU both read "you have tribulation" rather than "you will have tribulation."

John 17:2 M-text reads "shall give eternal life" rather than "should give eternal life."

John 17:11 M-text and NU both read "keep them through Your name which You have given me" rather than "keep through Your name those whom you have given me."

John 17:20 M-text and NU both read "those who believe" rather than "those who will believe."

John 18:15 M-text reads "the other" rather than "another."

John 19:28 M-text reads "seeing" rather than "knowing."

John 20:29 M-text and NU both lack "Thomas" (#87).

Acts 3:20 M-text and NU both read "Christ Jesus" rather than "Jesus Christ" and "ordained for you before" rather than "preached to you before."

Acts 5:23 M-text and NU both lack "outside."

Acts 5:25 M-text and NU both lack "saying."

Acts 5:41 M-text reads "the name of Jesus" rather than "His name" (NU reads "the name").

Acts 7:37 M-text and NU both lack "Him you shall hear."

Acts 8:37 M-text and NU both lack this entire verse.

Acts 9:5-6 M-text and NU both lack "'it is hard for you to kick against the goads.' So he, trembling and astonished, said, 'Lord, what do You want me to do?' Then the Lord said to him.'"

Acts 9:17 M-text lacks "Jesus."

Acts 10:5 M-text and NU both lack "He will tell you what you must do."

Acts 10:21 M-text and NU both lack "who had been sent to him from Cornelius."

Acts 10:39 M-text and NU both read "they also" rather than just "they."

Acts 12:25 M-text and NU both read "to Jerusalem" rather than "From Jerusalem."

Acts 13:17 M-text lacks "Israel."

Acts 13:23 M-text reads "salvation" rather than "a Savior—Jesus."

Acts 15:11 M-text and NU both lack "Christ."

Acts 15:22 M-text and NU both read "Barsabbas" rather than "Barsabas."

Acts 15:34 M-text and NU both lack this entire verse.

Acts 17:5 M-text lacks "becoming envious."

Acts 17:18 M-text and NU both read "Also" rather than "then."

Acts 19:16 M-text reads "and they overpowered them" rather than just "overpowered them."

Acts 20:8 M-text and NU both read "we" rather than "they."

Acts 20:28 M-text reads "of the Lord and God" rather than "of God."

Acts 20:34 M-text and NU both lack "Yes."

Acts 21:29 M-text omits "previously."

Acts 24:9 M-text and NU both read "joined the attack" rather than "assented."

Acts 24:20 M-text and NU both read "what wrongdoing they found" rather than "if they found any wrongdoing."

Acts 26:17 M-text and NU lack "now."

Acts 27:17 M-text reads "Syrtes" rather than "Syrtis" (#115).

M-text places Romans 16:25-27 between Romans 14:23 and 15:1.

Romans 15:7 M-text and NU both read "you" rather than "us."

Romans 15:14 M-text reads "others" rather than "one another."

Romans 16:18 M-text and NU both lack "Jesus."

1 Corinthians 11:15 M-text lacks "her."

1 Corinthians 11:27 M-text and NU read "the blood" rather than just "blood."

1 Corinthians 12:2 M-text and NU both read "that when you were" rather than just "that you were."

1 Corinthians 15:39 M-text and NU both lack "of flesh."

1 Corinthians 15:49 M-text reads "let us also bear" rather than "we shall also bear."

2 Corinthians 1:11 M-text reads "your behalf" rather than "our behalf."

2 Corinthians 2:17 M-text reads "the rest" rather than "so many."

2 Corinthians 8:4 M-text and NU both read "urgency for the favor and fellowship" rather than "urgency that we would receive the gift and the fellowship."

2 Corinthians 8:24 M-text and NU lack "and."

Galatians 4:24 M-text and NU both read "two covenants" rather than "the two covenants."

Ephesians 1:10 M-text and NU both lack "both."

Ephesians 1:18 M-text and NU read "hearts" rather than "understanding."

Ephesians 3:9 M-text and NU both read "stewardship" rather than "fellowship."

Ephesians 4:5 M-text reads "us" rather than "you" (NU has no pronoun here).

Philippians 1:23 M-text and NU both read "but" rather than "for."

Philippians 3:3 M-text and NU both read "in the spirit of God" rather than "God in Spirit".

Philippians 4:3 M-text and NU both read "Yes" rather than "and"

Colossians 1:5 M-text and NU both read "bringing forth fruit and growing" rather than just "bringing forth fruit."

Colossians 1:14 M-text and NU both lack "through His blood."

Colossians 1:27 M-text reads "who" rather than "which."

Colossians 2:20 M-text and NU both lack "therefore."

1 Thessalonians 2:2 M-text and NU both lack "even."

1 Thessalonians 2:11 M-text and NU read "implored" rather than "charged."

2 Thessalonians 1:10 M-text and NU read "have believed" rather than "believ.e"

2 Thessalonians 3:5 M-text and NU both read "they" rather than "he."

1 Timothy 5:4 M-text and NU both lack "good and."

1 Timothy 6:5 M-text and NU both read "constant friction" rather than "useless wrangling."

2 Timothy 1:1 M-text and NU both read "Christ Jesus" rather than "Jesus Christ."

2 Timothy 1:18 M-text and NU both lack "unto me."

2 Timothy 2:19 M-text and NU both read "the Lord" rather than "Christ."

Titus 2:8 M-text and NU both read "us" rather than "you" (150).

Philemon 6 M-text and NU read "us" rather than "you."

Philemon 7 M-text reads "thanksgiving" rather than "joy."

Hebrews 2:7 M-text and NU both lack "And set him over the works of Your hands."

Hebrews 4:2 M-text and NU both read "since they were not united by faith with those who heeded it" rather than "not being mixed with faith in those who heard it."

Hebrews 6:3 M-text reads "let us do" rather than "we will do."

Hebrews 6:18 M-text lacks "might."

Hebrews 10:9 M-text and NU both lack "O God."

Hebrews 11:13 M-text and NU both lack "were assured of them"

Hebrews 11:26 M-text and NU both read "of Egypt" rather than "in Egypt."

Hebrews 12:7 M-text and NU both read, "It is for discipline that you endure" rather than "If ye endure chastising."

Hebrews 12:20 M-text and NU both lack "or thrust through with a dart."

Hebrews 12:28 M-text lacks "may."

Hebrews 13:9 M-text and NU both read "away" rather than "about."

Hebrews 13:21 M-text and NU both read "us" rather than "you."

James 4:2 M-text and NU both lack "yet."

James 4:12 M-text and NU both read "but who" rather than just "who."

James 4:13 M-text reads "let us" rather than "we will."

James 5:9 M-text and NU both read "judged" rather than "condemned."

James 5:12 M-text reads "hypocrisy" rather than "judgment."

1 Peter 1:8 M-text reads "known" rather than "seen."

1 Peter 1:12 M-text and NU both read "you" rather than "us."

1 Peter 2:21 M-text and NU both read "you" rather than "us."

1 Peter 3:18 M-text and NU both read "you" rather than "us."

1 Peter 5:8 M-text and NU both lack "because."

1 Peter 5:10 M-text and NU both read "you" rather than "us."

2 Peter 2:3 M-text reads "will not" rather than "does not."

2 Peter 3:2 M-text reads "the apostles of your Lord and Savior" or "your apostles of the Lord and Savior" rather than "the apostles of the Lord and Savior."

1 John 1:4 M-text and NU both read "our" rather than "your."

1 John 3:1 M-text reads "you" rather than "us."

1 John 3:23 M-text lacks "us."

1 John 5:4 M-text reads "your" rather than "our."

1 John 5:7-8 M-text and NU both lack all of verse 7, begin verse 8 with "there are three" and lack the words "in earth."

2 John 1:2 M-text and NU both read "us" rather than "you."

3 John 1:11 M-text and NU both lack "but."

Jude 12 M-text and NU both read "along" rather than "about."

Jude 24 M-test reads "them" rather than "you" (#186).

Revelation 1:5 M-text reads "loves us and washed us" rather than "loved us and washed us" (NU reads "loves us and freed us).

Revelation 1:5 M-text and NU both read "a kingdom" rather than "kings."

Revelation 1:8 M-text and NU both lack "the beginning and the end" and read "the Lord God" rather than just "the Lord."

Revelation 1:9 M-text and NU both lack "both."

Revelation 1:11 M-text and NU both lack "'I am the Alpha and the Omega, the First and the Last,' and" and also lack "which are in Asia."

Revelation 1:19 M-text and NU both read "Therefore write" rather than just "Write."

Revelation 1:20 M-text and NU both lack "which you saw."

Revelation 2:15 M-text and NU both lack "which thing I hate."

Revelation 2:19 M-text and NU both read "faith, and service" rather than "service, and faith."

Revelation 2:20 M-text reads "your wife Jezebel" rather than "that woman Jezebel", M-test and NU both read "teaches and seduces" rather than "to teach and seduce."

Revelation 2:21 M-text and NU both read "and she does not want to repent of her sexual immorality" rather than "of her fornication; and she repented not."

Revelation 2:22 M-text and NU both read "her" rather than "their."

Revelation 2:24 M-text and NU both lack "and" before "unto the rest in Thyatira" and "will" before "put upon you."

Revelation 3:2 M-text and NU both read "My God" rather than just "God."

Revelation 3:4 M-text and NU both "Nevertheless, thou" rather than just "Thou" and lack "even" before "in Sardis."

Revelation 3:8 M-text and NU both read "which no one can shut" rather than "and no man can shut it."

Revelation 3:11 M-text and NU both lack "Behold."

Revelation 3:14 M-text and NU both read "in Laodicea" rather than "of the Laodiceans."

Revelation 3:16 M-text and NU both read "hot nor cold" rather than "cold nor hot."

Revelation 4:3 M-text lacks "And he that sat was" [thus making the description in the verse about the throne rather than the one sitting on it].

Revelation 4:4 M-text and NU both read "with crowns" rather than "and they had crowns."

Revelation 4:5 M-text and NU both read "voices and thunderings" rather than "thunderings and voices." M-text also lacks "the" before "seven Spirits of God."

Revelation 4:5 M-text and NU both read "something like a sea of glass" rather than just "a sea of glass."

Revelation 4:8 M-text has "holy" nine times rather than three.

Revelation 4:11 M-text and NU both read "our Lord and God" rather than "O Lord" and "existed" rather than "exist."

Revelation 5:4 M-text and NU both lack "and read."

Revelation 5:5 M-text and NU both lack "to loose."

Revelation 5:5 M-text and NU both read "I saw in the midst" rather than "and, lo, in the midst," and "a lamb standing" rather than "stood a lamb."

Revelation 5:10 M-text and NU both read "them" rather than "us" and "they" rather than "we."

Revelation 5:13 M-text concludes the verse with "Amen."

Revelation 5:14 M-text and NU lack "twenty-four" and "Him who liveth forever and ever."

Revelation 6:1 M-text and NU read "seven seals" rather than just "seals."

Revelation 6:3 M-text and NU both lack "and see."

Revelation 6:12 M-text and NU both lack "behold" and read "the whole moon" rather than just "the moon."

Revelation 6:15 M-text and NU both read "the chief captains, the rich men" rather than "the rich men, the chief captains."

Revelation 7:5-8 M-text and NU lack "were sealed" in all but the first and last instances.

Revelation 7:14 M-text and NU both read "my lord" rather than "sir."

Revelation 7:17 M-text and NU read "fountains of the water of life" rather than "living fountains of waters."

Revelation 8:7 M-text and NU both read, "and a third of the earth was burned up" after "and cast it into the earth."

Revelation 8:13 M-text and NU both read "eagle" rather than "angel."

Revelation 9:19 M-text and NU both read "the power of the horses" rather than "their power."

Revelation 9:21 M-text and NU both read "their drugs" or "their magic potions" rather than "their sorceries."

Revelation 10:4 M-text and NU both read "sounded" rather than "uttered" and also lack "unto me" after "from heaven saying."

Revelation 10:5 M-text and NU both read "right hand" rather than just "hand."

Revelation 10:11 M-text and NU both read "they" rather than "he."

Revelation 11:1 M-text and NU both lack "and the angel stood."

Revelation 11:4 M-text and NU both read "Lord" rather than "God."

Revelation 11:8 M-text and NU both read "their" rather than "our."

Revelation 11:9 M-text and NU both read "see" rather than "will see" and, on the other hand, read "will not allow" rather than just "not allow."

Revelation 11:12 M-text reads "I" rather than "they."

Revelation 11:17 M-text and NU both lack "and art to come."

Revelation 11:19 M-text reads "the testament of the Lord" rather than "His testament."

Revelation 12:8 M-text reads "him" rather than "them."

Revelation 12:17 M-text and NU both read "Jesus" rather than "Jesus Christ."

Revelation 13:1 M-text and NU both read "ten horns and seven heads" rather than "seven heads and ten horns."

Revelation 13:5 M-text reads "make war" rather than "continue."

Revelation 13:7 M-text and NU both read "kindred and people, tongue and nation" rather than just "kindreds, and tongues, and nations."

Revelation 13:14 M-text reads "my own people" rather than "those."

Revelation 13:17 M-text and NU both read "the mark, the name" rather than "The mark or the name."

Revelation 14:1 M-text and NU both read "the Lamb" rather than "a Lamb" and also "having His name and His Father's name" rather than just "having His Father's name."

Revelation 14:4 M-text reads "redeemed by Jesus" rather than just "redeemed."

Revelation 14:5 M-text and NU both read "falsehood" rather than "guile" and both lack the phrase "before the throne of God."

Revelation 14:8 M-text reads "Babylon the great is fallen. She has made" rather than "Babylon is fallen, is fallen, that great city, because she has made" (NU reads "Babylon the great is fallen, is fallen, which has made").

Revelation 14:12 M-text and NU both lack "here are they."

Revelation 14:13 M-text and NU both lack "unto me."

Revelation 14:15 M-text and NU both lack "for the.e"

Revelation 15:2 M-text and NU both lack "over his mark."

Revelation 15:3 M-text and NU both read "nations" rather than "saints."

Revelation 15:5 M-text and NU both lack "behold."

Revelation 16:1 M-text and NU both read "seven vials" rather than just "vials."

Revelation 16:5 M-text and NU both lack "O Lord" and both read "the Holy One" rather than "and shalt be" (as did all editions of the TR prior to Theodore Beza).

Revelation 16:5 M-text and NU both lack "For."

Revelation 16:7 M-text and NU both lack "another out of."

Revelation 16:14 M-text and NU both lack "of the earth and."

Revelation 16:16 M-text reads "Megiddo" rather than "Mount Megiddo."

Revelation 17:1 M-text and NU both lack "unto me."

Revelation 17:8 M-text and NU both read "shall be present" rather than "yet is."

Revelation 17:16 M-text and NU both read "and the beast" rather than "on the beast."

Revelation 18:2 M-text and M-text both lack "mightily."

Revelation 18:5 M-text and M-text both read "have been heaped up" rather than "have reached unto."

Revelation 18:5 M-text and NU both lack "you" after "she rewarded."

Revelation 18:8 M-text and NU both read "has judged" rather than "judgeth."

Revelation 18:14 M-text and NU both read "been lost to thee" rather than "are departed from thee."

Revelation 18:20 M-text and NU both read "saints and apostles" rather than "holy apostles and prophets."

Revelation 19:1 M-text and NU both say "something like a great voice" rather than just "a great voice" and they also both "our God" rather than "the Lord our God."

Revelation 19:5 M-text and NU both lack "both."

Revelation 19:5 M-text and NU both read "our Lord" rather than "the Lord."

Revelation 19:12 M-text reads "names written, and a name written" rather than just "a name written."

Revelation 19:14 M-text and NU both read "pure white linen" rather than "fine linen, white and clean."

Revelation 19:15 M-text reads "sharp two-edged sword" rather than just "sharp sword."

Revelation 19:17 M-text and NU both read "great supper of God" rather than "supper of the great God."

Revelation 19:18 M-text and NU both read "both free and slave" rather than just "free and slave."

Revelation 20:4 M-text reads "the thousand years" rather than "a thousand years."

Revelation 20:10 M-text and NU both read "where also" rather than just "where."

Revelation 20:12 M-text and NU both read "the throne" rather than "God."

Revelation 20:14 M-text and NU both read "death, the lake of fire" rather than just "death."

Revelation 21:2 M-text and NU both lack "John."

Revelation 21:5 M-text and NU both lack "unto me."

Revelation 21:5 M-text lacks "It is done."

Revelation 21:7 M-text reads "I shall give him these things" rather than "shall inherit these things."

Revelation 21:8 M-text adds "and sinners" between "unbelieving" and "abominable" (287).

Revelation 21:9 M-text and NU both lack "unto me," M-text also reads "woman, the Lamb's bride" rather than "bride, the Lamb's wife."

Revelation 21:10 M-text and NU both lack "great" before "city" and read "holy city, Jerusalem" rather than "holy Jerusalem."

Revelation 21:14 M-text and NU both read "twelve names" rather than just "the names."

Revelation 21:23 M-text reads "the very glory of God" rather than just "the glory of God."

Revelation 21:24 M-text and NU both lack "of them which are saved."

Revelation 21:26 M-text contains the phrase "that they may enter in" at the end of the verse, which is lacking in both the TR and the NU.

Revelation 21:27 M-text and NU both read "anything profane, nor one who causes an abomination" rather than "anything that defiles or causes an abomination."

Revelation 22:1 M-text and NU both lack "pure."

Revelation 22:5 M-text and NU both read "spirits of the prophets" rather than "holy prophets."

Revelation 22:8 M-text and NU both read "am the one who heard and saw" rather than just "saw and heard."

Revelation 22:11 M-text and NU both read "do right" rather than "be righteous still."

Revelation 22:13 M-text and NU both read "First and the Last, the Beginning and the End" rather than "the Beginning and the End, the First and the Last."

Revelation 22:15 M-text and NU both lack "But."

Revelation 22:18 M-text and NU both lack "For," M-text also reads "may God add" rather than "God will add."

Revelation 22:19 M-text reads "may God take away" rather than "God shall take away." M-text and NU both read "tree of life" rather than "book of life."

Revelation 22:21 M-text reads "with all the saints" rather than "with you all" (NU simply reads "with all") (#304).

BIBLIOGRAPHY

Aland, Kurt; Aland, Barbara. *The Text of the New Testament. An Introduction to the Critical Editions and to the Theory and Practice of Modern Textual Criticism*. Grand Rapids: William B Erdman Publishing Company, 1995.

Black, David Alan. *Rethinking New Testament Textual Criticism*. Grand Rapids: Baker Book House, 2002.

Borland, James A. "Re-examining the Textual-Critical Principles and Practices Used to Negate Inerrancy," The *Journal of the Evangelical Theological Society*, vol. 25, December 1982.

Burgon, John. *The Last Twelve Verses of Mark*. Grand Rapids: Associated Publishers and Authors, n. d.

_____ *The Revision Revised*. Paradise, Pa.: Conservative Classics, reprint, n. d.

_____ *Unholy Hands on the Bible*, vol. 1. The Complete Works of John W. Burgon. Lafayette, IN: Sovereign Grace Trust Fund, 1990.

Carson, D. A. *The King James Version Debate*. Grand Rapids: Baker Book House, 1979.

Farstad, Arthur L. *The New King James Version: In the Great Tradition*. Nashville: Thomas Nelson Publishers, 1989.

Fuller, David Otis. *Which Bible?* Grand Rapids: Grand Rapids International Publications, 1971.

Green, Sr., Jay. *Unholy Hands on the Bible. The Complete Works of John W. Burgon*. Volume 1. Lafayette, IN: Sovereign Grace Trust Fund, 1990. Green wrote the Preface.

Harrison, Everett F. *Introduction to the New Testament.* Grand Rapids: William B. Eerdmans Publishing Company, 1968.

Hills, *King James Version Defended.* Des Moines, Iowa: The Christian Research Press, 1956.

Hodges, Zane C. "Introduction to the Textus Receptus," Unpublished Notes, n.d.

_____ "The Angel at Bethesda—John 5:4." Bibliotheca Sacra 136:541 (January-March 1979)" 25-39.

_____ "The Greek Text of the King James Version." *Bibliotheca Sacra*, 125:500 (Oct -Dec 1968)" 334-345.

_____; Farstad, Arthur L. *The Greek New Testament According to the Majority Text.* Nashville: Thomas Nelson Publishers, 1982.

_____; Radmacher, Earl. The NIV reconsidered. Dallas" Redencion Viva, 1990.

Metzger, Bruce M. *The Text of the New Testament: Its Transmission, Corruption, and Restoration*, 3rd ed. 1992.

Pickering, Wilbur N. *The Greek New Testament According to Family 35.* Second Edition. Creative Commons Attribution-ShareAlike, 2015.

_____ and Freitas, Marcelo. *Family 35.* Creative Commons Attribution-ShareAlike, 2021.

Robinson, Maurice A. and Pierpont, William G. *The New Testament in the original Greek.* Nurnberg, Germany: VTR publishers, 2018.

Ruchman, Peter. *The Christian's Handbook Of Manuscript Evidence..* Pensacola: Bible Press, 1990.

Sorensen, David H. *Neither Oldest Nor Best*: Duluth, MN North Star Ministries, 2019.

Sturz, A. Harry. *The Byzantine Text type in New Testament Textual Criticism.* Nashville: Thomas Nelson Publishers, 1984.

The New Testament, The Greek Text Underlying the English Authorized Version of 1611. London: The Trinitarian Bible Society, 1976.

Wallace, Daniel. "Did the Original New Testament Manuscripts still exist in the Second Century?"

_____. article in *Bibliotheca Sacra* from the April-June '91.

_____. Speech on New Testament Manuscripts, 2013, posted at http://marturiamine.blogspot.com/2013/09/confession-of-ex-tr-evangelist.html.

Wayne, Luke. "Differences Between the Majority Text and the Textus Receptus."

Westcott, Brooke Foss and Hort, Fenton John Anthony. *New Testament in the Original Greek, Introduction and Appendix.* New York: Harper and Brothers, Franklin Square, 1882, reprint edition by Forgotten Books, 2012.

White, James R. *The King James Only Controversy.* Minneapolis: Bethany House Publishers, 1995.

Woudstra, Sierd. "A Teacher Looks at the NIV." *The Banner* 124 (April 10, 1989)" 8-9.

ABOUT THE AUTHOR

G. Michael Cocoris is a gifted communicator. He can make even complicated subjects simple, clear, and practical. His breadth of experience has enabled him to connect with a diverse range of audiences.

Michael received a Bachelor of Arts degree from Tennessee Temple University, a Master of Theology degree from Dallas Theological Seminary, and a Doctor of Divinity degree from Biola University. He traveled the United States for over a dozen years as a speaker. He has also served as a seminary professor, visiting lecturer, and world traveler, having hosted tours to Israel and China.

Michael has pastored three churches, including a rural church during his seminary years, an urban church, the historic Church of the Open Door, first located in downtown Los Angeles and later in Glendora, California, and a suburban church, the Lindley Church in Tarzana, California, a suburb of Los Angeles. While at the Church of Open Door, he had a daily radio broadcast.

Michael has written numerous magazine articles, mainly for Biblical Research Monthly. He has authored a number of books, including *Seventy Years on Hope Street, A History of The Church of the Open Door*; *The Spiritual Life, Clarifying the Confusion*; *Repentance, The Most Misunderstood Word in the Bible*; *Evangelism: A Biblical Approach*; *The Salvation Controversy*; *Lordship Salvation: Is It Biblical?*; *The Books of the Bible, the Subject, Structure, Situation, and Significant Verses of Each Book*; *Psalms, A Song for Every Situation, Each Summarized on One Page*; *Counseling Theories: A Simple Explanation and Biblical Evaluation,*

Proverbs, Autopsy of the United States, How to Study the Bible, and *Spiritual Basics, Basic Biblical Keys to Living a Spiritual Life.* In addition, he was a contributor to The NKJV Study Bible and *Nelson's New Illustrated Bible Commentary.*

Michael is the pastor of the Lindley Church in Tarzana, California. He and his wife, Patricia, live in Santa Monica, California.

See Michael's website at *insightsfromtheword.com.*

www.ingramcontent.com/pod-product-compliance
Lightning Source LLC
Chambersburg PA
CBHW081439070526
44586CB00019B/2175